THE COLLECTED WORKS OF
ISAAC ROSENBERG

This book is dedicated to
Joseph Leftwich
the author of the poem below,
in affection and gratitude

*

KILLED IN ACTION

Your 'Youth' has fallen from its shelf,
And you have fallen, you yourself.
They knocked a soldier on the head,
I mourn the poet who fell dead.
And yet I think it was by chance,
By oversight you died in France.
You were so poor an outward man,
So small against your spirit's span,
That Nature, being tired awhile,
Saw but your outward human pile:
And Nature, who would never let
A sun with light still in it set,
Before you even reached your sky,
In inadvertence let you die.

THE COLLECTED WORKS OF

ISAAC ROSENBERG

POETRY · PROSE · LETTERS
PAINTINGS AND DRAWINGS

With a Foreword by
SIEGFRIED SASSOON

Edited
with an Introduction and Notes
by
IAN PARSONS

CHATTO AND WINDUS

THE HOGARTH PRESS

LONDON

Published in 1984 by
Chatto and Windus · The Hogarth Press
40 William IV Street, London WC2N 4DF

Originally published by Chatto and Windus
in hardcover in 1979

British Library Cataloguing
in Publication Data

Rosenberg, Isaac
The collected works of Isaac Rosenberg
I. Parsons, Ian
821'.9'12   PR6035.067A/

ISBN 0 7011 2893 3

Printed in Great Britain by
Redwood Burn Limited,
Trowbridge, Wiltshire

Contents

List of Illustrations

I. PLATES IN COLOUR

Plates 1 to 8. Between pages 80 and 81

Plates 9 to 16. Between pages 208 and 209

II. MONOCHROME PLATES

FOREWORD

IT has been considered appropriate that I should say something about the poems of Isaac Rosenberg. I can only hope that what I say, inadequate though it may be, will help to gain for him the full recognition of his genius which has hitherto been delayed. In reading and re-reading these poems I have been strongly impressed by their depth and integrity. I have found a sensitive and vigorous mind energetically interested in experimenting with language, and I have recognised in Rosenberg a fruitful fusion between English and Hebrew culture. Behind all his poetry there is a racial quality—biblical and prophetic. Scriptural and sculptural are the epithets I would apply to him. His experiments were a strenuous effort for impassioned expression; his imagination had a sinewy and muscular aliveness; often he saw things in terms of sculpture, but he did not carve or chisel; he *modelled* words with fierce energy and aspiration, finding ecstasy in form, dreaming in grandeurs of superb light and deep shadow; his poetic visions are mostly in sombre colours and looming sculptural masses, molten and amply wrought. Watching him working with words, I find him a poet of movement; words which express movement are often used by him and are essential to his natural utterance.

Rosenberg was not consciously a 'war poet'. But the war destroyed him, and his few but impressive 'Trench Poems' are a central point in this book. They have the controlled directness of a man finding his true voice and achieving mastery of his material; words and images obey him, instead of leading him into over-elaboration. They are all of them fine poems, but 'Break of Day in the Trenches' has for me a poignant and nostalgic quality which eliminates critical analysis. Sensuous frontline existence is there, hateful and repellent, unforgettable and inescapable. And beyond this poem I see the poems he might have written after the war, and the life he might have lived when life began again beyond and behind those trenches which were the limbo of all sane humanity and world-improving imagination. For the spirit of poetry looks beyond life's trench-lines. And Isaac Rosenberg was naturally empowered with something of the divine spirit which touches our human clay to sublimity of expression.

Here, in this book, we have his immaturity and his achievement. Both are wonderful and manifold in richness. Having said what I can, I lay this reverent wreath upon his tomb.

1937   SIEGFRIED SASSOON

CHRONOLOGICAL SUMMARY OF ROSENBERG'S LIFE

1890 November 25	I.R. born at 5 Adelaide Place, Bristol, the eldest son and second child of Barnett and Anna Rosenberg. Their first, a daughter Minnie, had been born in Lithuania on March 23rd, 1887.
1892 October 25	Sister Annie born in Bristol.
1894 October 9	Sister Rachel born in Bristol.
1897 February 10	Brother David born in Bristol.
1897	Family move to 47 Cable Street, Stepney, London E1. R enrols at St. Paul's School, Wellclose Square, St. George's-in-the-East.
1899	Brother Elkon born.
1899 November 14	R enrols at Baker Street School, Stepney E.
1900?	Family move to 58 Jubilee Street, Stepney, becoming neighbours of the Amschewitz family; J. H. Amschewitz[1] is 8 years Isaac's senior, and at an early point in their friendship introduces him to Winifreda Seaton.[2]
1902-3	R begins special afternoon classes at the Stepney Green Art School, at the instigation of Mr. Usherwood, headmaster of Baker St. School.
1904	Family move to another flat in Jubilee St.
1904 May 14	R wins prize for an essay.
1904 December 23	R Leaves Baker Street School.
1905 Early January	Joins Carl Hentschel's[3], Engravers, of Fleet Street, EC4, as apprentice.
1907	Family move to 159 Oxford Street, London E.
1907	R starts evening classes at London School of Photo-Engraving and Lithography, 6 Bolt Court, Fleet Street. Attends till 1910.
1907	Attends evening classes at Birkbeck College, Chancery Lane, EC4, where instructed and befriended by Alice Wright.[4] Attends till 1909,

[1] See p. 44n.   [2] See p. 180n.
[3] Carl Hentschel was a friend of Jerome K. Jerome, and the original of 'Harris' in Jerome's best-selling novel *Three Men in a Boat* (1889).
[4] See p. 187n, 1.

	during which time he wins the Mason prize in 1908 for nude studies, and in 1909 the Pocock prize for a nude in oils.
1909?	Apprenticed to a Mr. Lascelles, process engraver, of Shoe Lane, EC4, though apparently still under the aegis of Hentschel.
1911 January 2	Meets Samuel Winsten, Joseph Leftwich and John Rodker in Whitechapel, in London's East End.[1]
1911 January	Sits for portrait by J. H. Amschewitz.
1911 Early March	Leaves Carl Hentschel's.
1911 March 17	Meets Lily Delissa Joseph (sister of Solomon J. Solomon, R.A.) at National Gallery.
1911 Early May	Starts as Tutor to Mrs. Joseph's son. Meets Mrs. Henrietta Löwy (sister of Mrs. Joseph) and Mrs. Herbert Cohen.
1911 July	Takes boat trip to St. Helena.
1911 October 3	Applies for entry to Slade School of Art, sponsored by Mrs. Delissa Joseph, Mrs. Herbert Cohen and Mrs. Henrietta Löwy.
1911 October 13	Fees of £21 for the 1911-12 session at the Slade paid by them, and Isaac joins.
1912 May 24	R's review of the J. H. Amschewitz/Henry Ospovat Exhibition at the Baillie Galleries, Bruton St., is printed in *The Jewish Chronicle*.[2]
1912 May/June	Moves to a studio at 40 Ampthill Square, Hampstead Road.
1912 Spring	Writes to and meets Laurence Binyon,[3] Keeper of Prints and Drawings at British Museum.
1912 Spring/Summer	*Night and Day*, a 24-page pamphlet of poems is printed by Israel Narodiczky,[4] who charges £2 for 50 copies.
1912 September	Moves to 32 Carlingford Road, Hampstead.
1912 Sept/October	R begins to fall out with Mrs. Cohen, who reduces his living allowance. Sees Ernest Lesser of the Jewish Educational Aid Society, requesting funds for continuing studies at The Slade. Returns home to 159 Oxford Street.

[1] See p. 266*n*, 1.   [2] See p. 286.   [3] See p. 192*n*.   [4] See p. 212*n*, 1.

1912 October	Painting 'Joy' wins First Class Certificate at Slade.
	New English Art Club exhibits and sells his 'Sanguine Drawing'. Another painting exhibited but unsold.
1912 Winter	Rosenberg family move to 87 Dempsey Street, Stepney E.
1912 December	Approval from J.E.A.S. to fund R till end March 1914.
1913 Early	Rents room at 1 St. George's Square, Chalk Farm, N. London.
	Submits group of paintings for Prix de Rome competition.[1] Fails to win it, but pictures exhibited at Imperial Institute Galleries, South Kensington.
1913 March	Leaves Slade.
	Seeks treatment (paid for by J.E.A.S.) for eye trouble.
1913 Spring	Health deteriorating. Moves back to Dempsey Street for care.
1913 Summer	Spends holiday at Sandown, Isle of Wight, with David Bomberg.[2]
	Returns to St. George's Square.
1913 August 24	Sister Minnie marries Wolf Horvitch.
1913 Sept 2	Minnie and husband depart for South Africa.
1913 Nov 10	Introduced by Gertler[3] to Edward Marsh and T. E. Hulme at Café Royal.
1914 Jan/Feb	Coughing and lungs worsen. Takes holiday (paid for by J.E.A.S.) in Bournemouth, Feb 20 to March 1.
1914 March	Returns to Dempsey Street, relinquishing St. George's Square studio.
	Requests funds ('£12 or £15') of J.E.A.S. for passage to South Africa for health reasons. Granted.
1914 May	Exhibits at Whitechapel Art Gallery's Exhibition of Twentieth Century Artists.
1914 Early June	Sails by Union Castle line from Tilbury for South Africa.
1914 End June	Reaches Cape Town, stays with sister Minnie at Hill House, 43 De Villiers St.

[1] See p. 197n, 3.   [2] See p. 194n, 1.   [3] See p. 204n, 4.

1914 July	Commissioned by Sir Herbert Stanley to paint two babies. Fee, £15.
	Lectures at studio of Madge Cook, daughter of Mrs. Agnes Cook, editor of *South African Women in Council*, who later publishes the lecture in two parts,[1] with his poems 'Beauty' and 'Our Dead Heroes'.
1914 August 4	England declares war against Germany.
	Meets Miss Molteno.[2] Spends fortnight at her home at Rondebosch. Returns to Cape Town.
1915 February	Sets sail for England. Reputedly loses most of his paintings overboard in Cape Town harbour.[3]
1915 March	Returns to 87 Dempsey Street.
1915 April	'*Youth*' printed at Narodiczky's, from type set (?) by Reuben Cohen.[4] 100 copies for £2.10s. Paid for by selling 3 pictures to Edward Marsh.
1915 May	Meets Sydney Schiff[5] at Café Royal.
1915 June	*Colour* Magazine, edited by T. M. Wood, prints 'Heart's First Word'.
1915 July 1	First and only edition of *The Jewish Standard*, a collaboration between Reuben Cohen and R, is issued.
1915 July	*Colour* Magazine prints 'A Girl's Thoughts'.
1915 August	*Colour* prints 'Wedded' (I).
	R apparently applies to Hentschel's, requesting work. Unsuccessful.
1915 Sept/Oct	Starts evening classes in block-making, in the hope of getting a job. No luck.
1915 End Oct	Enlists. Sent direct to Recruiting Depot at Bury St. Edmunds, Suffolk, to join Bantam Battalion of 12th Suffolk Regiment, 40th Division.
1915 Late Nov	In hospital with cut hands through falling.
1915 Nov	Lascelles Abercrombie,[6] shown R's poetry by Marsh, writes to him.
1915 Christmas	4 days leave at home.
1916 Jan 16	Transferred to 12th South Lancashires, at Blackdown Camp, Farnborough, Nr. Aldershot, Hants.

[1] See pp. 289-297. [2] See p. 207. [3] See Cohen, p. 112.
[4] Cohen was a journeyman compositor, and friend of R's, who worked for Narodiczky.
[5] See p. 212 *n*, 2 [6] See p. 208*n*, 3

1916 March	Again transferred, this time to 11th Battalion, King's Own Royal Lancasters Regiment, remaining at Blackdown Camp.
1916 May 19	6 days' pre-embarkation leave, during which Reuben Cohen, of Narodiczky's (using name 'Paragon Printing Works'), prints *Moses*.
1916 May 25	R back in barracks.
1916 ?June 2	Leaves for France (probably from Folkestone).
1916 ?June 3	Arrives? Le Havre en route for Somme trenches.
1916 June 23	R. C. Trevelyan writes.
1916 July 4	Gordon Bottomley writes.
1916 July	Arrives at front but remains behind the lines at 40th Division Salvage Office.
1916 End August	Sent into trenches.
1916 September	Sends 'Break of Day in the Trenches' to Harriet Monroe of *Poetry* (Chicago).
1916 Nov 25th	27th birthday.
1916 December	Harriet Monroe prints 'Marching' (sent by Rodker in Jan 1916) and 'Break of Day in the Trenches' in *Poetry* (Chicago).
1917 January	R reports sick and is relieved of trench duty.
1917 February	Re-assigned to 40th Division Works Battalion, behind the lines.
1917 Late Feb	Re-assigned to 229 Field Co., Royal Engineers, attached to 11th Battalion, King's Own Royal Lancasters.
1917 Sept 16	10 days leave spent at home.
1917 Sept 26	Back in France.
1917 Late Sept	*Georgian Poetry 1916-17* published, containing R's 'Ah Kolue' speech from *Moses*.
1917 October 10	R reports sick with influenza. Is sent to 51st General Hospital.
1917 Mid December	Leaves hospital and returns to trenches.
1918 Late Jan	Rest behind the lines.
1918 February 7	Transferred to 1st Battalion K.O.R.L., 40th Div.
1918 March 21	Recalled to trenches.
1918 April 1	Private I. Rosenberg, 22311, 1st K.O.R.L., is killed at dawn while on night patrol.

INTRODUCTION

ISAAC Rosenberg was born in Bristol on the twenty-fifth of
November 1890. His father, a cultured man and Hebrew
reader, came originally from Lithuania, but had moved to
Moscow where a brother was living, in the hope of finding work.
In Russia he found himself liable to be called up for military
service, and decided to emigrate. He came to England in 1887
or 1888, settling first in Yorkshire and then Bristol, where he
was joined in '88 by his wife and baby daughter. Nine years
later the family (there were now five children) moved to the
East End of London, where many Jewish families—refugees
from persecution in Eastern Europe—had settled. Anna and
Barnett Rosenberg were to have one further child after this,
and at one time were living seven-in-a-room in Cable Street,
Stepney. They had found a refuge in England from persecution,
but not from poverty. What saved them, and is an abiding
testimony to the generosity of their co-religionists, was the
practical help which they received from the charitable organisa-
tions set up by their predecessors in the flight from oppression,
some of whom, by their gifts and their industry, had become
affluent citizens. Barnett Rosenberg tried his hand at all sorts
of jobs, unsuccessfully, and ended up as an itinerant pedlar,
earning very little. His wife took in washing, and did needle-
work for neighbours, in order to keep the family going. But in
these early London days, and for many years to come, poverty
bordering on destitution was their lot. This needs to be said, for
poverty was a basic ingredient of Rosenberg's childhood and
youth, and it not only helped to mould his character but
influenced his whole life, and more especially his development
as a creative artist.

His all too short life, indeed, was a tantalizing mixture of
good and bad luck, of fortune and misfortune. He was lucky to
be born with creative gifts of a quite exceptional kind, and into
a family who not only cherished him, but one of whose members
early recognised and encouraged those gifts. He was unlucky
in that the same family was virtually without money and
doubted his ability to earn any. He was very lucky in two of the
teachers whom he encountered during his schooldays and
apprentice years: Miss Winifreda Seaton and Miss Alice
Wright. He was unlucky in that he was obliged to leave school
at fourteen and, in order to contribute something to the family's
exiguous income, to take a job as an engraver, which he found
frustrating and distasteful. On the other hand, he was extra-
ordinarily fortunate in his youthful companions. and it is

difficult to over-estimate the stimulus, emotional and intellectual, which he derived from his close friendships with Joseph Leftwich, John Rodker, and Samuel Winsten; or later, when he was at the Slade, with Mark Gertler and David Bomberg. With them he formed part of that extraordinary cultural explosion which took place between 1900 and 1914 in London's East End, and gave currency to the appellation 'The Whitechapel Boys'.

Rosenberg was not so fortunate with the patron to whom Gertler introduced him: Edward Marsh, a classical scholar and career Civil Servant with private means, whose five successive anthologies of *Georgian Poetry* sold thousands during the decade 1912 to 1922. True, Marsh conscientiously read Rosenberg's poems and encouraged him to go on writing, both by criticising his work and buying some of his pictures. But it is abundantly clear from both men's letters, as well as from the 'Georgian' anthologies, that Marsh (for all his goodwill and generosity as a patron) was about the last person to appreciate the originality and force of Rosenberg's poetry, which he found obscure, difficult, and lacking in form. By which he meant, of course, traditional form. Whereas Rosenberg was, as Robert Graves quickly saw, 'a born revolutionary'. His work was far too elemental, too imaginative, and too occupied with the struggle to give expression to the intangible, to appeal to Marsh's civilized but limited taste.

Nor was Rosenberg much more fortunate in the literary luminaries—Laurence Binyon, Lascelles Abercrombie and Gordon Bottomley—to whom Marsh showed his work. They were the leading members of the academic poetic 'establishment' of those days, and Rosenberg, whose letters show clearly how impressed he was by their works, came increasingly under their influence. It was not a very beneficial one, and it is tempting to speculate how differently he might have developed had his mentors been his fellow combatants—Owen, Sassoon and Graves. They would hardly, it seems safe to assume, have encouraged his interest in verse drama built round grandiose biblical themes; and we might have had, instead of *The Amulet* and *The Unicorn*, more of the great poems that were inspired by his personal experience of trench warfare.

All the same, it was from the former poets, with whose work Rosenberg's has almost nothing in common, that he received the encouragement he so anxiously sought, but did not really need. I say 'did not need' because one of the basic characteristics of genius, whenever and wherever it crops up (and it can crop up just as easily in Whitechapel as in Warminster), is that it is never in any real doubt about its own powers. Blake, who had a considerable influence on Rosenberg, had none; nor had D. H. Lawrence. But the latter, who found Marsh's criticism of his poetry just as irksome as Rosenberg sometimes did, at least got half-a-dozen poems into the Georgian anthologies, whereas Rosenberg is represented only by a single short extract from *Moses* in the 1916-17 volume.

That a good deal of Rosenberg's poetry, and especially his dramatic verse, is difficult to grasp, must be admitted. He himself was well aware of it. 'Most people', he wrote to Sydney Schiff in June 1915, 'find my poems difficult', and added, 'My technique in poetry is very clumsy I know.' 'My Moses', he told Ruth Löwy in Autumn 1916, 'is a hard pill to swallow', and in a later letter to Marsh, in August 1917, he spoke of 'my usual obscurity'. But in writing to Gordon Bottomley towards the end of July 1916, by which time Rosenberg had been on the Western Front for nearly two months, he elaborated on his poetic problems and aspirations.

'Simple *poetry*—that is where an interesting complexity of thought is kept in tone and right value to the dominating idea so that it is understandable and still ungraspable. I know it is beyond my reach just now, except, perhaps, in bits. I am always afraid of being empty. When I get more leisure in more settled times I will work on a larger scale and give myself room; then I may be less frustrated in my efforts to be clear, and satisfy myself too.'

And again, ten days later in a letter to Marsh dated August 4th, he wrote:

'I was most glad to get your letter and criticism. You know the conditions I have always worked under, and particularly with this last lot of poems. You know how earnestly one must wait on ideas, (you cannot coax real ones to you) and let as it were, a skin grow naturally round and through them. If you are not free, you can only, when the ideas come hot, seize them with the skin in tatters raw, crude, in some parts beautiful in others monstrous.'

It was typical of Rosenberg's modesty that he should react so mildly to Marsh's criticisms, harsh though these sometimes were. But then he had always welcomed criticism, right back to the days when he showed his early verses to Alice Wright. 'I should be much obliged for a criticism' he wrote to her in September 1912. But though he was grateful to Marsh for the considerable trouble he took over his poems, he was equally determined, like Lawrence, to go his own way, to find his own voice. And he was reluctant to the point of inflexibility about changing a word or an image if he felt instinctively that they were right—that they contributed to his constant effort 'to enrich the world of ideas'. The fact is that words flew into Rosenberg's mind as birds fly into a tree; they settled there, sometimes in patterns of indescribable beauty, but sometimes they failed to coalesce and remained disparate, glittering but inchoate.

But the difficulties and complexities, such as they are, sprang neither from confusion of thought nor any lack of the means of expression; still less, as Rosenberg himself said, 'from blindness or carelessness'; they were the result of an extraordinary compression of language ('I am always afraid of being empty'), and of his own particular and highly individual vision. Moreover he possessed, from very early on, the complementary gift of being able to clothe his ideas in language as original and startling as his vision. There are few poets whose work is more impressively free from the banal epithet and the dead phrase. Indeed, so many of his images are new and unfamiliar that one is apt at first to be puzzled by their strangeness; by the apparent abruptness, too, with which sometimes they are introduced. But gradually, with continued reading, one comes not only to appreciate their signal force and appropriateness, but to grasp the associations which link them to, and illuminate, their context.

One of the most astonishing statements made about the poets of the First World War, and by a Cambridge don at that, was that Owen and Rosenberg 'were killed before they had anything to write about except war'. It is not true of Owen, and it is ludicrously untrue of Rosenberg. For of the 154 poems in this book, 90 per cent. are not about war, and only one of the 55 fragments has anything to do with it. On the contrary, Rosenberg began writing poetry very early, in 1905 when he was barely 15 years old, and virtually never stopped. Moreover one cannot help being struck by the technical assurance of some of these juvenile poems, despite their occasional naïveté. They display, to a degree exceptional in so inexperienced a writer, what T. S. Eliot called 'an authoritativeness of manner'.

> She stood—a hill ensceptred Queen,
>   The glory streaming from her;
> While Heaven flashed her rays between,
>   And shed eternal summer. . . .
>
> And twilight's drowsy, half closed eyes,
>   Beheld that virgin splendour
> Whose orbs were as her darkening skies,
>   And as her spirit, tender.

Those are a couple of verses from a poem called 'Zion', written when Rosenberg was sixteen. And although in the immediately following years, his growing familiarity with English and other poets inevitably led him to reflect some of their accents and to echo some of their cadences, he fairly rapidly outgrew these influences. Swinburne is clearly present in a number of these early poems, including 'Dawn Behind Night', 'Lines Written in an Album', and 'Bacchanal'; Hardy is equally so in 'The

Dead Past', and Keats and Rossetti are certainly behind some of the 1911-12 love poems. But increasingly Rosenberg was finding his own idiom, and over the next two years produced a score of poems that are essentially *sui generis*. Among them were 'Glory of Hueless Skies', 'Apparition', 'A Warm Thought Flickers', 'At Night' and the superb 'Midsummer Frost'. Written in a variety of metres and rhyme-schemes, these poems have in common a peculiar freshness of outlook (no 'Georgian' echoes here), an originality of conception and imagery, and a command of metaphor that would be remarkable in a much older man. Above all they have already, as I have said, begun to take on the unmistakable tone and flavour of his mature poetry. Nobody but Rosenberg could be thought the author of these lines, the opening stanzas of 'Midsummer Frost':

> A July ghost, aghast at the strange winter,
> Wonders, at burning noon, (all summer seeming),
> How, like a sad thought buried in light words,
> Winter, an alien presence, is ambushed here.
>
> See, from the fire-fountained noon there creep
> Lazy yellow ardours towards pale evening,
> To thread dark and vain fire
> Over my unsens'd heart,
> Dead heart, no urgent summer can reach.
> Hidden as a root from air or a star from day;
> A frozen pool whereon mirth dances;
> Where the shining boys would fish.

To this period also belong several poems of marked originality, in both conception and form, such as 'The Mirror' and 'Significance':

> Chaos that coincides, form that refutes all sway,
> Shapes to the eye quite other to the touch,
> All twisted things continue to our clay
> Like added limbs and hair dispreaded overmuch.

These poems were followed or maybe shortly preceded—one can never be sure, for Rosenberg was an inveterate re-writer and much given to incorporating lines and whole passages of earlier drafts in a later composition, so that dating is often difficult ('The One Lost' is a classic example)—by a series of major poems written in South Africa or shortly after his return to this country in the Spring of 1915. They included love poems with a much broader range of emotion and depth of feeling than he could compass earlier, like 'I Have Lived in the Underworld too Long', 'Her Fabled Mouth' (written when he must have been reading the Elizabethan and Jacobean poets), 'The Exile', and the sensuous, almost erotic 'Sacred, Voluptuous Hollows Deep'. Perhaps the best, and certainly the most technically accomplished, was the first of the two poems he called 'Wedded', which begins:

> They leave their love-lorn haunts
> Their sigh-warm floating Eden;
> And they are mute at once;
> Mortals by God unheeden;
> By their past kisses chidden.
>
> But they have kist and known
> Clear things we dim by guesses—
> Spirit to spirit grown—
> Heaven, born in hand caresses—
> Love, fall from sheltering tresses.

Surely one of the most humanly revealing and moving poems of this kind ever written.

There were many other short poems—'A Girl's Thoughts', 'If You are Fire'—of a simplicity and lyric grace that give the lie to the assumption that all Rosenberg's middle period work was 'difficult'. Here, for example, are the first three verses of a poem he wrote in Cape Town in 1914, 'On Receiving News of the War':

> Snow is a strange white word;
> No ice or frost
> Have asked of bud or bird
> For Winter's cost.
>
> Yet ice and frost and snow
> From earth to sky
> This Summer land doth know,
> No man knows why.
>
> In all men's hearts it is.
> Some spirit old
> Hath turned with malign kiss
> Our lives to mould.

There are several others, written about the same time, of an equal simplicity and directness. Some of them (and many of the fragments) combine a bracing succinctness of diction with an exhilarating astringency. Such as:

> Pale mother night, suckling thy brood of stars,
> My fire, too, yearns for thy giant love,
> But they are calm, and mine is frenzy fire.

or:

> Even as a letter burns and curls
> And the mind and heart in the writing blackens,
> Words that wane as the wind unfurls—
> Obliteration never slackens.

And let nobody imagine that he was without humour. The prose piece called *On a Door Knocker* is proof of that, and the same cockney sense of comedy informs several of the poems. 'The Flea', or Fragment XXV for example, or this lighthearted quatrain:

> 'I live for you', says Ted to Jane
> 'And if you died, so I'd die too'.
> 'I'm sure you would', said working Jane
> 'You live for me—to live for you'.

Nor can one read far in Rosenberg's poetry without becoming aware of the fact that he was a painter-poet. Adjectives and images involving colour abound, and the sharp, observant eye of the draughtsman is everywhere apparent.

> Green thoughts are
> Ice block on a barrow
> Gleaming in July.
> A little boy with bare feet
> And jewels at his nose stands by.

A precise delineation of imaginative detail that reached its zenith, perhaps, in the lovely lyric which concludes:

> Your body is a star
> Unto my thought.
> But stars are not too far
> And can be caught—
> Small pools their prisons are.

It was on his return from staying with his married sister in Cape Town that Rosenberg embarked on his most ambitious work to date, his verse play *Moses*. The large number of extant drafts of it, or parts of it, show that it gave him many hours of labour, and when he published it the following year, at the end of May 1916, he was still not wholly satisfied with it. Understandably, in my view, for though it has always attracted critical attention at a high level and undoubtedly contains passages of surpassing beauty, it still seems to me a flawed work in which form and content never quite join hands.

Moreover it encouraged a misconception to which Laurence Binyon gave currency that Rosenberg 'aspired to become a representative poet of his own nation'. I do not believe that he did. Of course, he was a Jew, and was brought up in a conventional Jewish home, with all that that means in the way of traditional influence and cultural background. But he never really attempted to learn Hebrew, had only little Yiddish, and only small interest in Judaism as such. No, his vision was cosmic rather than sectarian, personal and unique rather than specifically Jewish. True, he was profoundly influenced by

Hebrew mythology and legend, especially as enshrined in the Bible; but it was his own myths that he wove round the archetypal characters that he drew from those sources. Siegfried Sassoon, it seems to me, put the matter in a nutshell in his 1937 Foreword:

'I have recognized in Rosenberg a fruitful fusion between English and Hebrew culture. Behind all his poetry there is a racial quality—biblical and prophetic. Scriptural and sculptural are the epithets I would apply to him.'

*   *   *   *

A painter-poet, or a poet-painter? Rosenberg could never quite make up his mind which. Writing to Winifred Seaton in 1910 he said 'I really would like to take up painting seriously; I think I might do something at that; but poetry—I despair of ever writing excellent poetry', and he went on to explain that this was because his mind was 'so cramped and dulled and fevered . . . by the fiendish persistence of the coil of circumstance'. In other words, by the frustrations of the last five years, during which he had been an apprentice engraver to Carl Hentschel; the cramped conditions at home (where the only place he could draw was at a corner of the kitchen table); and the perennial lack of money. Later, in 1912, after a chance meeting with Mrs. Lily Delissa Joseph in the National Gallery had enabled him to attend the Slade School of Art, sponsored by her and two other Jewish ladies of means, he told Laurence Binyon 'I spend most of my time drawing. I find writing interferes with drawing a good deal, and is far more exhausting'. But in a classic letter to Mrs. Herbert Cohen, one of the above-mentioned ladies, who had expressed dissatisfaction with his work, he remarked that 'Art is not a plaything, it is blood and tears, it must grow up with one; and I believe I have begun too late'.

In point of fact he had begun very early, and had quickly shown a marked talent for drawing. The two figure studies in pen and wash (Monochrome plates 2 (a) and 2 (b)), the chalk drawing of his Mother (3 (a)) and the oil painting of his Father (3 (b)) were all done before, or at the very outset of his joining the Slade. They are astonishingly accomplished work for a young man of twenty or so, more especially one brought up in his particular circumstances and surroundings. But at the Slade, where the approach to art was extremely serious, his latent talent for drawing developed rapidly under the strict discipline which the Slade tradition of drawing demanded, and the inspiring teaching of Professor Tonks.

His painting, too, showed remarkable promise, as is clear from the first seven works reproduced here in colour (Plates I to IV (b)), all of which were also produced before or immediately after he joined the Slade. Their sense of colour, of atmosphere, and of draughtsmanship are again exceptional. At the Slade he found himself the contemporary of such artists as C. R. W. Nevinson, William Roberts, Jacob Kramer and Stanley Spencer, as well as Gertler and Bomberg of whom mention has already been made. There, too, he was directed to pictures that he should study in the National collections and in contemporary exhibitions, so that he soon became enthusiastic about the work of Blake, Rossetti, Ingres and Degas, among the older draughtsmen, and of Stanley Spencer and Augustus John among the younger. Oddly enough, none of them seems to have much influenced him stylistically, although there is a touch of Boudin in 'People on the Seashore' and of Whistler in 'The Pool of London'. A more direct influence is visible in 'Sacred Love' (Colour Plate VIII, 1912) which owes a good deal to the two small panels in the National Gallery by Puvis de Chavannes.

It is a tragedy that so few of the other student drawings and paintings which Rosenberg must have done during his two and a half years at the Slade should have survived; also that some of the pictures he had painted in South Africa should allegedly have been lost overboard on his way home, and that no less than seven subjects that were included in the 1937 Whitechapel exhibition of his work have since disappeared. The paintings and drawings reproduced in this book are not, therefore, a selection chosen to show the best he could do: they are virtually all we have. If the missing works were equally good, and there is no reason to suppose they were not, then Rosenberg's standard of accomplishment as an artist was extremely high. As the late Maurice de Sausmarez has said, Rosenberg's works of the 1914-15 period 'have a quality that is intensely personal and suggests the probable direction of a later development. This quality is not easy to characterize, but it includes a simplification that moves towards compression of experience rather than towards the schematic, a design which is not arbitrarily imposed as in some of Stanley Spencer's work, but is distilled and inseparable from the content. The symbol always retains the sensuousness of the original experience and he mistrusts an art that uses 'symbols of symbols'. It is not through literary association that this work aims at evoking a response, but through purely pictorial forms, an essentially visual experience. By the time he produced these works he had clearly realised that 'an idea in painting is only one because it cannot be put into words', and that 'mere representation is unreal, is fragmentary. The bone taken from Adam remains a bone'. That this quality is more evident from his portraits and self-portraits than his landscapes is not surprising; like all young artists he was much given to painting himself and his family, if

xxiii

only because they were always there, and though we know from Leftwich's diary that he would take paints and a canvas out on their expeditions to Victoria Park or Epping Forest, he had far less opportunity of achieving finished works than he had at the Slade, or when he could borrow Amschwitz's studio.

On his return from South Africa in the Spring of 1915 Rosenberg was not only still engrossed with his play *Moses*, but in the preparation of his second small collection of privately printed poems *Youth*. He appears to have achieved relatively little in the way of pictures, apart from the sensitive drawing of his Father (Monochrome Plate 14 (b)), the well-known chalk drawing 'The First Meeting of Adam and Eve', both now in the Carlisle Art Gallery, and the splendid portrait in oils of Sonia Rodker (Colour Plate XV), probably his best surviving work. But neither the poems nor the pictures brought him enough money on which to keep himself, and as he refused to be a burden on his family, and his attempts to 'learn an honest trade' proved abortive, he decided to enlist. At the end of October 1915 he went to Whitehall and joined up, being posted immediately to Bury St. Edmunds, where, because he was such a very small, slight man, he was drafted into the so-called 'Bantam' battalion of the Suffolk Regiment. Thereafter he was increasingly deprived both of the opportunity and the wherewithal to paint, and once he had crossed to France at the beginning of June 1916, they ceased altogether. Rough pencil sketches, on the backs of envelopes or as part of a letter, some of which are reproduced in this volume, were all he could achieve. Understandably, he turned his attention almost exclusively to poetry, and by July was writing to Sydney Schiff 'I am convinced I am more deep and true as a poet than painter'.

Rosenberg did not enlist for patriotic reasons. He hated war, and had no wish to be a combatant. Killing people was as abhorrent to his natural instincts as it was to the faith in which he had been brought up. He enlisted purely in order to help his family, having been told that half his pay could be paid to his Mother as a 'separation allowance'.

But the radical change in his whole way of life that being in the Army entailed had a correspondingly profound effect on his character, and ultimately of course on his poetry. From the end of 1915 onward his poems increasingly reflect his changed circumstances and surroundings, and if some of them—like 'Marching—as seen from the left file' or 'The Troopship'—are about the Army rather than specifically about war, they were accurately designated 'Poems from Camp and Trench' by Gordon Bottomley in his 1922 selection. This was the period leading up to the great poems of 1916-17, half-a-dozen of which—including 'Break of Day in the Trenches', 'Returning,

Isaac Rosenberg his outer semblance? I have gone back to the trenches and send you this souvenir. Above is my new address. The line above the helmet is the Germans' front line, 100 yards away.

we Hear the Larks', and the superlative 'Dead Man's Dump'—
have been widely anthologised and form the basis on which,
for most people, Rosenberg's reputation as a poet rests.
Acclaimed by poets as far back as the twenties and the thirties
(Bottomley, Binyon, Sitwell, Sassoon, Muir) and by critics from
that day to this (Leavis, Harding, Isaacs, Silkin, Silk and
Hobsbaum) they are in no need of praise from me.

There are, in fact, only two or three things that I would like
to say about them. The first is that, splendid and deservedly
famous though they are, I do not think they should be allowed
to detract from the merits of the very large number of other
memorable poems which Rosenberg wrote, and which I hope
this book will make more familiar to readers generally.

Secondly, I do not think any useful purpose is served by making detailed comparisons between the war poems of Owen and Rosenberg. The differences are so great, not only because of differences in their circumstances (Owen was an officer, Rosenberg a private) though these to some extent conditioned the material on which they worked, but in the whole tone and idiom of their poems. So that what they had in common seems to me far less significant, in terms of poetry, than what distinguishes them. Like Owen, Rosenberg saw very clearly the horrific nature of the war in which they were both caught up, and the extent of the sacrifice that was to be incurred. But the bitter indignation, the *saeva indignatio* that, chastened and restrained by pity, is a dominant characteristic of Owen's war poems, has no place in Rosenberg's. In some extraordinary way, he managed to detach himself emotionally from the terrible things that were going on all round him, to expose himself to them and to record them minutely but objectively, and then to transmute them into poetry of the highest imaginative quality, set in a much broader context than his own personal plight. Thus it is that solicitude, rather than Owen's compassion, is the emotion they so movingly convey, as in these lines from 'Girl to Soldier on Leave':

> Pallid days arid and wan
> Tied your soul fast.
> Babel cities' smoky tops
> Pressed upon your growth
>
> Weary gyves. What were you,
> But a word in the brain's ways,
> Or the sleep of Circe's swine?
> One gyve holds you yet.
>
> It held you hiddenly on the Somme
> Tied from my heart at home.
> O must it loosen now? I wish
> You were bound with the old old gyves.
>
> Love! you love me—your eyes
> Have looked through death at mine.
> You have tempted a grave too much.
> I let you—I repine.

And what of the man himself? What was he like, the creator of these remarkable poems and verse dramas? I have referred in my Acknowledgments to the three biographies of Rosenberg that appeared in 1975; here I would only like to add the recommendation that anybody who wants to know the truth about Isaac Rosenberg's character should sit down and read his Letters straight through from beginning to end. They will find it a rewarding and ennobling experience. For Rosenberg was as incapable of duplicity as he was of meanness or malice, and his steadfastness and integrity shine through these letters with a brightness that increases as the years pass. They were features of his character that neither the rigours of life in the ranks (which were hurtful enough for a diminutive recruit, and a Jew to boot) nor the ardours and endurances of the trenches, could qualify or dim. Indeed, what one notices with growing admiration is the manner in which the hardships and dangers of life at the Front served only to heighten the intensity of his interest in poetry, other people's as well as his own, and his concern for the welfare of his friends. What has happened to Rodker, he asks; where is Bomberg? How dreadful that Bottomley should be ill, and does Marsh like his new job? His own miseries and misfortunes are retailed graphically but without a trace of self-pity. Through it all he retained, miraculously, not only his sense of humour but an unquenchable optimism. Writing to Marsh at the end of April 1917 about 'his mistress, the flighty Muse', he says that though she has absconded with luckier rivals 'surely I shall hunt her and chase her somewhere into the Summer and sweeter times'. And a few months later he writes to Bottomley, 'I live in an immense trust that things will turn out well'.

That trust, alas, was to prove ill-founded. On March 28th, 1918, he wrote once more to Marsh:

'I think I wrote you I was about to go up the line again after our little rest. We are now in the trenches again and though I feel very sleepy, I just have a chance to answer your letter so I will while I may. Its really my being lucky enough to bag an inch of candle that incites me to this pitch of punctual epistolary. I must measure my letter by the light. . . .'

When that letter was posted, on April 2nd, Rosenberg was already dead.

ACKNOWLEDGMENTS

MY first and deepest debt of gratitude is to the immediate past and present members of Rosenberg's family. I am thinking in particular of his brother David Burton, his sisters the late Annie Wynick and the late Rachel Lyons, his nephews Bernard Wynick and Isaac Horvitch, and his niece Betty Silver. Of them all, his sister Annie did more than anyone to preserve Isaac's manuscripts, paintings and drawings, and it is largely thanks to her unshakeable belief in his talents that the contents of the present volume are as representative as they are. But it would not have been possible to assemble, organise, and where possible date them without the active co-operation of other members of the family, and especially of Isaac Horvitch. I am greatly indebted to them all.

Anybody who works on Isaac Rosenberg's papers is bound to find themselves almost equally indebted to the editors of the 1937 *Collected Works*: Professor D. W. Harding and the late Gordon Bottomley. They were the pioneers in the difficult and exacting task of deciphering Rosenberg's numerous holographs, so many of which are confused or fragmentary and some almost illegible. I am particularly in their debt for their masterly reconstruction of the genesis and development of Rosenberg's last, unfinished work *The Unicorn*, which I have adopted virtually verbatim.

Others to whom I am grateful for help in tracking down, or for permission to print, unpublished Rosenberg materials are Mr. Roger Lancelyn Green (Gordon Bottomley's Literary Executor), Miss Livia Gollancz, Miss Jean Liddiard, Jon Silkin, Professor Joseph Cohen, the Henry W. and Albert A. Berg Collection of the New York Public Library (Astor, Lenox and Tilden Foundations), the Manuscript Department of the British Library, Dr. B. Winehouse and Dr. Richard Andersen. The last named amplified his assistance by allowing me to see his doctoral thesis on Rosenberg, and by kindly agreeing to read the present volume in proof. Last but very far from least, I must thank Joseph Leftwich for his constant willingness to answer every question put to him. Once a member of that phenomenal group of creative artists that sprang up in Whitechapel in the decade before the First World War, and today the doyen of Anglo-Jewish cultural leaders, his intimate knowledge of Rosenberg in his formative years has been invaluable to me;

while his 1911 Diary is an essential source-book for anybody working in this field.

This new edition of the *Collected Works* contains reproductions of more than fifty of Rosenberg's paintings and drawings, many of them never previously published in book form or reproduced in colour. This has only been made possible through the co-operation of their owners in allowing their possessions to be photographed. To all of them my warmest thanks are due. Acknowledgment of their courtesy is made alongside each individual picture, but I am especially grateful to Rosenberg's relatives overseas: Mrs. Edna Lee-Warden, Mrs. Ruth Garson, Mrs. Tilly Garson, Mrs. Kellman and Mrs. Sheila Lynn for the colour transparencies and documentation with which they provided me through Isaac Horvitch, and to the following individuals and institutions for their help: Miss Frances Carey, Miss Joan Rodker, Mr. and Mrs. S. Winsten, the Imperial War Museum, the National Portrait Gallery, the Tate Gallery, the Carlisle Art Gallery, and the Jewish Museum, Cape Town.

Finally I must acknowledge my obligation to the authors of the three biographies of Isaac Rosenberg which appeared in 1975: Joseph Cohen's *Journey to the Trenches*, Jean Liddiard's *Isaac Rosenberg: The Half Used Life*, and Dr. Jean Wilson's *Isaac Rosenberg, Poet and Painter*. Their combined extensive researches into Rosenberg's life story have been of great help to me in documenting and dating certain poems, letters and pictures, as well as absolving me from the need to include detailed bio-graphical information in my Introduction. Instead, I have provided a separate chronological summary of the principal events in Rosenberg's life, which I hope will enable readers who are unfamiliar with the story to find their way about this book without difficulty. I owe a similar debt to the compilers of the 1959 Leeds University Exhibition catalogue (Jon Silkin and Maurice de Sausmarez), and to those responsible for the cata-logue of the 1975 National Book League Exhibition (Clifford Simmons and Jean Liddiard).

I also wish to express my thanks to the Leverhulme Trust Fund for contributing towards my expenses during the final stages of my research.

I. M. P.

Abbreviations used in the following pages

ND: *Night and Day*, London, Privately printed, 1912. A copy kindly made available to me by Simon Nowell-Smith.

PIR: *Poems by Isaac Rosenberg*, selected and edited by Gordon Bottomley, with an Introductory Memoir by Laurence Binyon. London, William Heinemann, 1922.

CW: *The Collected Works of Isaac Rosenberg*, edited by Gordon Bottomley and Denys Harding, with a Foreword by Siegfried Sassoon. London, Chatto and Windus, 1937.

LBN: Rosenberg's large black notebook, in which many of the poems were copied out, mainly in ink.

SBN: Rosenberg's small black alphabetised notebook, in which, in addition to names and addresses, he made notes for poems and prose pieces, mainly in pencil.

MS: Holograph versions of the texts.

TS: Typescript versions of the texts.

BL: Versions of plays and poems in the Department of Manuscripts, the British Library.

N.B. Where more than one version of the same text exists in any of the above three forms, they are numbered BL1, BL2, etc. in their presumed order of composition and correction.

Cohen: *Journey to the Trenches*, the Life of Isaac Rosenberg 1890-1918, by Joseph Cohen. London, Robson Books, 1975. New York, Basic Books, 1975.

Liddiard: *Isaac Rosenberg: The Half Used Life*, by Jean Liddiard. London, Victor Gollancz, 1975.

Wilson: *Isaac Rosenberg Poet and Painter*, a biography by Jean Moorcroft Wilson. London, Cecil Woolf, 1975.

G.P.: *Georgian Poetry* (5 vols.), edited by Edward Marsh, The Poetry Bookshop, London, 1912-1922.

EDITOR'S NOTE

THOSE who are lucky enough to possess a copy of the 1937 *Collected Works*, now an extremely rare book, will know that it was arranged according to a plan which even at the time of its publication was described by Herbert Read as 'exasperating' and in the intervening years has come to seem increasingly unsatisfactory. For the editors, Gordon Bottomley and Denys Harding, printed Rosenberg's published poetry in chronological order, and his unpublished poetry (including fragments) in *inverse* chronological order. The same eccentric plan was followed with his prose works, while his letters to Edward Marsh were segregated from the rest of his surviving correspondence, both being given in chronological order, so that the reader was obliged to traverse the same ground twice.

I cannot now recall, after more than forty years, how or why this particular scheme was devised, although as the person who saw the book through the press I must take my share of responsibility for it. Nevertheless it undeniably reduced to a minimum the opportunities for tracing Rosenberg's development as a poet, and of relating his prose works and his letters to the facts and events of his life. I make no apology, therefore, for having abandoned it in favour of a straight chronological order (in so far as this can be determined) throughout.

In another, perhaps even more important direction, I have departed from Bottomley and Harding's editorial principles. They thought it right, in the case of letters which exist in their original form, to print them as it were *facsimile*, without emendation, on the grounds that 'irregularities in these are not such a distraction as they would have been in the poems and therefore less justify editorial intervention'. Virtually no attempt was therefore made to regularise them in grammar, punctuation or spelling, apart from changing Rosenberg's frequent use of an ampersand to 'and', and of 'thro' to 'through', both of which emendations I have followed.

With the poems, on the other hand, they considered it desirable that Rosenberg's inconsistent punctuation, sometimes questionable grammar, and occasional idiosyncratic spelling should be brought into line with conventional usage. Bottomley, in the 1922 *Poems of Isaac Rosenberg*, went a good deal further, and did not hesitate to change words which he thought archaic or obscure, to import others that appear nowhere in the sources, and generally to 'improve' certain poems in the matter of both sense and rhythm. Working as he did within a few years of Rosenberg's death, and in the full knowledge that Rosenberg thought the world of him as a poet, he can be forgiven for these well-meaning if misguided interventions. Many, though by no means all of them, were rescinded in the 1937 *Collected Works*, no doubt under the restraining hand of Professor Harding.

In this edition I have adopted exactly the opposite principles. On the ground that Rosenberg is now widely accepted as a major poet of the First World War, I have endeavoured to stick as closely as possible to the texts of the poems as he left them, only departing from them when there was some compelling reason for doing so, and always indicating the fact by square brackets or a footnote. With the Letters, on the other hand, I have thought it right to make them as easy as possible to read and understand. This has involved a certain (though very limited) amount of 'editing', in the matter of punctuation, spelling, and the occasional grammatical solecism. Rosenberg's formal education was strictly limited, but he was very far indeed from being illiterate, as anybody who reads the Letters will quickly discover. Indeed for somebody brought up in his circumstances he was astonishingly well read. So I have opted for clarity and consistency rather than textual exactitude, and have supplied apostrophes (which Rosenberg was apt to disregard) in order to avoid confusion between 'cant' and 'can't', 'Ill' and 'I'll', 'Id' and 'I'd' etc, and some missing commas and full stops where otherwise a sentence would be ambiguous or obscure. And when he occasionally spelt 'imagination' with two 'ms', or 'marvellous' with only one 'l', I have silently corrected the mistake. But I have kept 'Brown's Religion de Medici', 'Judas Macabeas', and 'Tolstoylians' as typical idiosyncrasies. I cannot believe that such superficial glosses to the Letters detract at all from their immediacy of impact, the individuality of their 'tone', or the moving culmination to which they so inexorably proceed. And it is surely a disservice to Rosenberg to perpetuate minor orthographical irregularities in letters that were nearly always hurriedly composed, often under difficulties of one kind or another, and for the last two years of his life were mostly written from the dugouts and trenches of Flanders.

POEMS
AND FRAGMENTS OF POEMS

ODE TO DAVID'S HARP

Awake! ye joyful strains, awake!
In silence sleep no more;
Disperse the gloom that ever lies
O'er Judah's barren shore.
5 Where are the hands that strung thee
With tender touch and true?
Those hands are silenced too.

The harp that faster caused to beat
The heart that throbbed for war,
10 The harp that melancholy calmed,
Lies mute on Judah's shore.
One chord awake—one strain prolong
To wake the zeal in Israel's breast;
Oh sacred lyre, once more, how long?
15 'Tis vain, alas! in silence rest.

Many a minstrel fame's elated
Envies thee thy harp of fame,
Harp of David—monarch minstrel,
Bravely—bravely, keep thy name.
20 Ay! every ear that listen'd,
Was charmed—was thrilled—was bound.
Every eye with moisture glisten'd
Thrilling to the harp's sweet sound.

Hark! the harp is pouring
25 Notes of burning fire,
And each soul o'erpowering,
Melts the rousing ire.
Fiercer—shriller—wilder far
Than the iron notes of war,
30 Accents sweet and echoes sweeter,
Minstrel—minstrel, steeds fly fleeter
Spurred on by thy magic strains.

There is an ink holograph in BL that differs markedly from the above version, which follows CW apart from minor changes in punctuation. The principal variants are:

l. 5: *that strung thy chords*
ll. 8-11: *Those chords whose tender strains awoke*
In hearts that throbbed for war,
The martial stir when glory calls
Lies mute on Judah's shore.

l. 17: *thy harp and fame.*
l. 29: *brazen notes*

Tell me not the harp lies sleeping,
Set not thus my heart aweeping,
35 In the muse's fairy dwelling
There thy magic notes are swelling.
But for list'ning mortals' ear
Vainly wait, ye will not hear.
So clearly sweet—so plaintive sad
40 More tender tone no harper had.
O! when again shall Israel see
A harp so toned with melody?

1905

BL adds 4 more lines to this stanza, which read:

> *Breasts are heaving, fate is weaving*
> *Other bonds than slavery's chains*
> *For her chosen's blood are frozen*
> *Icy fear in all their veins.*

For the last 4 lines of the poem, BL has:

> *The chords are rent—for years have bent*
> *Its living strings asunder.*
> *But harp and name—shall life proclaim*
> *In living voice of thunder.*

ZION

She stood—a hill-ensceptred Queen,
The glory streaming from her;
While Heaven flashed her rays between,
And shed eternal summer.

5 The gates of morning opened wide
On sunny dome and steeple.
Noon gleamed upon the mountain-side
Throng'd with a happy people.

And twilight's drowsy, half closed eyes
10 Beheld that virgin splendour
Whose orbs were as her darkening skies,
And as her spirit, tender.

Girt with that strength, first born of right,
Held fast by deeds of honour,
15 Her robe she wove with rays more bright
Than Heaven could rain upon her.

l: 13: CW has *first-born* but there is no hyphen in the TS subscribed by R
'16 years old when I wrote this', and as it alters the sense in a limiting
way I have omitted it.

Where is that light—that citadel?
That robe with woof of glory?
She lost her virtue and she fell,
20   And only left her story.

1906

DAWN BEHIND NIGHT

Lips! bold, frenzied utterance, shape to the thoughts that are
    prompted by hate
Of the red streaming burden of wrong we have borne and still
    bear;
That wealth with its soul-crushing scourges placed into its hands
    by fate,
Hath made the cement of its towers, grim-girdled by our despair.

5 Should it die in the death that they make, in the silence that
    follows the sob;
In the voiceless depth of the waters that closes upon our grief;
Who shall know of the bleakness assigned us for the fruits that
    we reap and they rob?
To pour out the strong wine of pity, outstretch the kind hand in
    relief.

In the golden glare of the morning, in the solemn serene of the
    night,
10 We look on each other's faces, and we turn to our prison bar;
In pitiless travail of toil and outside the precious light,
What wonder we know not our manhood in the curse of the
    things that are?

In the life or the death they dole us from the rags and the bones
    of their store,
In the blood they feed but to drink of, in the pity they feign in
    their pride,
15 Lies the glimpse of a heaven behind it, for the ship hath left the
    shore,
That will find us and free us and take us where its portals are
    opened wide.

1909

A BALLAD OF WHITECHAPEL

God's mercy shines,
And our full hearts must make record of this,
For grief that burst from out its dark confines
Into strange sunlit bliss.

5 I stood where glowed
The merry glare of golden whirring lights
Above the monstrous mass that seethed and flowed
Through one of London's nights.

I watched the gleams
10 Of jaggèd warm lights on shrunk faces pale.
I heard mad laughter as one hears in dreams,
Or Hell's harsh lurid tale.

The traffic rolled,
A gliding chaos populous of din.
15 A steaming wail at doom the Lord had scrawled
For perilous loads of sin.

And my soul thought,
'What fearful land have my steps wandered to?
God's love is everywhere, but here is naught
20 Save love His anger slew.'

And as I stood
Lost in promiscuous bewilderment,
Which to my mazèd soul was wonder-food,
A girl in garments rent

25 Peered 'neath lids shamed,
And spoke to me and murmured to my blood.
My soul stopped dead, and all my horror flamed
At her forgot of God.

Her hungered eyes,
30 Craving and yet so sadly spiritual,
Shone like the unsmirched corner of a jewel
Where else foul blemish lies.

I walked with her
Because my heart thought, 'Here the soul is clean,
35 The fragrance of the frankincense and myrrh
Is lost in odours mean.'

5

She told me how
The shadow of black death had newly come
And touched her father, mother, even now
40 Grim-hovering in her home,

Where fevered lay
Her wasting brother in a cold bleak room,
Which theirs would be no longer than a day,
And then—the streets and doom.

45 Lord! Lord! dear Lord!
I knew that life was bitter, but my soul
Recoiled, as anguish-smitten by sharp sword,
Grieving such body's dole.

Then grief gave place
50 To a strange pulsing rapture as she spoke,
For I could catch the glimpses of God's grace,
And desire awoke.

To take this trust,
And warm and gladden it with love's new fires,
55 Burning the past to ashes and to dust
Through purified desires.

We walked our way.
One way hewn for us from the birth of Time.
For we had wandered into Love's strange clime
60 Through ways sin waits to slay.

Love's euphony,
In Love's own temple that is our glad hearts,
Makes now long music wild deliciously,
Now Grief hath used his darts.

65 Love infinite,
Chastened by sorrow, hallowed by pure flame—
Not all the surging world can compass it,
Love—love—O! tremulous name.

God's mercy shines.
70 And my full heart hath made record of this.
Of grief that burst from out its dark confines
Into strange sunlit bliss.

1910

6

A BALLAD OF TIME, LIFE AND MEMORY

Hold wide the door and watch who passes here
From dawn through day to dawn,
Bravely as though their journey but begun,
Through change unchangèd still.
5 She, wild eyed, runs and laughs, or walks and weeps;
But him, swift footed, never can outrun,
Nor creep and he before.
And all she has and all she knows is his;
But not all his for her.

10 He gives her of the spices and the myrrh
And wonderful strange fruits,
He gives her more of tears, and girds her round
With yearning bitterness,
With fears that kill the hopes they feed upon,
15 With hopes that smile at fears and smile on her,
Till fears again prevail.
And as she goes the roses fall and die;
And as she goes she weeps.

But lo! behind, what dim processional?
20 What maiden sings and sighs?
And holds an urn, and as the roses fall,
And the wine pours and spills,
She gathers in her lap and breathes on them;
And in the urn the spilled wine glows again,
25 Lit by her eyes divine.
And all the roses at her touch revive,
And blush and bloom again.

And by her side, whose name is Memory,
The ghosts of all the hours,
30 Some smiling as they smiled within the sun,
Some, stained and wan with tears.
To those she gives the roses as they fall,
And bids them tune the praises of their prime.
To these their tears and dust.
35 And those are happy loves and wreathèd joys.
And these are sorrows pale.

Even as she sings so Time himself makes pause,
Even Time, Death's conqueror,
And Life's reverted face grows tenderer,
40 While the soul dreams and yearns,
Watching the risen faces of the hours,

And shrivelled Autumn change her face to June's,
And dead wine live again,
And dust discrowned know Life it knew before
45 Touched with a softened light.

There is no leaf upon the naked woods,
No bird upon the boughs,
And Time leads Life through many waste places,
And dreams and shapes of death.
50 Yet is the voice of Summer not quite dumb,
Although her lips be stilled and silenter.
For Memory bids her rise
To sing within the palace of the soul,
And Life and Time are still.

1910

An earlier version of the first half of verse 2 reads:

> *He gives her of the roses in his hand,*
> *He gives her of the wine,*
> *He gives her more of tears, and girds her round*
> *With shades of hopes and fears,*

In the same holograph, line 35 above had *heart crowned joys* and line 42 was changed from *And Autumned petals dying into June's*. The last line had *are dumb* for *are still*.

DEATH

Death waits for me—ah! who shall kiss me first?
No lips of love glow red from out the gloom
That life spreads darkly like a living tomb
Around my path. Death's gift is best not worst.
For even the honey on life's lips is curst.
And the worm cankers in the ripest bloom.
Yea, from Birth's gates to Death's, Life's travailed womb
Is big with Rest, for Death, her life, athirst.

Death waits, and when she has kissed life's warm lips
With her pale mouth, and made him one with her;
Held to him Lethe's wine whereof he sips;
And stilled Time's wings, earth shadowing sleepless whir;
Outside of strife, beyond the world's blood drips,
Shadowed by peace, Rest dwells and makes no stir.

1910

THE DEAD PAST

Ah! will I meet you ever—you who have gone from me,
You, the I that was then and a moment hath changed into you.
So many moments have passed and changed the I into we,
So many many times but alas I remember so few.

5 I know you are dead, long perished, the boy that babbled and
    played
With the toys like the wind with the flowers and the clouds play
    with the moon,
I know you are dead long ago and hid in the grove I made
Of regrets that were soon forgotten, as snow is forgotten by
    June.

You too are dead, the shining face that laughed and wept
    without thought
10 Uttered the words of the heart, wept or leapt as was right.
O, were you taken to heaven, by God in a whirlwind caught,
I do not know yours was best, you not conscious of your delight.

O my life's dead Springtime—why will you haunt me like
    ghosts,
You little buds that have died—and blossom in memory,
15 Will I meet you in some dead land and see your face in hosts,
Saying 'The past is the future and you and the future are we'?

An additional, unfinished verse, which R cancelled, read:

I in this workaday world, little joy do I know—
Books, pictures and sometimes friends, a girl's sweet sight and voice
Many sorrows have I, but each pleasure or pain is a throe
I can witness my own delight . . .

1911

'IN THE HEART OF THE FOREST'[1]

In the heart of the forest,
The shuddering forest,
The moaning and sobbing
Sad shuddering forest—
5 The dark and the dismal
Persistent sad sobbing
Throughout the weird forest.

---

[1] This was meant for an album. [Author's note on MS.]

9

Ah! God! they are voices—
Dim ghosts of the forest
10 Unrestfully sobbing
Through wistful pale voices,
Whose breath is the wind and whose lips the sad trees;

Whose yearning great eyes
Death haunted for ever
15 Look from the dark waters,
And pale spirit faces
Wrought from the white lilies.

The above text follows CW verbatim. A version in the possession of Mrs Frances Kletz, daughter of J. H. Amschewitz, has *forests* in line 9, and some variations in punctuation that also occur in another holograph, but are more confusing than helpful.

MY DAYS

My days are but the tombs of buried hours;
Which tombs are hidden in the pilèd years;
But from the mounds there springeth up such flowers
Whose beauty well repays its cost of tears.
Time, like a sexton, pileth mould on mould,
Minutes on minutes till the tombs are high;
But from the dust there falleth grains of gold,
And the dead corpse leaves what will never die.
It may be but a thought, the nursling seed
Of many thoughts, of many a high desire;
Some little act that stirs a noble deed,
Like breath rekindling a smouldering fire.
They only live who have not lived in vain,
For in their works their life returns again.

1911

The above follows CW and an early TS. Bottomley, in PIR, printed *spring up many flowers* in line 3 and *there fall some grains* in line 7, I suspect because he disliked the archaic usage of *springeth* and *falleth*. But there is no evidence that R intended this change.

'THE WORLD RUMBLES BY ME'

The world rumbles by me—can I heed?
The rose it is crimson—and I bleed.

The rose of my heart glows deep afar;
And I grope in the darkness 'twixt star and star.

5 Only in night grows the flower of peace,
  Spreading its odours of rest and ease.

It dies in the day like light in the night.
It revives like tears in the eyes of delight.

  For the youth at my heart beats wild and loud;
10 And raves in my ear of a girl and a shroud.

Of a golden girl with the soul in her eyes,
To teach me love and to make me wise.

With the fire on her lips and the wine in her hands,
To bind me strong in her silken bands.

15 For time and fate are striding to meet
  One unseen with soundless feet.

The world rustles by me—let me heed.
Clutched in its madness till I bleed.

  For the rose of my heart glows deep afar.
20 If I stretch my hand, I may clasp a star.

1911

TO MR. AND MRS. LÖWY, ON THEIR SILVER WEDDING

'Ye hearken as ye list', saith Time to all.
'Ye hear me as I pass or do not hear.
I gather all the fruits of all the year,
I hoard them when the barren seasons call.
Then, though I flew with Spring, with them I crawl.
To soothe their vacant eyes and feet of fear
I bid the Spring's sweet ghost rise from her bier,
And tender Memory come with light footfall.

'Then, when the seasons hang their heads in shame
And grief, I bring my store of hoarded fruit;
To warm the hands of age, youth's rosy flame;
And to old love the young love at the root,
Hallowed by me to silver sweet acclaim—
Hush—lo! the bride and bridegroom—hush!—be mute.'

1911

LINES WRITTEN IN AN ALBUM
TO J.L.[1]

The birds that sang in summer
Were silent till the spring;
For hidden were the flowers,
The flowers to whom they sing.
5 December's jewelled bosom—
Closed mouth—hill-hidden vale—
Held seed full soon to blossom;
Held song that would not fail.

I, silent all the winter,
10 No flower for me to praise,
For this rich wealth of roses
My song shall I not raise?
The lilies and the roses,
White hands and damask cheeks;
15 The eyes where love reposes
And laughs before he speaks.

Could this make music to thee,
The music of sweet thought;
Thy laughing eyes might hearken
20 To sounds sweet visions wrought,
Till the deep roses tingle
The cheeks they nestle in,
While music still would mingle,
And pleasure still begin.

25 Thus, hidden in these pages
My thoughts shall silent lie
Till gentle fingers find them,
When idly bent to pry.
I see them fondly linger,
30 And quicken with their breath
The music of the singer,
Whose silence was its death.

1911

[1] Joseph Leftwich

'GOD LOOKED CLEAR AT ME THROUGH HER EYES'

God looked clear at me through her eyes,
And when her fresh and sweet lips spake,
Through dawn-flushed gates of Paradise
Such silvern birds did wing and shake

5 God's fervent music on my soul,
And with their jewelled quivering feet
Did rend apart the quiet stole
That shades from girl-fanned pulsing heat.

Upon a gold branch in my breast
10 They made their nest, while sweet and warm
Hung wav'ring thoughts like rose-leaves drest;
My soul the sky to keep from harm.

In the heart's woods mysterious
Where feelings lie remote and far,
15 They fly with touch imperious,
And loose emotion's hidden bar.

And to dark pools of brooding care,
And blinding wastes of loneliness,
They gleam a Paradisal air,
20 And warm with a divine caress.

1912

BIRTHDAY SONG

To thy cradle at thy birth
Did not all the fairies come,
Genie of heaven and earth
While ogres stood afar and dumb,

5 And thy cradle to embower
Spun a roof of sun and flowers,
Gave thee for thy lifelong dower
Beauteous gifts and beauteous hours?

Time stood by, a gardener mild,
10 Watched the bud unfold to rose,
June's delight December's child,
Red rose of December snows.

Twenty years and one year more
Time here layeth at thy feet;
15 But thy friends bring twenty score
Wishes that the rest be sweet.

13

THE PRESENT

Time, leveller, chaining fate itself to thee—
Hope frets her eager pettings on thy sand,
Wild waves that strive to overreach command
Of nature, much in sight. Eternity
Is but thyself made shoreless. Toward thy sea
The streams-to-be flow from the shadowland
Of rootless flowers no earthly breeze has fanned,
Weave with the past thy restless apathy.

Thou art the link 'twixt after and before,
The one sole truth; the final ultimate
Endeavour of the ages. The loud roar
Of life around me is thy voice to fate
And Time—who looking on thee has grown hoar
While thou art yet—and freedom is so late.

NOCTURNE

Day, like a flower of gold fades on its crimson bed;
For the many chambered night unbars to shut its sweetness up;
From earth and heaven fast drawn together a heavy stillness is shed,
And our hearts drink the shadowy splendour from a brimming cup.

For the indrawn breath of beauty thrills the holy caves of night;
Shimmering winds of heaven fall gently and mysterious hands
   caress
Our wan brows with cooling rapture of the delicate starlight
Dropping from the night's blue walls in endless veils of loveliness.

A TS in the possession of Isaac Horvitch, R's nephew, gives *has come* for
unbars in line 2, and *fills* for *thrills* in line 5. But another TS shows the
former words changed to the latter in R's hand, and as there is an ink
fair-copy of the poem in LBN, also giving *unbars* and *thrills*, one is forced
to conclude, however reluctantly, that this is the later rendering.

THE KEY OF THE GATES OF HEAVEN

A word leapt sharp from my tongue,
Could a golden key do more
Than open the golden door
For the rush of the golden song?
5 She spoke, and the spell of her speech—
The chain of the heart linked song—
Was on me swift and strong,
And Heaven was in my reach.

A word was the key thereof;
10 And my thought was the hand that turned.
And words that throbbed and burned,
Sweet birds from the shine of love,
Flew clear 'tween the rosebud gate
That was parted beneath and above,
15 And a chain of music wove
More strong than the hand of fate.

A TS subscribed by Bottomley 'corrected by Miss Seaton's MS original'
has a full stop at the end of line 4, in place of the question mark that is
obviously more appropriate.

THE CAGE

Air knows as you know that I sing in my cage of earth,
And my mouth dry with longing for your winsome mouth of mirth,
That passes ever my prison bars which will not fall apart,
Wearied unweariedly so long with the fretful music of my heart.

If you were a rose, and I, the wandering invisible air
To feed your scent and live, glad though you knew me not there,
Or the green of your stem that your proud petals could never meet,
I yet would feel the caresses of your shadow's ruby feet.

O splendour of radiant flesh, O your heavy hair uncurled,
Binding all that my hopes have fashioned to crown me King of the
    world,
I sing to life to befriend me; she sends me your mouth of mirth,
And you only laugh as you pass me, and I weep in my cage of
    earth.

1912

BACCHANAL

If life would come to me
As she has never come,
The music of the spring,
The fullness of its prime;
5 With roses in her hair,
With laughter on her lips,
Ah! life!—we'd dance a tune.
Ah! life! we'd live—we'd live.

If life would come to me
10 With roses in her lap,
With wine between her hands,
And a fire upon her lips;
We would burn Time in that fire,
We would drown care in that wine,
15 And with music and with laughter
We would scare black death away.

If life would only come
As I would have her come,
With sweet breasts for my bed,
20 And my food her fiery wine;
If life would only come,
For we live not till it comes,
And it comes not till we feel
Its fire through all our veins.

1912

The TS which Bottomley subscribed 'Modifications in accordance with Miss Seaton's MS.' differs from the above text (apart from the spelling of Bachanal with one C) only in a few changes of punctuation that were clearly desirable.

'NOW THE SPIRIT'S SONG HAS WITHERED'

Now the spirit's song has withered
As a song of last year's June
That has made the air its tomb.
Shall we ever find it after
Sighing in some summer tune
That is sealèd now in gloom,
Safe for light and laughter?

l. 5: R originally wrote *in some ghostly tune.*

Now the sky blooms full of colour,
Houses glow and windows shine
Glittering with impatient wings.
Where they go to may I follow
Since mine eyes have made them mine?
Shall I ever find these things
Hid in hill or hollow?

1911-12

'SO INNOCENT YOU SPREAD YOUR NET'

So innocent you spread your net,
I knew not I was caught in it,
Till when I vainly tried to rise
I read the reason in your eyes.

Your silken smiles had bound me fast;
Your nestling speech had tangled more;
But when I started up at last
I shook the fetters to the floor.

THE NUN

So thy soul's meekness shrinks,
Too loth to show her face—
Why should she shun the world?
It is a holy place.

Concealèd to itself
If the flower kept its scent,
Of itself amorous,
Less rich its ornament.

Use—utmost in each kind—
Is beauty, truth in one,
While soul rays light to soul
In one God-linkèd sun.

'WE ARE SAD WITH A VAGUE SWEET SORROW'

We are sad with a vague sweet sorrow
Whose touch is a scent of sighs;

D

17

A flower that weeps to a flower
The old tale that beauty dies.

Our smiles are full of a longing,
For we saw the gold flash of the years.
They passed, and we know where they came from,
The deep—deep well of tears.

1912

PEACE

Where the dreamy mountains brood
Ever in their ancient mood
Would I go and dream with them
Till I graft me on their stem.

With fierce energy I aspire
To be thát the Gods desire
As the dreamy mountains are
And no God can break or mar.

Soon the world shall fade and be
One with still eternity
As the dreamy hills that lie
Silent to the passing sky.

1912

FLEET STREET

From north and south, from east and west,
Here in one shrieking vortex meet
These streams of life, made manifest
Along the shaking quivering street.
5 Its pulse and heart that throbs and glows
As if strife were its repose.

I shut my ear to such rude sounds
As reach a harsh discordant note,
Till, melting into what surrounds,
10 My soul doth with the current float,
And from the turmoil and the strife
Wakes all the melody of life.

The stony buildings blindly stare
Unconscious of the crime within,

15 While man returns his fellow's glare
 The secrets of his soul to win.
 And each man passes from his place,
 None heed. A shadow leaves such trace.

[?1912. Possibly 1906]

An earlier draft of the last verse reads:

The stony buildings blankly stare
While murder's being done within
While man returns his fellow's glare
The secrets of his soul to miss.
And each man's heart is foul with lust
Of women, or the blind gold dust.

THE GARDEN OF JOY

 In honey essenced bliss of sleep's deceit
 My sense lay drowned, and my soul's eyes saw clear,
 Unstranged to wonder, made familiar
 By instant seeing. Eden's garden sweet,
5 Shedding upon mine eyelids odorous heat
 Of the light fingered golden atmosphere
 Shaken through boughs whose whispering I could hear.
 Beneath, within the covert's cool retreat
 Of the spread boughs stood shapes who swayed the boughs,
10 And bright fruit fell, laughing to leave green house;
 While gleeful children dabbled with the sun
 Caught the strange fruit, then ran with smiles of love
 To earth, whose peoples as they ate thereof
 Soft sank into the garden, one by one.

15 They lie within the garden, outside Time.
 The ripened fulness of their soul's desire
 Glad on their tranquil faces. No fanged fire
 Of hot insatiate pleasure, no pulsed chime
 To summon to tusked orgy of earth's slime,
20 Flickers the throne of rapture's flushed empire
 That glows, mild rays of the divine attire
 Upon each face, sun of this day-spring clime.

 They seem forever wondering—listening
 Unto some tale of marvel, music told,
25 That the flowers weep in jewelled glistening
 With envy of the joy that they must hold,
 While in the dewy mirrors lady Spring
 Trims herself by their smiles, their happy mould.

1912

19

THE POET
(I)

The trouble of the universe is on his wonder travelled eyes.
Ah, vain for him the starry quest, the spirit's wistful sacrifice.
For though the glory of the heavens celestially in glimpses seen
Illumines his rapt gazing, still the senses shut him in.
No fellowship of suffering to meet his tear bewildered ways,
Alone he bears the burden of alienated days.
He is a part of paradise that all the earth has pressed between,
And when he calls unto the stars of paradise with heaven sweet
  songs
To his divided self he calls and sings the story of earth's wrongs.

Himself he has himself betrayed, and deemed the earth a path of
  heaven,
And wandered down its sunless days, and too late knew himself
  bereaven.
For swiftly sin and suffering and earth-born laughter meshed his
  ways,
And caught him in a cage of earth, but heaven can hear his dewy
  lays.

1912

MY SONGS

Deep into the great heart of things
My mood passed, as my life became
One with the mighty whisperings
That breathe the pure ineffable name.

A pulse of all the life that stirs
Through still deep shade and wavering light,
The flowing of the wash of years
From out the starry infinite.

And flowing through my soul, the skies
And all the winds and all the trees
Mixed with its stream of light, to rise
And flow out in these melodies.

l. 3: CW, following a holograph on the fly-leaf of Binyon's copy of
Night and Day, printed *vasty whisperings* but in a version that R sent to
Mrs Robert Solomon he wrote *mighty whisperings*, which seems a little
less portentous.

TO NATURE

Beneath the eternal wandering skies
O wilt thou rest awhile by me,
Immortal mother of mystery,
And breathe on my blind eyes!

Or is it that thou standest nigh,
And while I know that I am blind
I live, until thou passest by,
To leave me dead behind.

1912

DON JUAN'S SONG

The moon is in an ecstasy,
It wanes not nor can grow.
The heavens are in a mist of love,
And deepest knowledge know.
5 What things in nature seem to move
Bear love as I bear love?
And bear my pleasures so?

The moon will fade when morning comes,
The heavens will dream no more.
10 In our missed meetings are eyes hard?
What shadows fleck the door
Averted, when we part? What guard
Scents death in each vain word?
What haggard haunts the shore?

15 I bear my love as streams that bear
The sky still flow or shake.
Though deep within too far on high.
Light blossoms kiss and wake
The waters sooner than the sky.
20 And if they kiss and die!
God made them frail to break.

PIR has the first and third verses only, and, as usual, several punctuational variants from a fair-copy ink holograph.

YOU AND I

You and I have met but for an instant;
And no word the gate-lips let from out them.
But the eyes, voice audible—the soul's lips,
Stirr'd the depths of thought and feeling in me.

5 I have seen you somewhere, some sweet sometime,
Somewhere in a dim-remembered sometime.
Was it in the sleep-spun realm of dreamland?
In sweet woods, a faery flower of fancy?

If our hands touched would it bring us nearer?
10 As our souls touched, eyes' flame meeting eyes' flame.
If the lips spake would it lift the curtain
More than our mute bearing unaffected
Told the spirit's secrets eloquently?

Strange! this vast and universal riddle!
15 How perplexing! Manifold the wonder.
You and I, we meet but for an instant,
Pause or pass, reflections in a mirror.
And I see myself and wonder at it.
See myself in you, a double wonder.
20 With my thought held in a richer casket,
Clothed and girt in shape of regal beauty.
Strange! we pause! New waves of life rush blindly,
Madly on the soul's dumb silent breakers.

And a music strange is new awakened.
25 Fate the minstrel smites or holds the chord back.
Smites—new worlds undreamt of burst upon us.
All our life before was but embryo
Shaping for this birth—this living moment.

LOVE TO BE

When at that happy pause that holds sweet rest
As a hard burden, that it doth belate
And make him seem a laggard at the gate
Of long-wished night, while day rides down the west;
5 I, weighted from my toil, and sore distrest
In body and soul, the scourge of partial fate,
At such sweet pause, to silence consecrate,
Come thoughts swift changing fancy had bedrest

In colours of desire. I thought on her
10 I never yet have seen, my love to be.
   I conjured up all glorious shapes that were;
   And wondered what far clime, by what sad sea
   She roaming? And what spirits minister?
   What thoughts, and what vague shadowing of me?

15 By what far ways shall my heart reach to thine?
   We, who have never parted—never met,
   Nor done to death the joys that shall be yet,
   Nor drained the cup of love's delirious wine.
   How shall my craving spirit know for mine
20 Thine, self-same seeking? Will a wild regret
   For the lost days—the lonely suns that set,
   Be for our love a token and a sign?
   Will all the weary nights, the widowed days
   That sundered long, all point their hands at thee?
25 Yea! all the stars that have not heard thy praise
   Low murmur in thy charmèd ear of me?
   All pointing to the ending of the ways,
   All singing of the love that is to be?

l. 15: Cf. 'Day' ll. 201-214 (pp. 38-9) and 'Heart's First Word' I (p. 44)
ll. 21-22.

'LIKE SOME FAIR SUBTLE POISON'

Like some fair subtle poison is the cold white beauty you shed;
Pale flower of the garden I walk in, your scent is an amorous net
To lure my thoughts and pulses, by your useless phantom led
By misty hours and ruins with insatiate longing wet.

To lure my soul with the beauty of some enthralling sin.
To starve my body to hunger for the mystic rapture there.
O cruel; flesh and spirit your robe's soft stir sucks in,
And your cold unseeing glances, and the fantasies of your hair.

And in the shining hollow of your dream-enhaunted throat
My mournful thoughts now wander and build desire a nest,
But no tender thoughts to crown the fiery dreams that float
Around those sinuous rhythms and dim languors of your breast.

1912

TWILIGHT
(I)

A murmur of many waters, a moving maze of streams;
A doubtful voice of the silence from the ghosts of the shadows of
    dreams,
The far adieu of the day as it touches the fingers of night,
Wakes all to the eye and ear but seem wings spread for the soul for
    flight.

Can we look behind or before us, can we look on the dreams that
    are done?
The lights gleam dim in the distance, the distance is dimmer when
    won.
Soon that shall fade dimmer behind us, and when the night before
    us is here,
Ah! who of us shall wait for the dawn, while the shadows of night
    disappear?

AS WE LOOK

As they have sung to me,
So shall they sing to you?
One song have they.
Nay, when the old be new,
5 Nay, when the blind shall see,
Then, when the night is day,
Shall this thing be.

For this is truth, and still
Ever throughout be truth
10 While the world sings.
Gladly it sings to youth;
Sadly to age and ill.
To love sweet whisperings
Its songs fulfil.

15 One song the roses sing;
One song the chirping birds.
But whoso hears,
He makes within the words
To his soul murmuring.
20 High hopes or lowly fears
One song shall bring.

24

One song, one voice, the sky
The star, the moon, the cloud:
One song the trees.
25 But some will see a shroud,
And some will dim descry
Immortal harmonies
That never die.

Each looks with eyes that are
30 But the soul's curtain hung
Till thought draws clear.
One hears sweet songs, unsung
To some, and dumb the star,
To these while songs are near,
35 Fair things are far.

'EVEN NOW YOUR EYES ARE MIXED IN MINE'

Even now your eyes are mixed in mine.
I see you not, but surely, he—
This stricken gaze, has looked on thee.
From him your glances shine.

5 Even now I felt your hand in mine.
This breeze that warms my open palm
Has surely kist yours; such thrilled calm
No lull can disentwine.

The words you spoke just now, how sweet!
10 These grasses heard and bend to tell.
The green grows pale your speech to spell,
How its green heart must beat!

I breathe you. Here the air enfolds
Your absent presence, as fire cleaves,
15 Leaving the places warm it leaves.
Such warmth a warm word holds.

Bruised are our words and our full thought
Breaks like dull rain from some rich cloud.
Our pulses leap alive and proud.
20 Colour, not heat, is caught.

l. 8: Was originally the much more pedestrian *No lull shall ever untwine*, before R changed it on the otherwise fair-copy holograph. Curiously, he put question marks instead of exclamation marks at the end of lines 9 and 12, a slip which the 1937 editors were clearly right to amend.

PSYCHE'S LAMENT

O! love, my love! once, and not long,
Yet seems it dreams of ancient days,
When nights were passion's lips of song,
And thou his speech of honied praise.
5 'O love, my love', in murmurs low
Burnt in my ears. Then I was thine.
O! love, my love! 'twixt weepings now
The empty words are only mine.

O! sweetest love! O! cruel wings,
10 The darkening shadow of thy flight
Is all that dreary daylight brings
Of all that was so sweet at night.
O! sweetest love! once you called sweet,
Through kisses, her forlorn who weeps
15 That wings, too swift to hear their beat,
Of Time, flew with you . . . How he creeps.

O life, my life! I have no life
Whilst thou who hast my soul art far.
When night is not, while day has strife,
20 What life has the unwakened star?
O! life, my life, upon my brow
My tears like flowers are gathered up.
The fruit that sorrow did not sow
She turns to poison in her cup.

KNOWLEDGE

Within this glass he looks at he is fair.
Godlike his reach and shining in his eyes
The light that is the sun of Paradise.
Yet midst his golden triumph a despair
Lurks like a serpent hidden in his hair
And says 'Proud wisdom I am yet more wise'.
But swift before his look the serpent dies,
Before his glory's grandeur mirrored there.

This to himself, but what to us looks he?
A lank unresting spectre whose grey gaze
A moth by night—a ferret through the days—
A hunger that devours all it can see
And then feeds on himself but never slays
Insatiate with his own misery.

Lines 4 and 5 foreshadow the final couplet of 'Returning we Hear the Larks' (see p. 109).

RAPHAEL

Dear, I have done; it shall be done. I know
I can paint on and on, and still paint on.
Another touch, and yet another touch.
Yet wherefore? 'Tis Art's triumph to know this,
5 Long ere the soul and brain begin to flag,
And dim the first fresh flashes of the soul,
Before achievement, by our own desire
And loathing to desist in what we love,
Is wrought to ruin by much overtoil,
10 To know the very moment of our gain,
And fix the triumph with reluctant pause.
Come from the throne, sweet, kiss me on the cheek;
You have borne bravely, sweet, come, look with me.
Is it not well—think love—the recompense,
15 This binds the unborn ages at our feet.
Thus you shall look, my love, and never change
Throughout all changes. Time's own conqueror,
While worshippers of climes and time unknown
Lingeringly look in wonder—here—at us.

20 What have we done—in these long hours, my love?
Long—long to you—whose patient labour was
To sit, and sit, a statue, movelessly.
Love we have woven a chain more glorious
Than crowns or Popes—to bind the centuries.
25 You are tired. I should have thought a little.
But you said nothing, sweet, and I forgot,
In rapture of my soul's imaginings.
You—yes, 'twas thus you looked, ah, look again
That hint of smile—it was like wings for heaven,
30 And gave my spirit play to revel more
In dazzling visions. But ah! it mocked my hand.
There—there—before my eyes and in my brain
Limned perfect—but my fingers traitors were.
Could not translate, and heartsick was the strife.
35 But it is done—I know not how—perchance
Even as I, maddened, drew on hopelessly,
An angel taking pity—mayhap for thee—
Guided my hand and drew it easily.

And they will throng—admire with gaping mouth,
40 The students, 'Look, what ease, what grace divine.
What balance and what harmony serene.'
And some, 'Like noonday lakes to torrents wild,
After titanic Mighty Angelo.'
Ah, Angelo, he has no sweetness—true.

27

45 But ah, I would I had his breadth of wing.
Jove's Thunders, and the giant craggy heights
Whose points cleave the high heavens, and at whose feet
The topmost clouds have end, afraid to soar.

And I too, shake my brow amongst the stars.
50 And this I know and feel, what I have done
Is but the seed plot of a mightier world.
Yea, world on world is forming in my brain.
I have no space to hold it. Time will show
I could draw down the Heavens, I could bend
55 Yon hoar age-scorning column with my hand
I feel such power. But where there's sun there's shade!
And these thoughts bring their shadow in their train.
Who lives?—see this, it is my hand—my name.
But who looks from the canvas, no—not me.
60 Some doubt of God—but the world lives who doubts?
Even thus our own creations mock at us.
Our own creations outlive our decay.

What do I labour for if all is thus?
I triumph, but my triumph is my scorn.
65 'Tis true I love my labour, and the days
Pass pleasantly,
But what is it I love in it—desire
Accomplished? Never have I reached
The halfway of the purpose I have planned.
70 A hardship conquered?—a poor juggler's feat
And his elatement mayhap betters mine.
The adoration of the gaping crowd,
Who praise, with jest, not knowing why they praise,
Then turn, and sing a lewd and smutty song.
75 Or kneel—bate breath—to my Lord Cardinal.
Or is it the approval of the wise?
I take it—sadly knowing what I know,
And feeling that this marvel of their world
Is little triumph to me, it being my world.
80 Their deeds being circumscribed—proportionate,
Within their limits; and mine loftier,
But (God how bounded yet) to do as thus
Is but my nature—therefore little pride
Their praises give me. Ah, but this gives pride
85 To know that there is one that does feel pride
When they praise me, and cannot hide the glow
Upon her cheeks to hear me spoken of.
Love—this is better—here to be with you,
My head upon your bosom while your hair
90 A loosened fire falls all about my face,

And through its tangles—like a prison bar
To shut my soul in—watch the shadows creep,
The long grey shadows creeping furtively.
I would I were a poet—love—this once.
95 I cannot tell my feelings . . .
How effable in this half-light you look,
Love, I would dream—the shadows thickly press.
You fade into my fancy—and become
A thought—a smile—a rapture of the brain,
100 A presence that embraces all things felt.
A twilight glamour—faery fantasy.
Your two eyes in the shadow, stars that dream
In quiet waters of the evening, draw
My spirit to them and enfold me there,
105 Love. I would sleep, dear love I would forget.
Love I would sleep, you watching, covering me,
Charmed by your love and sheltered 'neath love's wing,
Sweet, let the world pass as this day has passed,
What do you murmur—sleeping? Then will I.

1912

'O'ER THE CELESTIAL PATHWAYS'

O'er the celestial pathways the mortal and immortal strays;
For earth is a swift dream of God, and man one shape within His
brain.
And there man meeteth sun and moon, immortal shapes of nights
and days,
And in God's glad mood he is glad and in God's petulance has pain.

And there he dreams his dreamer's face; forgets, nor knows himself
a dream,
Until some shadow wavers by and leaves him but a trembling shade
To murmur in his impotence that nothing is, but all things seem,
And what they seem like man shall know when man beneath the
dust is laid.

1912

29

NIGHT AND DAY

ARGUMENT

NIGHT. The Poet wanders through the night and questions of
the stars but receives no answer. He walks through the crowds
of the streets, and asks himself whether he is the scapegoat
to bear the sins of humanity upon himself, and to waste his
5 life to discover the secret of God, for all.

DAY. He wakes, and sees the day through his window. He feels
endowed with a larger capacity to feel and enjoy things, and
knows that by having communed with the stars, his soul has
exalted itself, and become wiser in intellectual experience.
10 He walks through the city, out into the woods, and lies under
the trees, dreaming through the sky-spaces.
   He hears Desire sing a song of Immortality,
   Hope, a song of love,
   And Beauty, a song of the Eternal rhythm.
15   Twilight comes down and the poet hearkens to the song of the
evening star; for Beauty has taught him to hear, Hope to feel,
and Desire, a conception of attainment.
   By thinking of higher things we exalt ourselves to what
we think about.
   Striving after the perfect—God, we attain nearer to
perfection than before.

TS1 and TS2 have 'thro' for 'through' in line 1, but as they also have
'through' in lines 2, 10 and 11, I have followed the 1937 editors in using
this spelling throughout the poem. However, I have restored the capital I
for Immortality in line 12, as being more consonant with R's use of
capitals elsewhere in this prologue, as well as the semi-colon which TS1
has after *star* in line 16.

NIGHT

When the night is warm with wings
Invisible, articulate,
Only the wind sings
To our mortal ears of fault.
5 And the steadfast eyes of fate
Gleam from Heaven's brooding vault,
Through dull corporeal bars
We drink in the proud stars.

These, my earth-sundered fantasy
10 On pillared heights of thought doth see
In the dark heaven as golden pendulous birds,
Whose tremulous wings the wind translates to words,
From the thrilled heaven which is their rapturous nest.
Still, though they sleep not, thoughtful to illume,
15 They are not silent, only our sundering gloom
Makes their songs dumb to us—a tragic jest.

Sing to me, for my soul's eyes
Anguish for those ecstasies
And voluptuous mysteries
20 That must somewhere be,
Or we could not know of them.
Sing to me, O sing to me,
Is your light from sun of them,
Or from boughs of golden stem
25 Trickling over ye,
That your nest is hanging on?

Though the sun's face be on high,
Yet his fiery feet do lie
Fixed on earth, to give the sky
30 In our hands a while.
So our mortal hearts make bliss,
And we may a little smile.
Wherefore keep ye all your bliss?
What your gain for gain we miss?
35 Wherefore so beguile
With your shining, heard of none?

How can I burst this trammel of my flesh,
That is a continent 'twixt your song and me?
How can I loosen from my soul this mesh
40 That dulls mine ears and blinds mine eyes to see?

When I had clambered over the walls of night,
Lo! still the night lay unperturbed behind.
Only in Heaven the starry birds of light
Swarmed as arrested in their showery flight.
45 O! could I bind your song as night can bind.

*　　*　　*

l. 18: TS1, TS2 and ND all have *those ecstasies*, which seems to me preferable to CW's *these ecstacies*.

l. 36: The interval here follows TS1, which clearly has a query at the end
of the line and a stanza-break thereafter. ND has the query; the break is
indeterminate.

Sudden the night blazed open at my feet.
Like splintered crystal tangled with gold dust
Blared on my ear and eye the populous street.

Then, like a dark globe sprinkled with gold heat
50 Wherein dark waters move—dark gleaming seas,
So round the lit-faced shadows seemed the street.

They feel the skeleton rattle as they go.
'Let us forget', they cry, 'soon we shall know,—
Drown in life's carnival fate's whisperings.'

55 Foul heat of painted faces, ribald breath,
Lewd leer, make up the pageant as they flow
In reeking passage to the house of death.

Then said I, what divides love's name from lust?
Behold, what word can name the life for these?
60 For starven and not hungered, O! what crust?

Lean—starven, and they hunger not increase.
Starven of light, barriered 'gainst purity,
A bruten lust of living their life's lease.

A dream-empearled ladder to the moon,
65 A thought enguarded heavenly embassy
To treat with God for a perpetual June,

Colours my youth's flower for them, for me.
One flower whose ardent fragrance wastes for all.
Fed with the sobbings of humanity.

70 The sobbing of the burden of their sins
Is all the guerdon strife to ease them wins.
Who seeks heaven's sign, earth's scapegoat must he be?

God gives no June, and Heaven is as a wall.
No symboled answer to my questionings—
75 Only the weak wind yearns, the stars wink not at all.

l. 73: CW has: *Heaven is a wall*, but both TSS and ND clearly have: *Heaven is as a wall.*

1. (a) Rabbi Peretz Rosenberg. Oil. Whereabouts and dimensions unknown. Very early

Courtesy The Imperial War Museum

1. (b) Studies of nude children. Sanguine. 1908 or earlier $6\frac{3}{4}'' \times 6\frac{1}{2}''$ and $7'' \times 4''$

2. (a) Two figures at a
Table. Pen and wash.
c. 1910   6″ × 4″

2. (b) Figures seated round a Table. Pen and wash. c. 1910 $5\frac{1}{2}″ × 7″$

DAY

The fiery hoofs of day have trampled the night to dust;
They have broken the censer of darkness and its fumes are lost
  in light.
Like a smoke blown away by the rushing of the gust
When the doors of the sun flung open, morning leaped and
  smote the night.

5 The banners of the day flame from the east.
Its gorgeous hosts assail the heart of dreams.
They brush aside the strange and cowled priest
Who ministers to our pillows with moonbeams
And restful pageantry or lethe draught,
10 Sleep—who by day dwells in invisibleness—
Their noising stirs the waking veils of thought,
Ah! I am in the midst of their bright press.

I went to sleep in the night,
In the awed and shadowy night,
15 Pleading of those birds delight.
Where has the morning borne me to?
What has she done with the night?
And those birds flown whereto?

Surely some God hath breathed upon mine eyes
20 Between awake and waking, or poured strange wine
Of some large knowledge—for I am grown wise
And big with new life—eager and divine.

Last night I stripped my soul of all alloy
Of earth that did ensphere and fetter it.
25 I strove to touch the springs of all the night.
My brow felt spray, but hands and eyes were dry.

Last night my soul thought God—my soul felt God.
I prayed the stars this for my body's dole.
Through prayer and thought to purified desires.
30 Through hallowed thought I was made half divine.

Shall I dream of shadow
Now I have the light;
Spoil the sunny meadow
To think of night?

l. 9: R originally wrote *restful luxury.*

E   33

35 Forth into the woods I will fare.
I will walk through the great clanging city
To seek what all have sought to find.
No face shall pass me
But I will question therein
40 Some mirrored subtlety,
Some wandering gleam that straggled through
Nativity, from the forgotten shelter of God's skirts.
In all that Time has harvested,
Whether a seed from Heaven has sprung;
45 In all God has made mutable and swift
Some lustre of his smile to see.
And the dun monstrous buildings be a book
To read the malediction of lucre
That spreads a shade and shelter for a plague.

50 Noon blazes in the city, tumult whirled.

Flame crowned and garmented
With robes that flaunt
The splash of gold he throws
About my feet,
55 He weaves above my head
A golden chaunt,
A song that throbs and glows
Through all the noon-day heat.

No Pan-pipe melodies
60 Of wind and boughs.
No tired waves listless wash,
No silence deep
With spirit harmonies
Night only knows;
65 No tender breaking flush,
Dawn's voice of dreams-asleep.

But buildings glorified,
Whose windows shine
And show the heaven, while far
70 Down the throng'd street

ll. 56-7: ND has: *he weaves a golden song/above my head* in place of these
2 lines.

l. 61: CW has: *no tired wave's listless wash,* making 'wash' a noun, but both
TSS and ND have: *no tired waves listless wash,* making 'wash' a verb,
followed by a comma instead of CW's colon.

l. 66: CW has *dream-asleep.* ND has *dreams-asleep.*

Mingles man's song of pride
With the divine
Song of the day's great star
Struck from the noon-day heat.

*   *   *

75 Shall I turn me to this tavern
And so rest me from the sultriness?

*   *   *

Dim-watery-lights, gleaming on gibbering faces,
Faces speechful, barren of soul and sordid.
Huddled and chewing a jest, lewd and gabbled insidious,
80 Laughter, born of its dung, flashes and floods like sunlight,
Filling the room with a sense of a soul lethargic and kindly.
Touches my soul with a pathos, a hint of a wide desolation.

*   *   *

Green foliage kisses my heart's sight
Before I yet have left the street,
85 My heart feels summer-leaping light
These summer silent guests to greet.
The grassy plot with rows of trees,
Like some sweet pallisaded land
From off some land outcast of these,
90 Whose air you breathe is grinding sand.

These are the outskirts of the woods,
The shore of mighty forest seas,
Where Pan plays to the solitudes
His deep primordial melodies.
95 Where night and day like ships sail by,
And no man knoweth this miracle;
Eternal as the eternal sky
That is the earth's dumb oracle.

*   *   *

I saw the face of God to-day,
100 I heard the music of his smile,
And yet I was not far away,
And yet in Paradise the while.

There is a typescript version of lines 77 to 82 entitled 'In the Workshop'. They
were included in PIR under that title, having first appeared in *A Piece of Mosaic*
for a Jewish Bazaar. Verbally the TS is identical with CW, but the punctuation
is so much clearer that I have adopted it, apart from the comma at the end of
l. 79, which R inserted on the only copy of ND I have seen.

35

I lay upon the sparkling grass,
And God's own mouth was kissing me,
105 And there was nothing that did pass
But blazèd with divinity.

Divine—divine—upon my eyes,
Upon my hair—divine—divine,
The fervour of the golden skies,
110 The ardent gaze of God on mine.

Let me weave my fantasy
Of this web like broken glass
Gleaming through the fretted leaves
In a quaint intricacy,
115 Diamond tipping all the grass.

Hearken as the spirit heaves
Through the branches and the leaves
In the shudder of their pulse.
Delicate nature trembles so
120 To a ruder nature's touch,
And of peace that these convulse
They have little who should [have] much.
Life is so.
Let me carve my fantasy
125 Of the fretwork of the leaves.

Then the trees bent and shook with laughter,
Each leaf sparkled and danced with glee.
On my heart their sobs came after,
Demons gurgling over me.
130 And my heart was chilled and shaken,
And I said through my great fear,
When the throat of tears is slaken
Joy must come for joy will hear.

Then spake I to the tree,
135 'Were ye your own desire
What is it ye would be?'

ll. 107-8: TS1, as well as a separate holograph version consisting only of lines 99-110 above, and entitled 'In Kensington Gardens', has *upon mine eyes* and *upon mine hair*, but R wisely abandoned this archaism in ND.

l. 114: CW has *In quaint intricacy*, omitting 'a', though the word appears in all the original sources as well as in *Youth*, where R reprinted lines 111-125 as a separate poem entitled 'In the Park'. A holograph version of these lines, entitled 'In the Woods', has *carve my fantasy* in line 111 and *From the fretwork* in line 125.

l. 122: I have retained CW's *have much* though the second verb does not appear in ND.

Answered the tree to me,
'I am my own desire
I am what I would be.

140 If ye were your desire
Would ye lie under me,
And see me as you see?'

'I am my own desire
While I lie under you,
145 And that which I would be
Desire will sing to you.'

Through the web of broken glass
I knew her eyes looked on me.
Soon through all the leaves did pass
150 Her trembling melody.
Yea! even the life within the grass
Made green stir
So to hear
Desire's yearned song of immortality.

155 'Mortals—ancient syllables
Spoken of God's mouth,
Do spirits them chronicle
So they be not lost?

'Music, breathed ephemeral—
160 Fragrant maid and child;
Bellow, croak and droning—
Age and cumbrous man.

'Music that the croaking hears:
Croak, to mate the music:
165 Do Angels stand and throw their nets
For you, from banks Eterne?

'Surely the speech of God's mouth
Shall not be for naught!
Music wrought of God's passion
170 Less than vanished dew?

l. 157: CW has: *Lo! what spirits chronicle* and *Lo! Angels stand and throw
their nets* for line 165, but TS1 and ND clearly read 'Do' for 'Lo' in both
cases, followed by a question mark, which seems preferable.

l. 170: TS1 and ND have *withered dew*, but in *Youth* R changed this when
reprinting lines 155-174 under the title 'Desire Sings of Immortality.'

37

'As the sea through cloud to sea,
Thought through deed to thought,
Each returneth as they were,
So man to God's mouth?'

175 So man to God's mouth,
Mouth whose breath we are.
How far—O—how far!
Spring of the soul's drouth?

I heard a whisper once
180 Of a way to make it near,
And still that whisper haunts
Like a wonder round my ear.

Hope whispered to me,
I could not hear
185 The meaning to subdue me
Of the music most clear.

*   *   *

'Music that the croaking hears,
Croak, to mate the music.'

Was it lorn Echo babbling to herself,
190 That none would mate and none would hear her?

'I wander—I wander—O will she wander here?
Where'er my footsteps carry me I know that she is near.
A jewelled lamp within her hand and jewels in her hair,
I lost her in a vision once and seek her everywhere.

195 'My spirit whispers she is near, I look at you and you.
Surely she has not passed me, I sleeping as she flew.
I wander—I wander, and yet she is not here,
Although my spirit whispers to me that she is near.'

Verily my heart doth know the voice of Hope.
200 What doth he in these woods singing this wise?

'By what far ways shall my heart reach to thine?
We, who have never parted—never met,
Nor done to death the joys that shall be yet,
Nor drained the cup of love's delirious wine.
205 How shall my craving spirit know for mine
Thine, self-same seeking? Will a wild regret
For the lost days—the lonely suns that set,
Be for our love a token and a sign?
Will all the weary nights, the widowed days

38

210 That sundered long, all point their hands at thee?
Yea! all the stars that have not heard thy praise
Low murmur in thy charmed ear of me?
All pointing to the ending of the ways,
All singing of the love that is to be?'

215 Of love to be, wherefore of love to be?
I never have heard the stars though they look wistfully at me.
I have cried to them and they showed me Desire.
She brought me a passionate wistful dream of eternity.
I cried to them, and they showed me Hope—a fire.
220 He brought me a dream of love—he made my heart to feel
Vague shadowy longings—whereon loneliness had put a seal.
Wherefore? because love is the radiant smile of God,
Because love's land is a heaven only by angels trod.
Where beauty sings and teaches her fair song
225 Of the eternal rhythm—ah! teach me.

'Close thine eyes and under the eyelids that hide,
The glory thine eyes have seen in thy soul shall abide.
The beauty thy soul has heard shall flow into thy soul.
Lordship of many mysteries will be thine being beauty's thrall.

230 'Close thine eyes and under the eyelids that hide,
A bridge build from Heaven as the earth is—wide,
For the bright and dense shapes that 'twixt earth and heaven
    do pass,
Lutanists of day and even, to the pool and to the grass.

'To the cloud and to the mountains, to the wind and to the
    stars,
235 Silvern tongued din of fountains, golden at the sunset bars.

'So they sing the songs I taught them, and they lute the songs
    I made
For the praise of Him who wrought them lauders of his sun
    and shade.

'How may there be a silence? for the cosmic cycle would cease.
I am but the voice of God and these do lute my litanies.'

*   *   *

l. 230: CW has no comma after *hide*, which makes it a transitive verb with
bridge as its object; but TS1 has a clear comma, making *build* an impera-
tive, and this seems more likely to have been R's intention. ND is obscure
at this point.
l. 235: TS1 has *at heavy sunset bars*.

39

240 One night and one day and what sang Desire?
All that God sings betwixt them is not lost.
One night and one day, what did Beauty choir?
If our souls hearken little is the most,
And nothing is which is not living sound,
245 All flowing with the eternal harmony
That with creation's first day was unwound.
One night and one day—what sang Hope to me?
That the next night and day love's song must fill.
He showed me in a mirror, ecstasy,
250 And a new dawn break over the old hill.

Twilight's wide eyes are mystical
With some far off knowledge;
Secret is the mouth of her,
And secret her eyes.

255 Lo! she braideth her hair
Of dim soft purple and thread of satin.
Lo! she flasheth her hand—
Her hand of pearl and silver in shadow.
Slowly she braideth her hair
260 Over her glimmering eyes,
Floating her ambient robes
Over the trees and the skies,
Over the wind-footing grass.
Softly she braideth her hair
265 With shadow deeper than thought.

To make her comely for night?
To make her meet for the night?

Slowly she heaveth her breast,
For the night to lie there and rest?

270 Hush, her eyes are in trance
Swooningly raised to the sky.
What heareth she so to enthral?
Filleth her sight to amaze?

'From the sweet gardens of the sky
275 Whose roots are pleasures under earth,
Whose atmosphere is melody
To hail each deathless minute's birth,
Between frail night and frailer day
I sing what soon the moon will say,
280 And what the sun has said in mirth.

'I sing the centre of all bliss.
The peace like a sweet-smelling tree
That spreads its perfumed holiness
In unperturbed serenity.
285 Between the darkness and the light,
I hang above my message bright
The clamour of mortality.

'Here, from the bowers of Paradise
Whose flowers from deep contentment grew,
290 To reach his hand out to the wise
My casement God's bright eyes look through.
For him whose eyes do look for Him
He leans out through the seraphim
And His own bosom draws him to.'

300 I heard the evening star.

[1912 and earlier]

DUST CALLETH TO DUST

A little dust whispered—a little grey dust,
As it whirled round my knees in the arms of the wind,
'O wind lift me higher, sweet wind, lift me higher
To see through his eyes to the vast of his mind.'

Then I soon heard it murmur—'O brother, dear brother
How long must you guard that fierce temple of God?
So fixt to the earth and a foe to the wind—
O haste and with me kiss the cloud and the clod.'

1912

TO MICHAEL SHERBROOKE
ON HEARING HIS RECITATION OF 'THE RAVEN'

O! Keen magnificent pangs, luxurious opulent doom,
The exquisite tortures of death, felt, seen from the fullness of life,
A harrowing soul despair wrought out of a jewelled gloom,
My overcharged heart can endure not this pinnacled orient strife.

O master—take thought of our weakness, be not like God in his
　　might;
He may forget—He is God, but why should you play with our
　　hearts?
Lift them to ecstasy's sunblaze, steep them in tear-dripping night.

1912

The above poems were written in the back of Michael Sherbrooke's copy of *Night and Day*, now in the University Library at Jerusalem. As R 'broke with' Sherbrooke in the Autumn of 1912 (see R's letter to Mrs Cohen on pp. 195-6) and *Night and Day* was only published that year, it is reasonably safe to assume that they were composed in the Spring or Summer of 1912.

Michael Sherbrooke was an actor of Polish origin (his parents' name was originally Czevzik) and the son of an East End Rabbi. He made some reputation on the stage in Ibsen's plays, and was a friend of J. H. Amschewitz, in whose studio R met him. For a time Sherbrooke helped and befriended R, but eventually the older man's patronage became irksome, as the above-mentioned letter indicates.

ASPIRATION

The roots of a dead universe are shrunken in my brain;
And the tinsel leafed branches of the charred trees are strewn;
And the chaff we deem'd for harvest shall be turned to golden
  grain,
While May no more will mimic March, but June be only June.

5 Lo! a ghost enleaguer'd city where no ghostly footfall came!
And a rose within the mirror with the fragrance of it hid;
And mine ear prest to the mouth of the shadow of a name;
But no ghost or speech or fragrance breathing on my faint eyelid.

I would crash the city's ramparts, touch the ghostly hands
  without.
10 Break the mirror, feel the scented warm lit petals of the rose.
Would mine ears be stretched for shadows in the fading of the
  doubt?
Other ears shall wait my shadow,—can you see behind the
  brows?

For I would see with mine own eyes the glory and the gold.
With a strange and fervid vision see the glamour and the dream.
15 And chant an incantation in a measure new and bold,
And enaureole a glory round an unawaken'd theme.

1912

ll. 2-3: CW, following the text in *Youth* and a corrected TS, gives the
above reading. The only holograph has a full stop at the end of line 2,
and no *And* at the beginning of line 3.

TO J. H. AMSCHEWITZ[1]

In the wide darkness of the shade of days
Twixt days that were, and days that yet will be,
Making the days that are, gloom'd mystery,

[1] John Henry Amschewitz R.B.A. His parents became friends of R's
parents, and advised them to send him to evening classes at Birkbeck
College; which they did. Amschewitz remained a friend of R's, and one
of the three surviving typescripts of this poem has a superscription in
Annie Wynick's hand which reads: 'This gentleman is an artist and the
first friend who helped my poor brother in his Art—a good friend he was
too'. This TS has *dark mystery* in l. 3, but ND and the others give *gloom'd*,
one of which is an ink correction by R. The punctuation of the first 3
lines follows all 3 TSS, not CW. A striking portrait of R by Amschewitz,
painted in January 1911, is the earliest likeness of him we have, and was
presented to the Jews' College, London, by Michael Sherbrooke.

What starshine glimmers through the nighted ways
Uplifting? and through all vain hope's delays
What is it brings far joy's foretaste to me?
A savour of a ship-unsullied sea,
A glimpse of golden lands too high for praise.

Life holds the glass but gives us tears for wine.
But if at times he changes in his hand
The bitter goblet for the drink divine,
I stand upon the shore of a strange land.
And when mine eyes unblinded of the brine
See clear, lo! where he stood before, you stand.

HEART'S FIRST WORD
(I)

To sweeten a swift minute so
With such rare fragrance of sweet speech,
And make the after hours go
In a blank yearning each on each;
5 To drain the springs till they be dry,
And then in anguish thirst for drink,
So but to glimpse her robe thirst I,
And my soul hungers and I sink.

There is no word that we have said
10 Whereby the lips and heart are fire;
No look the linkèd glances read
That held the springs of deep desire.
And yet the sounds her glad lips gave
Are on my soul vibrating still.
15 Her eyes that swept me as a wave
Shine my soul's worship to fulfil.

Her hair, her eyes, her throat and chin;
Sweet hair, sweet eyes, sweet throat, so sweet,
So fair because the ways of sin
20 Have never known her perfect feet.
By what far ways and marvellous
May I such lovely heaven reach?
What dread dark seas and perilous
Lie 'twixt love's silence and love's speech?

[1911-12]

l. 13: R originally wrote *tranced lips.*

'WHEN I WENT FORTH'

When I went forth as is my daily wont
Into the streets, into the eddying throng,
Lady—the thought of your sweet face was strong,
The grace of your sweet shape my ways did haunt.
About this spell clangoured the busy chaunt
Of traffic, like some hundred-throated song
Of storm set round some moon-flashed isle in wrong.
But soon usurped your robe's undulant flaunt—
Your last words said—your ruby gaolers' loss—
The instant and unanchored gleams across
My soul's mirror that holds you there for aye;
The sounds that beat the guard down of sound's gates,
But memory mastereth not, behind who waits,
Your speech—your face—his text by night and day.

[1911-12]

l. 14: R originally wrote *night or day*.

IN NOVEMBER

Your face was like a day in June
Glad with the raiment of the noon,
And your eyes seemed like thoughts that stir
To dream of warm June nights that were.

5 The dead leaves dropped off one by one,
All hopeless in the withered sun.
Around, the listless atmosphere
Hung grey and quiet and austere.

As we stood talking in the porch
10 My pulse shook like a wind kissed torch,
Too sweet you seemed for anything
Save dreams whereof the poets sing.

Your voice was like the buds that burst
With latter spring to slake their thirst,
15 While all your ardent mouth was lit
With summer memories exquisite.

[1911-12]

45

'LADY, YOU ARE MY GOD'

Lady, you are my God—
Lady, you are my heaven.

If I am your God
Labour from your heaven.

Lady, you are my God,
And shall not love win heaven?

If Love made me God
Deeds must win my heaven.

If my love made you God,
What more can I for heaven?

1912

In PIR Bottomley printed couplets 2 and 4 in italics, but there is no authority for this. The comma at the end of the penultimate line follows ND and *Youth*, not CW.

SPIRITUAL ISOLATION

Fragment

My Maker shunneth me.
Even as a wretch stricken with leprosy
So hold I pestilent supremacy.
Yea! He hath fled far as the uttermost star,
5 Beyond the unperturbed fastnesses of night,
And dreams that bastioned are
By fretted towers of sleep that scare His light.

Of wisdom writ, whereto
My burdened feet may best withouten rue,
10 I may not spell—and I am sore to do.

l. 4: This follows PIR and the only TS I have seen in printing *far as* rather than CW's *as far as*.

l. 5: R. originally wrote *imperturbable*.

l. 9: PIR gives *may hasten* for *may best*, which certainly makes better sense, but I cannot find the authority for this reading, any more than the 1937 editors could.

l. 10: R originally wrote *and love is sore to do*.

46

Yea! all seeing my Maker hath such dread,
Even mine own self-love wists not but to fly
To Him, and sore besped
Leaves me, its captain, in such mutiny.

15 Will, deemed incorporate
With me, hath flown ere love, to expiate
Its sinful stay where he did habitate.
Ah me! if they had left a sepulchre;
But no—the light hath changed not and in it
20 Of its same colour stir
Spirits I see not but phantasm'd feel to flit.

Air legioned such stirreth,
So that I seem to draw them with my breath.
Ghouls that devour each joy they do to death.
25 Strange glimmering griefs and sorrowing silences,
Bearing dead flowers unseen whose charnel smell
Great awe to my sense is
Even in the rose-time when all else is well.

In my great loneliness,
30 This haunted desolation's dire distress,
I strove with April buds my thoughts to dress,
Therewith to reach to joy through gay attire;
But as I plucked came one of those pale griefs
With mouth of parched desire
35 And breathed upon the buds and charred the leaves.

[1911-12]

l. 11: R originally wrote *Yea! love.* PIR inserted parentheses round *seeing my Maker hath such dread,* and a comma after *self-love* in the next line, no doubt in an attempt to clarify the text; but there is no sign of them in the TS or ND.

l. 15: CW gives a comma after *incorporate,* which is not in the TS and alters the sense.

l. 22: PIR gives *Air, legioned with such, stirreth,* and prints commas instead of full stops at the end of the next 2 lines. I cannot discover the source of these emendations and have followed CW, except in hyphenating *rose-time* in line 28, as in the TS.

l. 35: The TS has *leafs,* to rhyme with *griefs,* but CW (rightly I think) changed this to *leaves.* ND and PIR omit this last stanza altogether.

TESS

The free fair life that has never been mine, the glory that might have
    been,
If I were what you seem to be and what I may not be!
I know I walk upon the earth but a dreadful wall between
My spirit and your spirit lies, your joy and my misery.

The angels that lie watching us, the little human play—
What deem they of the laughter and the tears that flow apart?
When a word of man is a woman's doom do they turn and wonder
    and say,
'Ah! why has God made love so great that love must burst her
    heart?'

l. 8: CW, following ND, printed a comma after *Ah*, but I think Bottomley
was right in PIR to follow the TS from which *Night and Day* was almost
certainly set up, and print an exclamation mark.

[1911-12]

'O! IN A WORLD OF MEN AND WOMEN'

    O! in a world of men and women
    Where all things seemed so strange to me,
    And speech the common world called human
    For me was a vain mimicry,

5 I thought—O! am I one in sorrow?
    Or is the world more quick to hide
    Their pain with raiment that they borrow
    From pleasure in the house of pride?

    O! joy of mine, O! longed for stranger,
10 How I would greet you if you came!
    In the world's joys I've been a ranger,
    In my world sorrow is their name.

[1911-12]

l. 1: PIR gives a comma in lieu of an exclamation mark after *O* here,
and throughout; as well as a colon at the end of line 10, where ND had
one of R's eccentric question marks.

3. (a) The Artist's Mother.
Black Chalk. 1911   10″ × 8″

3. (b) The Artist's Father. Oil.
1911   16″ × 12″

4. (a) Portrait of the Artist's Father, 1911. Whereabouts and size unknown

Courtesy Joseph Cohen Collection

4. (b) Self-Portrait. Pencil. 1911–12 13″ × 11½

TWILIGHT
(II)

Mist-like its dusky panic creeps in the end to your proud heart:
O you will feel its kisses cold while it rends your limbs apart.
Have you not seen the withering rose and watched the lovely moon's
   decay,
And more than mortal loveliness fade like the fainting stars away?

I have seen lovely thoughts forgot in wind, effacing dreams;
And dreams like roses wither leaving perfume not nor scent;
And I have tried to hold in net like silver fish the sweet starbeams,
But all these things are shadowed gleams of things beyond the
   firmament.

1913

AS A BESIEGED CITY

   In the hushed pregnancy
   And gleaming of hope,
   When a joy's infancy
   Fills our stars' horoscope,
5 Flowering like a mist
   Heaven mixed but light unkist,
   The soul is mixed in anguish,
   For joy has not yet burst.

   Expectant is the fear—
10 O! why the doubt?
   Surely our friends are near,
   And the strong foe cast out.
   Ah! but if we are dead
   In their loving fears, and shed
15 The tears for us in anguish,
   And they turn from gates not burst.

l. 10: R made several attempts at this line, changing it from *O! torture the doubt* to *O! end, end the doubt* and *Hang on the walls the doubt* before arriving at its final form.

CREATION

As the pregnant womb of night
Thrills with imprisoned light,
Misty, nebulous-born,
Growing deeper into her morn,
5 So man, with no sudden stride
Bloomed into pride.

In the womb of the All-spirit
The universe lay; the will
Blind, an atom, lay still.
10 The pulse of matter
Obeyed in awe
And strove to flatter
The rhythmic law.
But the will grew; nature feared
15 And cast off the child she reared,
Now her rival, instinct-led,
With her own powers impregnated.

Brain and heart, blood-fervid flowers,
Creation is each act of yours.
20 Your roots are God, the pauseless cause,
But your boughs sway to self-windy laws.
Perception is no dreamy birth
And magnifies transfigured earth.
With each new light, our eyes receive
25 A larger power to perceive.

If we could unveil our eyes,
Become as wise as the All-wise,
No love would be, no mystery.
Love and joy dwell in infinity.
30 Love begets love; reaching highest
We find a higher still, unseen
From where we stood to reach the first.
Moses must die to live in Christ,
The seed be buried to live to green.
35 Perfection must begin from worst.
Christ perceives a larger reachless love
More full, and grows to reach thereof.
The green plant yearns for its yellow fruit.
Perfection always is a root.
40 And joy, a motion that doth feed
Itself on light of its own speed,
And round its radiant circle runs,
Creating and devouring suns.

l. 21: One draft has *swing* for *sway*.

Thus human hunger nourisheth
45 The plan terrific—true design—
Makes music with the bones of death,
And soul knows soul to shine.
What foolish lips first framed 'I sin'?
The virgin spirit grows within
50 To stature its eyes know to fail.
And all its edges weaken and pale
Where the flesh merges and is one;
A chalice of light for stagnation
To drink, but where no dust can come
55 Till the glass shatters and light is dumb.

Soul grows in freedom natural.
When in wild growths eventual
Its light casts shadow on other light,
All cry 'That spirit is not white'.
60 As when God strides through the wrack of skies,
The plunging seas welcome paradise,
They say not 'This dark period
Sheweth our bitter wrong to God'.
But revel in a dark delight,
65 And day is sweet and night is bright.
The jewelled green laughs myriadly.
The yearning pits swing and draw down
The rainbow-splintered mountains thrown
By wrestling giants beneath the sea.

70 An emanation like a voice
Spreads up, the spirits of our joys.
The sky receives it like an ear
Bent o'er the throbbing atmosphere.
Our thoughts like endless waterfalls
75 Are fed—to fill life's palace halls
Until the golden gates do close
On endless gardens of repose.
A sun, long set, again shall rise,
Bloom in annihilation's skies
80 Strong—strong—past ruin to endure,
More lost than bliss—than life more sure.
This universe shall be to me
Millions of years beneath the sea
Cast from my rock of changelessness
85 The centre of eternity.
And uncreated nothingness,
Found, what creation laboured for
The ultimate silence—Ah, no more
A happy fool in paradise,
90 But finite—wise as the All-wise.

1913

Glory of hueless skies
What pallid splendour flies
Like visible music touched
From the lute of our eyes.

5 The stars are sick and white
Old in the morning light
Like genius in a rabble
The obscure mars their might.

The forest of the world
10 Lights scattering hands have uphurled
The branches of thought are driven
The vapours of act are uncurled.

Deed against strenuous deed
Dark seed choking the seed
15 The impulses blind that blacken
The ways of life's rough need.

Mountain and man and beast
Live flower and leaf diseased
Riot or revel in quiet
20 At the broad day's feast.

1913

The above follows the punctuation of the only holograph, which has none of the terminal commas printed in CW.

A QUESTION

What if you shut your eyes and look,
Yea, look with all the spirit's eyes,
While mystic unrevealèd skies
Unfold like pages of a book

Wherein new scenes of wonder rare
Are imaged, till the sense deceives
Itself, and what it sees believes—
Even what the soul has pictured there?

APPARITION

From her hair's unfelt gold
My days are twined.
As the moon weaves pale daughters
Her hands may never fold.

Her eyes are hidden pools
Where my soul lies
Glimmering in their waters
Like faint and troubled skies.

Dream pure, her body's grace,
A streaming light
Scatters delicious fire
Upon my limbs and face.

A CARELESS HEART

A little breath can make a prayer,
A little wind can take it
And turn it back again to air:
Then say, why should you make it?

An ardent thought can make a word,
A little ear can hear it,
A careless heart forget it heard:
Then why keep ever near it?

THE POET
(II)

He takes the glory from the gold
For consecration of the mould,
He strains his ears to the clouds' lips,
He sings the song they sang to him
And his brow dips
In amber that the seraphim
Have held for him and hold.

So shut in are our lives, so still,
That we see not of good or ill—
A dead world since ourselves are dead.
Till he, the master, speaks and lo!
The dead world's shed,
Strange winds, new skies and rivers flow
Illumined from the hill.

THE BLIND GOD

Streaked with immortal blasphemies,
Betwixt his twin eternities
The shaper of mortal destinies
Sits in that limbo of dreamless sleep,
Some nothing that hath shadows deep.

The world is only a small pool
In the meadows of Eternity,
And the wise man and the fool
In its depths like fishes lie.
When an angel drops a rod
And he draws you to the sky
Will you bear to meet your God
You have streaked with blasphemy?

1913

ll. 2-3: CW printed:

Betwixt twin eternities
Shaper of mortal destinies

I have reverted to the pencil holograph in LBN, which PIR followed, as being clearer and more euphonious.

The same manuscript originally had *And the angels drop their nets* for line 10, and *Streaked with all your blasphemies* for the last line, before R altered them. He made several starts on this poem, with alternative openings, one of which read:

Streaked with Immortal blasphemies
Betwixt His twin eternities
The blind God sits sinister
Time leading man he knows
Streaked with Eternal woes.

l. 13: BL has a pencil holograph which reads *Streaked over with your blasphemy.*

'WALK YOU IN MUSIC, LIGHT OR NIGHT'

Walk you in music, light or night,
Spelled on your brows, plain to men's sight
Is death and darkness written clear.
God only can neither read nor hear.

Ah men, ye are so skilled to write
This doom so dark in letters bright.
But how can God read human fear
Who cannot dry a human tear?

1913

TWILIGHT
(III)

A sumptuous splendour of leaves
Murmurously fanning the evening heaven;
And I hear
In the soft living grey shadows,
In the brooding evanescent atmosphere,
The voice of impatient night.

The splendour shall vanish in a vaster splendour;
Its own identity shall lose itself,
And the golden glory of day
Give birth to the glimmering face of the twilight,
And she shall grow into a vast enormous pearl maiden
Whose velvet tresses shall envelop the world—
Night.

The punctuation of the above follows CW and a holograph copy of the poem which R sent to Mrs Robert Solomon. But in another holograph R changed *lambent* in line 10 to *glimmering*—a favourite adjective of his—and added the word *shall* to the penultimate line. This is the version I have adopted.

'O, BE THESE MEN AND WOMEN'

O, be these men and women
That pass and cry like blowing flakes,
Seeking the parent cloud,
Seeking the parent sea?
5 Or like famished flames that fly
On a separate root of fire
Far from the nurturing furnace.
Or like scent from the flower
That hovers in doubt afar,
10 Or the colour of grasses
That flies to the spirit and spreads.

Are these things your dreams
That I too can watch?
When I dream my dreams
15 Do you see them too?
When the ghosts depart
Can you follow them,
Though I see them not.

55

A warm thought flickers
An idle ray—
Being is one blush at root.

For the hours' ungentle doom
5 Where one forsaking face
Hides ever—hides for our sighing
Is a hard bright leaf over clover
And bee-bitten shade.

What moons have hidden
10 Their month-long shine,
What buds uncover
And plead in vain,
While one opaque thought wearies
The weary lids of grief?

15 One thought too heavy
For words to bear,
For lips too tired
To curl to them.

1913

SONG

A silver rose to show
Is your sweet face,
And like the heavens' white brow,
Sometime God's battle place,
Your blood is quiet now.

Your body is a star
Unto my thought.
But stars are not too far
And can be caught—
Small pools their prisons are.

l. 3: An earlier draft reads *As quiet as the heavens' whitest brow.*

SPRING

I walk and I wonder
To hear the birds sing—
Without you my lady
How can there be Spring?
5 I see the pink blossoms
That slept for a year,
But who could have woke them
While you were not near?

Birds sing to the blossoms,
10 Blind, dreaming your pink;
These blush to the songsters,
Your music they think.
So well had you taught them
To look and to sing,
15 Your bloom and your music,
The ways of the Spring.

ON A LADY SINGING

She bade us listen to the singing lark
In tones far sweeter than its own.
For fear that she should cease and leave us dark
We built the bird a feignèd throne,
Shrined in her gracious glory-giving ways
From sceptred hands of starred humility.
Praising herself the more in giving praise
To music less than she.

1913

There are two pencil drafts and an ink fair-copy of this poem, the text of the last being followed here. The earlier draft has *lark* for *bird* in line 4, and both have *Watching her gracious glory-giving ways* for line 5.

l. 6: R originally had *pure humility*. Both PIR and CW have a dash at the end of this line, but R used a full stop in all three holographs.

'AS A SWORD IN THE SUN—'

As a sword in the sun—
A glory calling a glory—
Our eyes seeing it run
Capture its gleam for our story.

57

Singer, marvellous gleam
Dancing in splendid light,
Here you have brought us our dream—
Ah! but its stay is its flight.

The original draft had a third verse reading:

A splendour of moving wings
Drifting the infinite
Like a procession of starry kings
Passing us out of the light.

which R wisely omitted in the fair-copy that he sent to Miss Seaton.
The exclamation mark has been restored to its original position after
'Ah', instead of at the end of the line, as in CW.

AT SEA-POINT

Let the earth crumble away,
The heavens fade like a breath,
The sea go up in a cloud,
And its hills be given to death.

5 For the roots of the earth are old,
And the pillars of heaven are tired.
The hands that the sea enfold
Have seen a new desired.

All things upon my sense
10 Are wasted spaces dull,
Since one shape passed like a song
Let God all things annul.

A lie with its heart hidden
Is that cruel wall of air
15 That held her there unbidden,
Who comes not at my prayer.

Gone who yet never came.
There is the breathing sea,
And the shining skies are the same,
20 But they lie—they lie to me.

For she stood with the sea below,
Between the sky and the sea,
She flew ere my soul was aware,
But left this thirst in me.

1914

l. 11: R originally had *flame* for *a song*, and, curiously, *rook* for *lie* in line 13.

'O HEART, HOME OF HIGH PURPOSES'

O heart, home of high purposes,
O hand with craft and skill,
Say, why this meagre dalliance
To do such greatness ill?

5 Marshal the flame-winged legions, yours,—
The thunder and the beauty;
Sweeten these sunsoiled days of ours,
We need your wizard duty.

Our parched lips yearn for music yet.
10 Find us some gate in air
To leave our world-stained lives behind,
And live a life more fair.

The vagrant clouds are alive with light
When the sun shines and sings,
15 When the wind blows they race in flight
So happy in their wings.

Help us, the helpless, breathe thy breath,
Show us new flowers, new ways to live,
Thy glory thaw our lips of death,
20 To you your feel of power we'll give.

1914

R very seldom used hyphens in his compound adjectives, and did not
do so in lines 5 and 11 above when making a fair-copy of this poem. But
CW inserted them, surely with good reason, to avoid ambiguity.

OF ANY OLD MAN

Wreck not the ageing heart of quietness
With alien uproar and rude jolly cries,
Which satyr-like to a mild maiden's pride
Ripens not wisdom, but a large recoil.
Give them their withered peace, their trial grave,
Their past youth's three-scored shadowy effigy.
Mock them not with your ripened turbulence,
Their frost-mailed petulance with your torrid wrath,
While edging your boisterous thunders shivers one word,
Pap to their senile sneering, drug to truth.

The feigned ramparts of bleak ignorance.
'Experience'—crown of naked majesties,
That tells us nought we know not—but confirms.
O think! you reverend, shadowy, austere,
Your Christ's youth was not ended when he died.

1914

The above text follows an ink holograph. CW has a number of punctuational variants, including two sets of parentheses in lines 3 and 10-11,
and *When* for *While* at the beginning of line 9.

'INVISIBLE ANCIENT ENEMY OF MINE'

Invisible ancient enemy of mine
My house's foe
To rich my pride with wrongful suffering
Your vengeful gain
5 Coward and striker in the pit lined dark
Lie to my friends
Feed the world's jealousy and pamper woe.

When I had bowed
I felt your smile, when my large spirit groaned
10 And hid its fire
Because another spirit leaned on it,
I knew you near.

O that the tortured spirit could amass
All the world's pains,
15 How I would cheat you, leaving none for life,
You would recount
All you have piled on me, self-tortured count
Through all eternity.

1914

CW printed commas or dashes at the end of every line in verse 1, but as
none appears in the holograph from which this text was taken, and they
do not seem to clarify the poet's meaning, they have been omitted here.
Moreover, R's punctuation of the other two verses is perfectly clear and
normal.

l. 9: This originally began *I saw you smile.*

AT NIGHT

Crazed shadow from no golden body
That I can see, embraces me warm;
All is purple and closed
Round by night's arm.

5 A brilliance wings from dark-lit voices,
Wild lost voices of shadows white.
See the long houses lean
To the weird flight.

Star-amorous things that wake at sleep-time
10 (Because the sun spreads wide like a tree
With no good fruit for them)
Thrill secrecy.

Pale horses ride before the morning
The secret roots of the sun to tread,
15 With hoofs shod with venom
And ageless dread,

To breathe on burning emerald grasses,
And opalescent dews of the day,
And poison at the core
20 What smiles may stray.

1914

BL has one TS, with the last verse in ink holograph. It omits the hyphens in lines 5 and 9, as well as the parentheses in lines 10 and 11, which both PIR and CW give. In line 1 of it R changed *white* to *crazed* and in line 6 to *lost*. A later holograph fair-copy, and what appears to be a contemporaneous TS, agree with CW, except that neither of them, nor the BL TS, shows a comma after *shadow* in line 1. So I have omitted it.

SUBJECTIVITY

At my eyes' anchoring levels
The pigmy skies foam over
The flat earth my senses see;
A vapour my lips might stir—
5 The heat of my breath might wither.
Strong eyes unfed, not baffled.
Yon bright and moving vapour
In a moment fades.

The beamy air, the roofless silence,
10 The smoke-throated, man-thundered street,
Die to an essence, a love spirit.
Whose feet [?compounded] are
As my own breath back brought.
All things, that, brooding, are still,
15 Speak to me, untwist and twine
The shifting links of consciousness,
Speak to the all-eyed soul,
And tread its intricate infinities.
Immured in two hands' breadth
20 Behind the mask of man.

1914

There are 2 early versions of the above, written in pencil on the backs of
letters R received from Marsh and C. M. Khan, shortly before leaving
for S. Africa. These have an additional line before line 2 above, which
reads: *Like a vapour blown from me*, and diverge markedly both from the
CW text and a corrected ink holograph of that text which is followed here.
The later of the early versions has, for lines 4-13, the following:

> *The houses uttermost edges*
> *Mountains under eyes desiring*
> *Strong eyes that chafe to be hindered*
> *By yon bright moving vapour.*
>
> *The lights, the eddying silence,*
> *The noised quivering street*
> *Dissolve into an essence like a spirit.*
> *Some subtle compound is poured*
> *Which my life feels to stir*

On the above-mentioned ink holograph R changed the title of the poem
from 'The Poet' (The Poet III in CW) to 'Subjectivity'; he also omitted
line 12 of CW and changed the wording of CW's next 2 lines from:

> *Some subtle compound wrought*
> *By no wonder-list'ning sleep.*

and the final couplet from:

> *Pass through the ward of our immured immensity*
> *Into the secret God, behind the mask of man.*

'WISTFULLY IN PALLID SPLENDOUR'

Wistfully in pallid splendour
Drifts the lonely infinite,
A wan perfume vague and tender,
Dim with feet of fragile light.

5 Drifts so lightly through the spirit,
Breathes the torch of dreams astir
Till what promised lands lie near it
Wavering are betrayed to her.

Ghostly foam of unheard waters,
10 And the gleam of hidden skies,
Footsteps of Eve's whiter daughters
Tremble to our dreaming eyes.

O! sad wraith of joy lips parted,
Hearing not a word they say—
15 Even my dreams make broken hearted
And their beauty falls away.

1914

'HAVE WE SAILED AND HAVE WE WANDERED'

Have we sailed and have we wandered,
Still beyond, the hills are blue.
Have we spent and have we squandered,
What's before us still is new.

See the foam of unheard waters
And the gleam of hidden skies,
Footsteps of Eve's whiter daughters
Flash between our dreaming eyes.

Soundless waning to the spirit,
Still—O still the hills are blue,
Ever and yet never near it,
There where our far childhood grew.

1914

l. 8: R originally wrote *Tremble to our dreaming eyes*, and for the last line, *The far home which once we knew.*

FAR AWAY

By what pale light or moon-pale shore
Drifts my soul in lonely flight?
Regions God had floated o'er
Ere He touched the world with light?

63

Not in Heaven and not in earth
Is this water, is this moon;
For there is no starry birth,
And no dawning and no noon.

Far away—O far away,
Mist-born—dewy vapours rise
From the dim gates of the day
Far below in earthly skies.

GIRL'S SONG

The pigmy skies cover
No mood in my eyes,
The flat earth foams over
My pallour's moonrise.
5 Thin branches like whips
Whiten the skies
To gibbous lips
Calling for my mad lover.

What is his knowledge
10 Knowing not this?
I'll send him a message,
My life in a kiss.
Why is he mad?
I hold fire for him, bliss
15 He has not had
And dare not aspire.

1914-1915

BL has an early draft in which the first 4 lines read:

The pigmy skies cover
The mood in my simple eyes,
The flat earth foams over
With pallor when I first rise.

Two later holographs exist, the first of which has: *The roots of my eyes* for
line 2 and *The shores of moonrise* for line 4. The second gives the version
CW printed, which is followed above except for the spelling of *pallour* in
line 4, and *fire* for *fires* in line 14, two corrections which R made to it. In
all three scripts R mis-spelt *gibbous* as *gibbuous* in line 7, perhaps thinking
it was a tri-syllable, which would have suited the rhythm better.

'I KNOW YOU GOLDEN'

I know you golden
As summer and pale
As the clinging sweetness
Of marvels frail.

A touch of fire,
A loitering thrill,
My dancing spirit
Has passed the will.

And love and living
And Time and space—
My naked spirit
Hath seen its face.

l. 3: R tried two other adjectives, *fading* and *lidded*, before apparently deciding on *clinging*.

l. 12: R originally wrote *Is God's own face*.

'SACRED, VOLUPTUOUS HOLLOWS DEEP'

Sacred, voluptuous hollows deep
Where the unlifted shadows sleep
Beneath inviolate mouth and chin.
What virginal woven mystery
5 Guarding some pleadful spiritual sin
So hard to traffic with or flee,
Lies in your chaste impurity?

Warm, fleshly chambers of delights,
Whose lamps are we, our days and nights.
10 Where our thoughts nestle, our lithe limbs
Frenzied exult till vision swims
In fierce delicious agonies;
And the crushed life bruised through and through,
Ebbs out, trophy no spirit slew,
15 While molten sweetest pains enmesh
The life sucked by dissolving flesh.

l. 16: R originally wrote *entwining* flesh.

O rosy radiance incarnate,
O glowing glory of heaven-dreamt flesh,
O seraph-barred transplendent gate
20 Of paradisal meadows fresh.
O read—read what my pale mouth tells.
God! could that mouth be but the air
To kiss your chasteness everywhere
Bound with lust's shrivelling manacles!

25 As weary water dreams of land
While waves roll back and leave wet sand,
Their white tongues fawning on its breast,
But turns it to the thing that prest,
Though my thoughts crown you sweet, and cover,
30 Your shape in me is my mad lover.

1914

l. 19: CW has *resplendent* for *transplendent*. The 1937 editors evidently distrusted R's portmanteau epithet.

THE EXILE

A northern spray in an all human speech
To this same torrid heart may somewhat reach,
Although its root, its mother tree
Is in the North.
5 But O! to its cold heart, and fervid eyes,
It sojourns in another's paradise,
A loveliness its alien eyes might see
Could its own roots go forth.

O! dried up waters of deep hungering love!
10 Far, far, the springs that fed you from above,
And brimmed the wells of happiness
With new delight.
Blinding ourselves to rob another's sun
Only its scorching glory have we won,
15 And left our own homes in bleak wintriness
Moaning our sunward flight.

Here, where the craggy mountains edge the skies,
Whose profound spaces stare to our vain eyes;
Where our thoughts hang, and theirs, who yearn
20 To know our speech.
O! what winged airs soothe the sharp mountains' brow?
From peak to peak with messages they go,
Withering our peering thoughts that crowd to learn
Words from that distant beach.

1914

'MY SOUL IS ROBBED'
(I)

My soul is robbed by your most treacherous eyes
Treading its intricate infinities,
Some pale light hidden in light and felt to stir
In listening pulse, an audible wonder
5 Delighting me with my immortal loss;
While you stay in its place, rich robbers, that is dross.
Wine of the Almighty who got drunk with thee.
(The reason sin—God slumbering then—flew free.)
Alas! if God thus, what will hap to me?
10 Ah! even now drunken while your sweet light beams,
You, far as Heaven, I am drunk on my dreams.
Not yet, that glance engendered ecstasy,
That subtle, unspaced, mutual intimacy,
Whereby two spirits of one thought commune,
15 Like separate instruments that play one tune.
The music of my playing is lost in thine.
Does the sun see when noonday torches shine?
Mine is not yours though you have stolen mine.
Beautiful thieves, I cannot captive ye,
20 Being so bound even as ye rifle me.
My limbs that moved in trembling innocence
You harden to knowledge of experience
Till honour rings upon the ear as crime.

There are 3 TSS of the above, in one of which (conjecturally the last to
be corrected) R changed *viols* to *music* in line 16. It shows, additionally,
some variations in punctuation which have been followed here. R later
rewrote the poem in a different, more concentrated mode (see p. 90).

NIGHT

With sleek lascivious velvety caresses
The nestling hair of night strays on my cheeks.
My heart is full of brimless fervid fancies
Ardent to hear the imperious word she speaks.

5 O purple-hued—O glimmering mouth that trembles!
O monstrous dusky shoulders lost above,
Wrapt in bleak robes of smoke from eye, star embers;
You smouldering pyres of flaming aeons of love.

The straining lusts of strenuous amorists,
10 Smoking from crimson altars of their hearts,
In burning mists are shed upon my dreaming.

Relax—relax. I have not strength to withstand thee;
My soul will not recoil, so full of thee.
Thy loathsomeness and beauty fill my hunger,
15 O! splendid, thy lithe fingers gripping me.

Naked and glorious, like a shining temple
I fill with adorations, fervent psalm,
Anoint with honey of kisses, while thy bosom
Throbs music to my unprofaning palm.

20 See! how thy breasts, those two white grapes of passion,
Look mixed in mine, like globed fruit mixed with leaves.
Lo! where I press, what crimson stains come leaping,
Bright juice of inexhaustible dreams lust weaves.

'WHAT IF I WEAR YOUR BEAUTY'

What if I wear your beauty as this present
Wears infinite aeons yet is only now.
The spirit opens but to receive,
Close hid, nought yet departing—
5 But the world's gaze lessens love.

O softer pearl whose iridescent fountain
Hath been my sky, my sun, my stream of light
From the first dazzling dayspring, the enfolden
Sweet thirst, a mother prattle
10 To a new babbled birth.

I like an insect beautiful wings have gotten,
Shed from you. Let me hide, O like a vessel
That you have marvel laden, burdened
With new rich fears of pirates
15 I droop dark penurous sails.

1914

An earlier draft of verse 1 reads:

What if I wear my beauty as an hour
Wears infinite aeons yet is only one.
The spirit opens but to take in
Nothing departs but this,
To show the world you lessen, somewhat lose.

l. 8: CW has *daystream* for *dayspring*, although the holograph script is clear and it seems unlikely that R would have repeated *stream* in 2 consecutive lines.
l. 15: CW has *pendulous* sails, which is certainly more appropriate than the obsolete adjectival form of 'penury'; but *penurous* could hardly have been a slip of the pen for *pendulous*, and penury was well known to R.

DAWN

O tender, first cold flush of rose,
O budded dawn, wake dreamily;
Your dim lips as your lids unclose
Murmur your own sad threnody.
5 O as the soft and frail lights break
Upon your eyelids, and your eyes
Wider and wider grow and wake,
The old pale glory dies.

And then, as sleep lays down to sleep
10 And all her dreams lie somewhere dead,
(While naked day digs goldly deep
For light to lie uncovered),
Your own ghost fades with dream-ghosts there,
Our lorn eyes see mid glimmering lips,
15 Pass through the haunted dream-moved air,
Slowly, their laden ships.

1914

There are three ink holographs of the above, the earliest of which has
different concluding lines that Bottomley printed in PIR. They read:

> *The iron shepherd leads his sheep*
> *To pastures parched whose green is shed.*
> *Still, O frail dawn, still in your hair*
> *And your cold eyes, and sad sweet lips,*
> *The ghosts of all the dreams are there,*
> *To fade like passing ships.*

The second holograph is a fragment of only 6 lines, of which two differ
from the version given here. They read, after line 12:

> *Unbreathe your swan song of despair*
> *While your ghost fades with dream ghosts there*

'UNDER THESE SKIES'

Under these skies, that take the hues
Of metals locked beneath earth,
According as the spirit woos
What changing mood to birth.
Delicate silver gleaming
In threads of tender thought;
Gold in a proud dreaming
Our dream ships have brought;

69

But the skies of lead
When our hearts are dead,
And the skies relentless
Of an iron petal scentless,
That brooding like a shadow
Weighs down the sunless meadow.

[?1914]

The 1937 editors classified this as a fragment, because R wrote the first five words of a second stanza. But he may well have desisted because he thought the first said all he wanted to say. In any case, it seemed a pity to relegate so original and virtually complete a poem to the relative obscurity of 'Fragments'.

THE FEMALE GOD

We curl into your eyes.
They drink our fires and have never drained.
In the fierce forest of your hair
Our desires beat blindly for their treasure.

5 In your eyes' subtle pit
Far down, glimmer our souls.
And your hair like massive forest trees
Shadows our pulses, overtired and dumb.

Like a candle lost in an electric glare
10 Our spirits tread your eyes' infinities.
In the wrecking waves of your tumultuous locks
Do you not hear the moaning of our pulses?

Queen! Goddess! animal!
In sleep do your dreams battle with our souls?
15 When your hair is spread like a lover on the pillow,
Do not our jealous pulses wake between?

You have dethroned the ancient God.
You have usurped his sabbath, his common days,
Yea! every moment is delivered to you.
20 Our Temple, our Eternal, our one God.

Our souls have passed into your eyes
Our days into your hair.
And you, our rose-deaf prison, are very pleased with the
world.
Your world.

1914

There are 2 holograph versions of this poem, one included in a letter to
Marsh from S. Africa in late 1914 (see p. 206), the other an ink copy
made later. In it R changed *soundless* to *subtle* in line 5 and deleted the
three exclamation marks that originally appeared in the last line of verse
5. Punctuation and use of capitals follow this holograph rather than the
varied emendations of PIR and CW.

'HER FABLED MOUTH'

Her fabled mouth, love hath from fables made.
She tells the same old marvels and sweet stories.
Chaos within her eyes his jewels laid.
Our lips and eyes dig up the antique glories.

The wonder of her heavy coloured hair
Still richly wears the hues of faded Eden;
There, where primeval dream hath made its lair,
Joy subtly smiles, in his arms sorrow hidden.

O! as her eyes grow wide and starlight wanes,
Wanes from our hearts that grow into her splendour,
We melt with wronging of love's fabled pains,
Her eyes so kind, her bosom white and tender.

1914

l. 10: R originally wrote *Fades* for *Wanes*, and in line 12 had *her breast so
soft and tender.*

'A BIRD TRILLING ITS GAY HEART OUT'

A bird trilling its gay heart out
Made my idle heart a cage for it
Just as the sunlight makes a cage
Of the lampless world its song has lit.

71

I was half happy and half vexed
Because the song flew in unasked
Just as the dark might angry be
If sudden light her face unmasked.

I could not shut my spirit's doors
I was so naked and alone,
I could not hide and it saw that
I would not to myself have shown.

1914

'SUMMER'S LIPS ARE AGLOW'

Summer's lips are aglow, afresh
For our old lips to kiss,
The tingling of the flesh
Makes life aware of this.

Whose eyes are wild with love?
Whose hair a blowing flame
I feel around and above
Laughing my dreams to shame?

My dreams like stars gone out
Were blossoms for your day;
Red flower of mine I will shout,
I have put my dreams away.

1914-1915

'I HAVE LIVED IN THE UNDERWORLD TOO LONG'

I have lived in the underworld too long
For you, O creature of light,
To hear without terror the dark spirit's song
And unmoved hear what moves in night.

I am a spirit that yours has found
Strange, undelightful, obscure,
Created by some other God, and bound
In terrible darkness impure.

Creature of light and happiness,
Deeper the darkness when you
With your bright terror eddying the distress
Grazed the dark waves and shivering further flew.

1914

The above reproduces CW verbatim, and is based on an ink holograph. PIR, following an early pencil holograph slightly re-punctuated by Bottomley, had a different first verse which read:

> *I have lived in the underworld so long:*
> *How can you, a creature of light,*
> *Without terror understand the song*
> *And unmoved hear what moves in night?*

and a different line 8 reading: *In terrible darkness, breathing breath impure.*

l. 10: PIR has *the darkness was* . . . but the verb does not occur in either holograph, and was presumably imported by Bottomley in the interest of rhythm.

'I AM THE BLOOD'

I am the blood
Streaming the veins of sweetness; sharp and sweet,
Beauty has pricked the live veins of my soul
And sucked all being in.

I am the air
Prowling the room of beauty, climbing her soft
Walls of surmise, her ceilings that close in.
She breathes me as her breath.

I am the death
Whose monument is beauty, and forever
Although I lie unshrouded in life's tomb,
She is my cenotaph.

BEAUTY
(I)

An angel's chastity
Unfretted by an earthly angel's lures.
The occult lamp of beauty
Which holds? Is truth? Whose spreaded wing endures?

73

5 Say—beauty springs and grows
From the flushed night of the nun solitude
And the deep spirit's throes.
Unconscious as in Eden—chaste and nude.

His self-appointed aim
10 Whose bloodless brows bloom with austere delight,
O'er his entombèd fame,
Whose ghost, an unseen glory, walks in hidden light.

Her sire and her lover.
He burns the world to gloat on the bright flame,
15 Her absence doth him cover.
Her silence is a voice that calls his name.

From the womb's antechambers
He list'ning, moves through life's wide presence-hall,
Blindly its turret clambers,
20 Then searches his own soul for the flying bacchanal.

Is she an earthly care
Moulding our needs unto her gracious ends,
Making the rough world fair,
With softer meanings than its rude speech lends?

1914

l. 6: originally read *From the flushed arms of star-packed solitude.*

AUGURIES

Fading fire that does not fade
Only changing its nest,
Sky-blown words of cloudlike breath
Live in another sky.
5 Days that are scrawled hieroglyphs
On thunder stricken barks,
First our souls have plucked the fruit.
Here are Time's granaries.
Were we not fed of summer, but warmth and summer sang to us.
10 Has my soul plucked all the fruit?
Not all the fruit that hung thereon—
The trees whose barks were pictured days,
One waits somewhere for me
Holding fresh the fruit I left,

15 And I hold fruit for one.
What screen hid us gathering
And lied unto our thirst,
While two faces looked singly to the moon?
But the moon was secret and chill.

20 Will my eyes know the fruit I left?
Will her eyes know her own?
This broken stem will surely know
And leap unto its leaf.
No blossom bursts before its time
25 No angel passes by the door
But from old Chaos shoots the bough
While we grow ripe for heaven.

1914

ON RECEIVING NEWS OF THE WAR

Snow is a strange white word;
No ice or frost
Have asked of bud or bird
For Winter's cost.

5 Yet ice and frost and snow
From earth to sky
This Summer land doth know,
No man knows why.

In all men's hearts it is.
10 Some spirit old
Hath turned with malign kiss
Our lives to mould.

Red fangs have torn His face.
God's blood is shed.
15 He mourns from His lone place
His children dead.

O! ancient crimson curse!
Corrode, consume.
Give back this universe
20 Its pristine bloom.

Cape Town, 1914

l. 3: PIR and CW emended *have* to *has*, but the former avoids a double
's', and R's slightly elliptical grammar here is surely acceptable.

75

BEAUTY
(II)

Far and near, and now, from never,
My calm beauty burns for ever,
Through the forests deep and old
Which loose their miser secrets hold,
5 Unto the fountains of the sky,
Whose showers of radiant melody
Delight the laughter-burdened ways,
And dress the hours to light the days,
While hand in hand they reel their round;
10 For the burning bush is found.
Joy has blossomed, joy has burst;
And earth's parched lips and dewy thirst
Have found a shroud of summer mirth,
And Eden covers all the earth
15 Whose lips love's kisses did anoint,
And straight our ashes fell away.
Our lives are now a burning point,
And faded are their walls of clay,
Purged of the flames that loved the wind
20 Is the pure glow that has not sinned.

1914

THE FLEA

A flea whose body shone like bead
Gave me delight as I gave heed.

A spider whose legs like stiff thread
Made me think quaintly as I read.

10 A rat whose droll shape would dart and flit
Was like a torch to light my wit.

A fool whose narrow forehead hung
A wooden target for my tongue.

A meagre wretch in whose generous scum
15 Himself was lost—his $\left\{\begin{array}{l}\text{dirty}\\\text{living}\end{array}\right\}$ tomb.

But the flea crawled too near
His blood the smattered wall doth smear

76

And the spider being too brave
No doctor now can him save.

20 And when the rat would rape my cheese
He signed the end of his life's lease.

O cockney who maketh negatives,
You negative of negatives.

1914

This interesting pastiche of Blake's 'Auguries of Innocence' was included among *Fragments* in CW, but appears to be complete, since the wheel comes full circle. R later used the same adjective *droll* for the rat in 'Break of Day in the Trenches' (see p. 103).

'A WOMAN'S BEAUTY'

A woman's beauty is a strong tree's roots.
The tree is space, its branches hidden lutes,
Wherefrom such music spreads into the air
That all it breathes on doth its spirit share,
5 And all men's souls are drawn beneath and lie
Mixed into her as words mix with the sky.
And as some words before they mix are stayed
And old thoughts live new spirits by their aid,
So souls of some men meet the spirit of love
10 That sentinels.

A woman's beauty is like kisses shed,
A colour heard, or thoughts that have been said.
It covers, with infinity between.
The memory sees, but 'twixt you and that seen
15 A million ages lie. It is a wave
That in old time swept Gods, and did enslave
As the broad sea imprisons, savage lands.
It is a wind that blows from careful hands
The grains of gathered wheat, and golden grains
20 To others bears.

It is a diver into seas more strange
Than fishes know. No poison makes such change
As her swift subtle alchemy.

CW treated this also as a fragment, but the closing triplet appears to be the intended conclusion of the poem.

'BUT I AM THROWN WITH BEAUTY'S BREATH'

But I am thrown with beauty's breath
Climbing my soul, driven in
Like a music wherein is pressed
All the power that withers the mountain
And maketh trees to grow.

From the neck of a God your hands are odorous.
Now I am made a God and he without you is none.
Your eyes still wear the looks of Paradise.
I look upon its shining fields and mourn for the outcast angels
Who have no Eden now since it shines in your eyes.

*   *   *

My soul is a molten cup with brimming music of your mouth;
Somewhere is a weeping silence and I feel a happy thief.

1914

CW treated this as a fragment, I do not know why, since it appears complete and there is no indication that R intended to add to it.

'IN HALF DELIGHT OF SHY DELIGHT'

In half delight of shy delight,
In a sweetness thrilled with fears,
Her eyes on the rich storied night,
Reads love and strangely hears
Love guests with wintered years.

We know the summer-plaited hours,
O maiden still plaiting
Your men-unruffled curls
For fierce loving and hating—
No trap to keep you girls.

She walks so delicately grave
As lovely as her unroofed fancies
Of love's far-linked dances
In waters of soft night they lave
Through measureless expanses.

1914

CW treated this as a fragment, and printed the first 9 lines only. But a just decipherable holograph has yielded a further 6 lines, which appear to complete the poem. So it has been treated accordingly.

'PAST DAYS ARE HIEROGLYPHS'

Past days are hieroglyphs
Scrawled behind the brows
Scarred deep with iron blows,
Upon the thundered tree
Of memory.

Marvellous mad beliefs
(To believe that you believed!),
Plain and time-unthieved,
Scratched and scrawled on the tree
Of memory.

Time, good graver of griefs,
Those words sapped with my soul,
That I read as of old and whole,
What eye in the world shall see
On this covered tree?

1915

'WHO LOSES THE HOUR OF THE WIND?'

Who loses the hour of the wind
Where the outer silence swings?
But frail—but pale are the things
We seek and the seekers blind.
They seek us on broken wings.

No cold kiss blown from the surge
Of the dark tides of the night.
We sleep and blind is their flight
The dreams of whose kisses urge
The soul to endure its plight.

Blown words, whose root is the brain,
Live over your ruined root.
For other mouths is the fruit
And the songs so rich with pain
Of a splendour whose lips were mute.

1915

A holograph in R's hand on the last page of a copy of *Youth* in the Ewelme
Collection is entitled 'Epilogue', and for the first line has *Not lost is the hour
of the wind*, as well as minor punctuational variants.

An earlier version had a different opening verse, reading:

Who loses the door that the wind
Of the after silence swings?
But lost—lost—lost, are the things
We seek, and the seekers blind
And broken are all our wings.

and the first two lines of the second verse were in the form of a question, beginning: *Is a cold kiss blown* . . .

DUSK AND THE MIRROR

Where the room seems pondering,
Shadowy hovering,
Pictured walls and dove-dim ceiling,
Edgeless, lost and spectral,
5 In a quaint half farewell
Away the things familiar fall
In some limbo to a spell.
Mutation of slipped moment
When nothing and solid is blent.
10 O! dusk palpitant!
Prank fantastical!
You hide and steal from morning
What you give back from hiding,
You prank before the dawning
15 And run from her frail chiding,
And all my household Gods
When he who worships nods
You tweak and pinch and hide
And dabble under your side
20 To drop upon the shores
Of an old tomorrow
Shut with the same old doors
Of sleep and shame and sorrow.

But naked you have left
25 One jewel, dripping still
From plundering plashless fingers.
Lying in a cleft
Of your own surging bosomed hill,
It dreams of dreams bereft
30 And warm dishevelled singers,
Safe from your placeless will.

l. 4: R changed *traceless* to *edgeless* here, and *wash* to *drop* in line 200.

l. 19: originally read *In your heart and tide*, and lines 30-31:

And lovely singers
Safe from your dark browed will.

80

I. Self Portrait. 1910 $19\frac{1}{2}'' \times 15\frac{1}{2}''$

II. (a) People on the Seashore. 1910 $8\frac{1}{2}'' \times 14\frac{1}{2}''$

II. (b) Sea and Beach. 1910 $8\frac{1}{2}'' \times 12\frac{1}{2}''$

III. (a) Blackfriars Bridge. 1911   8″ × 12″

III. (b) The Pool of London. 1911   8¼″ × 12⅝″

IV. (a) Highgate. 1911 $8\frac{3}{4}'' \times 12\frac{1}{2}''$

IV. (b) Landscape with Three Figures. 1910 $10\frac{1}{2}'' \times 14\frac{1}{4}''$

V. Self Portrait. 1912 $17\frac{3}{4}'' \times 15\frac{3}{4}''$

VI. (a) Landscape. ? Springfield Park. 1911   7¼″ × 11″

VI. (b) Landscape with River. 1911–12   8″ × 11⅞″

VII. Head of a Woman "Grey and Red". 1912   16″ × 12″

VIII. Sacred Love. 1911–12 19″ × 23½″

Or you are like a tree now,
And that is like a lake,
Sinister to thee now
35 Its glimmer is awake.
Like vague undrowning boughs
Above the pool
You float your gloom in its low light
Where Narcissian augurs browse,
40 Dreaming from its cool
Apparition a fear;
Behind the wall of hours you hear
The tread of the arch light.

                                        1915

THE MIRROR

It glimmers like a wakeful lake in the dusk narrowing room.
Like drowning vague branches in its depth floats the gloom,
The night shall shudder at its face by gleams of pallid light
Whose hands build the broader day to break the husk of night.

No shade shall waver there when your shadowless soul shall pass,
The green shakes not the air when your spirit drinks the grass,
So in its plashless water falls, so dumbly lies therein
A fervid rose whose fragrance sweet lies hidden and shut within.

Only in these bruised words the glass dim-showing my spirit's face,
Only a little colour from a fire I could not trace,
To glimmer through eternal days like an enchanted rose,
The potent dreamings of whose scent are wizard-locked beneath its
    glows.

l. 1: CW has *dark* for *dusk*, although the latter is clearly written in R's hand
in an ink fair-copy which appears to be the only manuscript source;
and it is perhaps not without significance that the preceding poem is called
'Dusk and the Mirror', and has verbal similarities—*glimmer, plashless,
lake* etc.—with the above. The first 2 lines of the second verse clearly
foreshadow the opening of the 5th stanza of 'Dead·Man's Dump'.

SIGNIFICANCE

The cunning moment curves its claws
Round the body of our curious wish,
But push a shoulder through its straitened laws—
Then are you hooked to wriggle like a fish.

5 Lean in high middle 'twixt two tapering points,
Yet rocks and undulations control
The agile brain, the limber joints
The sinews of the soul.

Chaos that coincides, form that refutes all sway,
10 Shapes to the eye quite other to the touch,
All twisted things continue to our clay
Like added limbs and hair dispreaded overmuch.

And after it draws in its claws
The rocks and unquiet sink to a flat ground.
15 Then follow desert hours, the vacuous pause
Till some mad indignation unleashes the hound.

And those flat hours and dead unseeing things
Cower and crowd and burrow for us to use,
Where sundry gapings spurn and preparing wings—
20 And O! our hands would use all ere we lose.

[1914-15]

l. 1: R originally wrote *the knotted moment*.

This poem was originally entitled 'Interest', and had only 4 verses. The 3rd verse occurs in a later, holograph fair-copy entitled 'Significance', as well as in an untitled BL draft of this verse that has an alternative version, written above it, which reads:

> *Surprise that stops sharp breath and things to touch*
> *Giving a shape quite other to the eye,*
> *Form that refutes all sway, chaos that coincides*
> *Freedom manacled to passion overmuch.*

See *Moses* p. 154.

NONE HAVE SEEN THE LORD OF THE HOUSE

Stealth-hushed, the coiled night nesteth
In woods where light has strayed;
She is the shadow of the soul—
A virgin and afraid,
5 That in the absent Sultan's chamber resteth,
Sleepless for fear he call.

Lord of this moon-dim mansion,
None know thy naked light.
O! were the day, of Thee dim shade,
10 As of the soul is night,
O! who would fear when in the bourne's expansion,
With Thy first kiss we fade.

But the sad night shivers,
And palely wastes and dies;
15 A wraith under day's burning hair,
And his humid golden eyes.
He has browsed by immortal meadowed rivers;
O! were she nesting there!

An alternative version of the second stanza reads:

> Lord of this moon-dim mansion
> Hid is thy imminent face
> O! were Apollo thy weak shade
> Who would not leave this place,
> And ever to infinity's expansion
> Dream that our bodies fade!

l. 18: Two TSs have *resting*, but *Youth* gives *nesting*.

A GIRL'S THOUGHTS

Dim apprehension of a trust
Comes over me this quiet hour,
As though the silence were a flower,
And this, its perfume, dark like dust.

My individual self would cling
Through fear, through pride, unto its fears.
It strives to shut out what it hears,
The founts of being, murmuring.

O! need, whose hauntings terrorize;
Whether my maiden ways would hide,
Or lose, and to that need subside,
Life shrinks, and instinct dreads surprise.

1914

l..6: R originally wrote: *Through fear, unto a self which fears;* and corrected
this to: *Through fear, and dreaming to its fears;* before arriving at the final
text.

WEDDED
(I)

They leave their love-lorn haunts,
Their sigh-warm floating Eden;
And they are mute at once;
Mortals by God unheeden;
5   By their past kisses chidden.

But they have kist and known
Clear things we dim by guesses—
Spirit to spirit grown—
Heaven, born in hand caresses—
10   Love, fall from sheltering tresses.

And they are dumb and strange;
Bared trees bowed from each other.
Their last green interchange
What lost dreams shall discover?
15   Dead, strayed, to love-stranged lover.

l. 7: R made several attempts at this line, progressing from *What palest fancy guesses*, through *What we but know by guesses* and *Clear what we glimpse by guesses*, to the splendid final version.

l. 15: a puzzling anomaly here. An early ink holograph of the poem (LBN), a typed fair-copy, and the printed text in *Youth* all three of them give *love-stranged*, and when the poem was reprinted in *Moses* without the terminal 'd', R inserted it in indelible pencil on his copy. Yet both PIR and CW printed *love-strange*.

WEDDED
(II)

The knotted moment that untwists
Into the narrow laws of love,
Its ends are rolled round our four wrists
That once could stretch and rove.

See our confined fingers stray
O'er delicate fibres that recoil,
And blushing hints as cold as clay;
Love is tired after toil.

But hush! two twin moods meet in air;
Two spirits of one gendered thought.
Our chained hands loosened everywhere
Kindness like death's have caught.

MIDSUMMER FROST

A July ghost, aghast at the strange winter,
Wonders, at burning noon, (all summer seeming),
How, like a sad thought buried in light words,
Winter, an alien presence, is ambushed here.

5 See, from the fire-fountained noon there creep
Lazy yellow ardours towards pale evening,
To thread dark and vain fire
Over my unsens'd heart,
Dead heart, no urgent summer can reach.
10 Hidden as a root from air or a star from day;
A frozen pool whereon mirth dances;
Where the shining boys would fish.

My blinded brain pierced is,
And searched by a thought, and pangful
15 With bitter ooze of a joyous knowledge
Of some starred time outworn.
Like blind eyes that have slinked past God,
And light, their untasked inheritance,
(Sealed eyes that trouble never the Sun)
20 Yet has feel of a Maytime pierced.
He heareth the Maytime dances;
Frees from their airy prison, bright voices,
To loosen them in his dark imagination,
Powered with girl revels rare
25 And silks and merry colours,
And all the unpeopled ghosts that walk in words.
Till wave white hands that ripple lakes of sadness,
Until the sadness vanishes and the stagnant pool remains.

Underneath this summer air can July dream
30 How, in night-hanging forest of eating maladies,
A frozen forest of moon unquiet madness,
The moon-drunk haunted pierced soul dies;
Starved by its Babel folly, lying stark,
Unvexed by July's warm eyes.

1914-15

l. 5: CW, following the printed text in *Youth*, printed a comma after
noon, but as it does not appear in two of the three holographs, or the TS,
and weakens the line, I have omitted it.

An earlier version, which R sent to Marsh in April or early May 1914,
was markedly different from line 7 onwards. It is given overleaf. Marsh
criticized the poem in some detail, and R revised it in the light of some of
these criticisms before it appeared in *Youth* the following year. He clarified
and improved it in places, but in the process the original lines 7 to 11 were
damagingly condensed to the new lines 7 to 9 inclusive.

MIDSUMMER FROST

A July ghost, aghast at the strange winter,
Wonders, at burning noon, (all summer seeming),
How, like a sad thought buried in light words,
Winter, an alien presence, is ambushed here.
5 See, from the fire-fountained noon there creep
Lazy yellow ardours towards pale evening,
Dragging the sun across the shell of thought.
A web threaded with fading fire.
Futile and fragile lure!
10 All July walks her floors that roof this ice,
My frozen heart the summer cannot reach,
Hidden as a root from air, or star from day.
A frozen pool whereon mirth dances
Where the shining boys would fish.

15 Amorous to woo the golden kissing sun,
Your flaunting green hoods bachic eyes
And flower-flinging hands,
Show quaint as in some frolic masker's whim,
Or painted ruby on a dead white rose.
20 Deriding those blind who slinked past God
And their untasked inheritance,
(Whose sealed eyes trouble not the sun)
With a thought of Maytime once,
And Maytime dances;
25 Of a dim pearl-faery boat
And golden glimmerings;
Waving white hands that ripple lakes of sadness
Until the sadness vanishes and the stagnant pool remains.
Pitiless I am, for I bind thee, laughter's apostle,
30 Even as thy garland's glance, and thy soul is merry, to see
How in night-hanging forest of eating maladies,

Another (typewritten) version of the above draft has 3 additional lines
between lines 9 and 10, which read:

> *A rainbow smiling on a sodden wretch:*
> *Like those deaf cherubim whose bright shadows fell*
> *From Eden on the joy beleaguered waste*

It also has *Your flaunting green apparel* for line 16, and omits lines 25, 26 and
34 entirely. A still earlier holograph version of the opening lines, entitled
'In the season of rejoicing', has:

> *Dragging the day across my spirit's shell*
> *To thread a cunning web of fading fire*

in lieu of lines 7 and 8 above.

A frozen forest of moon-unquiet madness
The moon-drunk, haunted, pierced soul, dies.
Tarnished and arid, dead before it dies.
35 Starved by its Babel folly, stark it lies,
Stabbed by life's jealous eyes.

1914

LOVE AND LUST

No dream of mortal joy;
Yet all the dreamers die.
We wither with our world
To make room for her sky.

O lust! when you lie ravished,
Broken in the dust,
We will call for love in vain,
Finding love was lust.

IN PICCADILLY

Lamp-lit faces! to you
What is your starry dew?
Gold flowers of the night blue!

Deep in wet pavement's slime,
Mud rooted, is your fierce prime,
To bloom in lust's coloured clime.

The sheen of eyes that lust,
Dew, time made your trust,
Lights your passionless dust.

l. 8: PIR gives *which dew-time made your trust*, a much more intelligible
reading that makes *Lights* a verb instead of a plural noun. But the above is
the text printed in *Youth* and CW, which in the absence of other evidence
I have felt bound to follow.

87

A MOOD

You are so light and gay,
So slight, sweet maid;
Your limbs like leaves in play,
Or beams that grasses braid;
5 O! joys whose jewels pray
My breast to be inlaid.

Frail fairy of the streets;
Strong, dainty lure;
For all men's eyes the sweets
10 Whose lack makes hearts so poor;
While your heart loveless beats,
Light, laughing, and impure.

O! fragrant waft of flesh
Float through me so—
15 My limbs are in your mesh,
My blood forgets to flow.
Ah! lilied meadows fresh,
It knows where it would go.

In LBN and a TS the last 3 lines of verse 1 read:

Or beams blue grasses braid;
More sweet than I can say
The joy your glances shed.

R was uncertain whether to call this poem 'A Mood' or 'His Mood'.
Bottomley opted for the former.

APRIL DAWN

Pale light hid in light
Stirs the still day-spring;
Wavers the dull sight
With a spirit's wing.

Dreams, in frail rose mist,
Lurking to waylay,
Subtle-wise have kist
Winter into May.

Nothing to the sight . . .
Pool of pulseless air.
Spirits are in flight,
And my soul their lair.

1914

IF YOU ARE FIRE

If you are fire and I am fire,
Who blows the flame apart
So that desire eludes desire
Around one central heart?

A single root and separate bough,
And what blind hands between
That make our longing's mutual glow
As if it had not been?

BREAK IN BY SUBTLER WAYS[1]

Break in by subtler nearer ways;
Dulled closeness is too far.
And separate we are
Through joined days.

The shine and strange romance of time
In absence hides and change.
Shut eyes and hear the strange
Perfect new chime.

[1] Originally entitled 'Friendship', perhaps a more explanatory name for this obscure poem. LBN has an unmistakable comma after 'chime', which suggests that it is really an unfinished fragment.

THE ONE LOST

I mingle with your bones.
You steal in subtle noose
This lighted dust Jehovah loans
And now I lose.

5 What will the Lender say
When I shall not be found,
Safe sheltered at the Judgment Day,
Being in you bound?

He'll hunt thronged wards of Heaven,
10 Call to uncoffined earth
'Where is this soul unjudged, not given
Dole for good's dearth?'

And I, lying so safe
Within you, hearing all,
15 To have cheated God shall laugh,
Freed by your thrall.

l. 9: PIR gives *through wards*, but I cannot trace this variant elsewhere.

For early drafts of the first two verses of this poem, the first untitled, see R's letters to Marsh on pp. 208 and 212. There are still earlier, weaker drafts of these two verses, in LBN and an untitled TS, which serve to show how hard R worked on a poem until it satisfied him.

'MY SOUL IS ROBBED'
(II)

My soul is robbed by your most treacherous eyes
Treading its intricate infinities.
Stay there, rich robbers! what I lose is dross;
Since my life is your dungeon, where is loss?

5 Ah! as the sun is prisoned in the heaven,
Whose walls dissolve, of their own nature bereaven,
So do your looks, as idly, without strife,
Cover all steeps of sense, which no more pasture life.
Which no more feel, but only know you there,
10 In this blind trance of some white anywhere.

Come—come—that glance engendered ecstasy—
That subtle unspaced mutual intimacy
Whereby two spirits of one thought commune
Like separate instruments that play one tune,
15 And the whole miracle and amazement of
The unexpected flowering of love
Concentres to an instant that expands
And takes unto itself the strangest of strange lands.

For an earlier, very different, and less successful version of this poem see
p. 67.

GOD MADE BLIND

It were a proud God-guiling, to allure
And flatter, by some cheat of ill, our Fate
To hold back the perfect crookedness, its hate
Devised, and keep it poor,
5 And ignorant of our joy—
Masked in a giant wrong of cruel annoy,
That stands as some bleak hut to frost and night,
While hidden in bed is warmth and mad delight.

For all Love's heady valour and loved pain
10 Towers in our sinews that may not suppress
(Shut to God's eye) Love's springing eagerness,
And mind to advance his gain
Of gleeful secrecy
Through dolorous clay, which his eternity
15 Has pierced, in light that pushes out to meet
Eternity without us, heaven's heat.

And then, when Love's power hath increased so
That we must burst or grow to give it room,
And we can no more cheat our God with gloom,
20 We'll cheat Him with our joy.
For say! what can God do
To us, to Love, whom we have grown into?
Love! the poured rays of God's Eternity!
We are grown God—and shall His self-hate be?

l. 6: In *Youth*, *masked* is spelt *masqued*, which has a slightly different nuance;
but as the former fits the sense rather better I have followed CW in
printing it.

THE DEAD HEROES

Flame out, you glorious skies,
Welcome our brave,
Kiss their exultant eyes;
Give what they gave.

5 Flash, mailed seraphim,
Your burning spears;
New days to outflame their dim
Heroic years.

Thrills their baptismal tread
10 The bright proud air;
The embattled plumes outspread
Burn upwards there.

Flame out, flame out, O Song!
Star ring to star,
15 Strong as our hurt is strong
Our children are.

Their blood is England's heart;
By their dead hands
It is their noble part
20 That England stands.

England—Time gave them thee;
They gave back this
To win Eternity
And claim God's kiss.

                                    1914

In *S. African Women in Council* (Dec. 1914) the last verse read:

England, they live in thee,
In thy proud fame,
They died to keep thee free,
And thy pure name.

THE CLOISTER[1]

Our eyes no longer sail the tidal streets,
Nor harbour where the hours like petals float
By sensual treasures glittering through thin walls
Of women's eyes and colour's mystery.

The roots of our eternal souls were fed
On the world's dung and now their blossoms gleam.
God gives to glisten in an angel's hair
These He has gardened, for they please His eyes.

[1] Originally entitled 'The Saint' (LBN), which also clearly reads *women's*
in line 4, (CW: *woman's*).

EXPRESSION

Call—call—and bruise the air:
Shatter dumb space!
Yea! We will fling this passion everywhere;
Leaving no place

5 For the superb and grave
　Magnificent throng,
The pregnant queens of quietness that brave
　And edge our song

Of wonder at the light,
10 (Our life-leased home),
Of greeting to our housemates. And in might
　Our song shall roam

Life's heart, a blossoming fire
　Blown bright by thought,
15 While gleams and fades the infinite desire,
　Phantasmed naught.

Can this be caught and caged?
　Wings can be clipt
Of eagles, the sun's gaudy measure gauged,
20 But no sense dipt

In the mystery of sense:
　The troubled throng
Of words break out like smother'd fire through dense
　And smouldering wrong.

l. 16: In an incomplete draft (LBN) this line reads *gleams and is nought.*

GOD

In his malodorous brain what slugs and mire,
Lanthorned in his oblique eyes, guttering burned!
His body lodged a rat where men nursed souls.
The world flashed grape-green eyes of a foiled cat
5 To him. On fragments of an old shrunk power,
On shy and maimed, on women wrung awry,
He lay, a bullying hulk, to crush them more.
But when one, fearless, turned and clawed like bronze,
Cringing was easy to blunt these stern paws,
10 And he would weigh the heavier on those after.

ll. 1-2: R originally framed the opening lines as a question, not an exclamation.

l. 5: Two earlier versions of this line read: *on fragments of a skull of power,* and *on fragments of a doom like dower.*

l. 8: R had difficulty with this line too, re-wording it from *But when one will waxed cruel and clawed in bronze* to *But when a wheel waxed cruel* etc.

Who rests in God's mean flattery now? Your wealth
Is but his cunning to make death more hard.
Your iron sinews take more pain in breaking.
And he has made the market for your beauty
15 Too poor to buy, although you die to sell.
Only that he has never heard of sleep;
And when the cats come out the rats are sly.
Here we are safe till he slinks in at dawn.

But he has gnawed a fibre from strange roots,
20 And in the morning some pale wonder ceases.
Things are not strange and strange things are forgetful.
Ah! if the day were arid, somehow lost
Out of us, but it is as hair of us,
And only in the hush no wind stirs it.
25 And in the light vague trouble lifts and breathes,
And restlessness still shadows the lost ways.
The fingers shut on voices that pass through,
Where blind farewells are taken easily . . .

Ah! this miasma of a rotting God!

[1916 or earlier]

l. 15: The text of the poem, as it appeared in the publication *Moses*, ended with this line. Both this and the preceding line were incorporated in the text of the play, in Scene II at ll. 351-2.

FIRST FRUIT

I did not pluck at all,
And I am sorry now.
The garden is not barred,
But the boughs are heavy with snow,
The flake-blossoms thickly fall,
And the hid roots sigh, 'How long will our flowers be marred?'

Strange as a bird were dumb,
Strange as a hueless leaf,
As one deaf hungers to hear
Or gazes without belief,
The fruit yearned 'fingers, come'.
O, shut hands, be empty another year.

[1915-1916]

BL has an ink holograph whose punctuation I have followed rather than CW's, as it seems to me clearer. Both it and another MS give: *And the hid roots sigh, 'no daisies of ours are starred,'* for line 6, and *O shut hands, be empty open a year* for the final line.

94

CHAGRIN

Caught still as Absalom,
Surely the air hangs
From the swayless cloud-boughs,
Like hair of Absalom
5 Caught and hanging still.

From the imagined weight
Of spaces in a sky
Of mute chagrin, my thoughts
Hang like branch-clung hair
10 To trunks of silence swung,
With the choked soul weighing down
Into thick emptiness.
Christ! end this hanging death,
For endlessness hangs therefrom.

15 Invisibly—branches break
From invisible trees—
The cloud-woods where we rush,
Our eyes holding so much,
Which we must ride dim ages round
20 Ere the hands (we dream) can touch,
We ride, we ride, before the morning
The secret roots of the sun to tread,
And suddenly
We are lifted of all we know
25 And hang from implacable boughs.

[1915-1916]

BL 2 has one draft with minor punctuational variations from CW, but also
(*we believe*) for (*we dream*) in line 20, and *suddenly to the end of the world*,
for line 23. The poem appears among fragments of *Moses*.

MARCHING
(AS SEEN FROM THE LEFT FILE)

My eyes catch ruddy necks
Sturdily pressed back—
All a red brick moving glint.
Like flaming pendulums, hands
5 Swing across the khaki—
Mustard-coloured khaki—
To the automatic feet.

We husband the ancient glory
    In these bared necks and hands.
10 Not broke is the forge of Mars;
    But a subtler brain beats iron
    To shoe the hoofs of death,
    (Who paws dynamic air now).
    Blind fingers loose an iron cloud
15 To rain immortal darkness
    On strong eyes.

[1915-16]

R sent a copy of this poem in a letter to Marsh from Bury St. Edmunds late in 1915 (see p. 227) and there is a TS of it, signed (but not dated) over his regimental particulars at Blackdown Camp; therefore in 1916. Both versions differ from PIR and CW in giving *mustard colored* for *mustard-coloured* in line 6, and a clear comma at the end of line 12, which I have restored. The poem was first published by Harriet Monroe in *Poetry* (*Chicago*) December 1916, and from this the 1937 editors doubtless assumed that *colored* was American spelling. In fact it was common usage among radical intellectuals of that era, like Shaw and Wells, with whose work R was familiar; and he used it elsewhere.

SLEEP

Godhead's lip hangs
When our pulses have no golden tremours,
And his whips are flicked by mice
And all star-amorous things.

5 Drops, drops of shivering quiet
Filter under my lids.
Now only am I powerful.
What though the cunning gods outwit us here
In daytime and in playtime,
10 Surely they feel the gyves we lay on them
In our sleep.

O, subtle gods lying hidden!
O, gods with your oblique eyes!
Your elbows in the dawn, and wrists
15 Bright with the afternoon,

Do you not shake when a mortal slides
Into your own unvexed peace?
When a moving stillness breaks over your knees

5. (a) The Fountain. Oil. 1911 $6\frac{3}{8}'' \times 10\frac{1}{4}''$

5. (b) Landscape with Flowering Trees. Oil. 1911–12 $6'' \times 10\frac{1}{4}''$

6. (a) Head of a Woman, possibly
the Artist's sister Minnie. Pencil.
c. 1914   15″ × 11″

6. (b) Ruth Löwy as the Sleeping Beauty. Sanguine. 1912 $10\frac{1}{2}″ × 13\frac{3}{4}″$

(An emanation of piled aeons' pressure)
20 From our bodies flat and straight,
   And your limbs are locked,
   Futilely gods',
   And shut your sinister essences?

[1915-1916]

A TS in the possession of Patric Dickinson has, in pencil in R's hand, the following in place of the first 4 lines in the above version, which follows the CW text.

> *Godheads lip hangs*
> *Whenever our pulses have no golden tremors*
> *And his whips hang uselessly.*

The last 3 lines of the poem, also written in R's hand on the same TS, replaced an earlier draft which read:

> *An emanation petrified. From our bodies flat and straight,*
> *And you are chained, fooled gods!*
> *And cannot wreak your hate.*

There are, in fact, no less than 3 other typescript versions of the poem extant, all starting at the equivalent of line 5 above, and all differing from each other. What appears to be the latest version of the most different draft is given below, since it is virtually another poem.

SLEEP
(another version)

   A spray of shivering quiet
   Filters under my lid.
   Thinnest veils are shaken, are dropt—
   Silver is tarnished from whispers hid.
5 Outside the world, their twilight stone,
   Our unfamiliar ghosts are known . . .
   Though the cunning Gods outwit us, nay,
   We have dear gyves and torpor as they.

   The Gods with their oblique eyes,
10 The subtle Gods lying hid,
   Elbowed in dawn their twilight wrists
   Shake where sudden a mortal slid
   Into their own unvexed peace,
   And the moving stillness breaks over their knees
15 Far from our bodies flat and straight,
   That bear like a stone the whole night's weight.

Upon my lips, like a cloud
To burst on the peaks of light,
Sit cowled lost impossible things
20 To tie my hands at the noon's height.
And breath floats like a twilight old
Of some spent words pale shredded gold;
And soft hair laid on a feathered fur
Sinks dim as a thought of a sound astir.

ll. 17-20 were incorporated almost verbatim into the play *Moses* at
    Scene 1, ll. 106-9.
ll. 20-24: Another version has, for these 4 lines:

But here is noon and sheltering ease,
And shadow from death rooted trees:
The kind cool shadow where Keats had rest,
And wide eyed Eve soothed her dark breast.

HEART'S FIRST WORD
(II)

And all her soft dark hair,
Breathed for him like a prayer.
And her white lost face,
Was prisoned to some far place.
Love was not denied—
Love's ends would hide.
And flower and fruit and tree
Were under its sea.
Yea! its abundance knelt
Where the nerves felt
The springs of feeling flow
And made pain grow.
There seemed no root or sky
But a pent infinity
Where apparitions dim
Sculptured each whim
In flame and wandering mist
Of kisses to be kist.

[1915-1916]

'GREEN THOUGHTS ARE'

Green thoughts are
Ice block on a barrow
Gleaming in July.
A little boy with bare feet
And jewels at his nose stands by.

CW classes this as a fragment, but it seems to me a wholly self-contained and vivid glimpse of a street scene.

LUSITANIA[1]

Chaos! that coincides with this militant purpose.
Chaos! the heart of this earnest malignancy.
Chaos! that helps, chaos that gives to shatter
Mind-wrought, mind-unimagining energies
For topless ill, of dynamite and iron.
Soulless logic, inventive enginery.
Now you have got the peace-faring *Lusitania*,
Germany's gift—all earth they would give thee,
    Chaos.

[?1915]

An earlier draft of this unsatisfactory poem, which Bottomley omitted from PIR, reads:

> *Chaos that coincides with this military purpose*
> *Iron evolving, all the intersubtled malignancy*
> *Of gases, the shattering nature from her womb[,]*
> *Now she has taken the Lusitania and her people*
> *Under the waters[:] let them ask the reason.*

[1] The S.S. *Lusitania* was a British passenger ship of the Cunard Line, on the trans-atlantic run. On 7th May 1915 she was sunk by a German submarine with the loss of 1,198 lives, of which 128 were Americans. Although it was nearly two years (6th April 1917) before America declared war on Germany, it is generally conceded that the sinking of the *Lusitania* was the first violation of neutral rights to swing American opinion away from isolationism.

THE TROOP SHIP

Grotesque and queerly huddled
Contortionists to twist
The sleepy soul to a sleep,
We lie all sorts of ways
And cannot sleep.
The wet wind is so cold,
And the lurching men so careless,
That, should you drop to a doze,
Winds' fumble or men's feet
Are on your face.

1916

The above text follows CW, which in turn followed PIR verbatim. R included the poem in 3 letters from France, to Marsh and R. C. Trevelyan, all of which have *is* for *are* in the last line, which presumably Bottomley silently emended in the interests of grammar. Additionally the Marsh letter has *but* for *and* at the beginning of line 5.

AUGUST 1914

What in our lives is burnt
In the fire of this?
The heart's dear granary?
The much we shall miss?

Three lives hath one life—
Iron, honey, gold.
The gold, the honey gone—
Left is the hard and cold.

Iron are our lives
Molten right through our youth.
A burnt space through ripe fields,
A fair mouth's broken tooth.

1916

THE JEW

Moses, from whose loins I sprung,
Lit by a lamp in his blood
Ten immutable rules, a moon
For mutable lampless men.

The blonde, the bronze, the ruddy,
With the same heaving blood,
Keep tide to the moon of Moses,
Then why do they sneer at me?

l. 4: R originally repeated *immutable*.
l. 6: R originally wrote *flowing blood*.
l. 7: CW has a full stop after *Moses*, but a holograph version and a TS corrected by R both show a comma.

FROM FRANCE

The spirit drank the café lights;
All the hot life that glittered there,
And heard men say to women gay,
'Life is just so in France'.

The spirit dreams of café lights,
And golden faces and soft tones,
And hears men groan to broken men,
'This is not Life in France'.

Heaped stones and a charred signboard shows
With grass between and dead folk under,
And some birds sing, while the spirit takes wing.
And this is Life in France.

[1916]

l. 9: CW gives *show*, which is more grammatical; but the only holograph I have seen (seemingly a fair-copy) clearly has *shows*. As I have a feeling that R was thinking of the signboard rather than the stones at this point I have kept the singular form.

SPRING 1916

Slow, rigid, is this masquerade
That passes as through a difficult air;
Heavily—heavily passes.
What has she fed on? Who her table laid
5 Through the three seasons? What forbidden fare
Ruined her as a mortal lass is?

I played with her two years ago,
Who might be now her own sister in stone,
So altered from her May mien,
10 When round vague pink a necklace of warm snow
Laughed to her throat where my mouth's touch had gone.
How is this, ruined Queen?

Who lured her vivid beauty so
To be that strained chilled thing that moves
15 So ghastly midst her young brood
Of pregnant shoots that she for men did grow?
Where are the strong men who made these their loves?
Spring! God pity your mood.

1916

l. 2: CW, following all the holograph sources as well as the printed text in *Moses*, has *through granite air*, but on the verso of the missing title page to R's own copy of *Moses*, which has only recently come to light among Bottomley's papers, R corrected this to *a difficult air*. This explains why PIR had this reading, and since it is presumably the latest, I have reverted to it.

l. 10: PIR had *When round the pink a necklace of warm snow*, again accepting R's pencilled correction to the *Moses* text, while CW, following the latter, printed *When round pink neck a necklace of warm snow*. But in a letter to Schiff from Blackdown Camp, shortly before he left for France, R copied out the poem and changed *pink neck* to *vague pink*, presumably to avoid the repetition of 'neck' and 'necklace', and I have adopted this reading.

l. 18: None of the above holographs, including the one enclosed in the letter to Schiff, which was almost certainly written after the text of *Moses* had been proofed, has an exclamation mark at the end of this line, though the printed version has.

IN THE TRENCHES

I snatched two poppies
From the parapet's ledge,
Two bright red poppies
That winked on the ledge.

5 Behind my ear
I stuck one through,
One blood red poppy
I gave to you.

The sandbags narrowed
10 And screwed out our jest,
And tore the poppy
You had on your breast . . .
Down—a shell—O! Christ,
I am choked . . . safe . . . dust blind, I
15 See trench floor poppies
Strewn. Smashed you lie.

1916

R sent this poem in a letter to Sonia Rodker from France, probably in June or July 1916, with the comment 'here's a little poem, a bit commonplace I'm afraid.'

BREAK OF DAY IN THE TRENCHES[1]

The darkness crumbles away.
It is the same old druid Time as ever,
Only a live thing leaps my hand,
A queer sardonic rat,
5 As I pull the parapet's poppy
To stick behind my ear.
Droll rat, they would shoot you if they knew
Your cosmopolitan sympathies.
Now you have touched this English hand
10 You will do the same to a German
Soon, no doubt, if it be your pleasure
To cross the sleeping green between.
It seems you inwardly grin as you pass
Strong eyes, fine limbs, haughty athletes,
15 Less chanced than you for life,
Bonds to the whims of murder,
Sprawled in the bowels of the earth,
The torn fields of France.
What do you see in our eyes
20 At the shrieking iron and flame
Hurled through still heavens?
What quaver—what heart aghast?
Poppies whose roots are in man's veins
Drop, and are ever dropping;

25 But mine in my ear is safe—
Just a little white with the dust.

June 1916

[1] First published in *Poetry Magazine*, Chicago, December 1916, where line 8 is followed by the line, in parentheses, (*And God knows what antipathies*). The punctuation of lines 13-15 in the American version differs unimportantly from the above, but the former printed four totally different lines between line 19 and the final couplet, as follows:

> *At the boom, the hiss, the swiftness,*
> *The irrevocable earth buffet—*
> *A shell's haphazard fury.*
> *What rootless poppies dropping?*

a quatrain which R immeasurably improved in the later version, handwritten on a TS signed and dated June 1916, on which he also deleted the line in parentheses mentioned above. Both PIR and CW, apparently following *Poetry* (Chicago), printed dashes at the end of lines 1, 3, 4 and 10, a form of punctuation which R only occasionally used, and as none appears in either of the signed and emended TSS, I have followed them. A TS once in Bottomley's possession has: *it seems, odd thing, you grin as you pass* for line 14, and *is* corrected by R to *are* in line 25.

HOME-THOUGHTS FROM FRANCE

Wan, fragile faces of joy!
Pitiful mouths that strive
To light with smiles the place
We dream we walk alive.

To you I stretch my hands,
Hands shut in pitiless trance
In the land of ruin and woe,
The desolate land of France.

Dear faces startled and shaken,
Out of wild dust and sounds
You yearn to me, lure and sadden
My heart with futile bounds.

'A WORM FED ON THE HEART OF CORINTH'

A worm fed on the heart of Corinth,
Babylon and Rome:
Not Paris raped tall Helen,
But this incestuous worm,
Who lured her vivid beauty
To his amorphous sleep.
England! famous as Helen
Is thy betrothal sung
To him the shadowless,
More amorous than Solomon.

1916

THE DYING SOLDIER

'Here are houses', he moaned,
'I could reach but my brain swims.'
Then they thundered and flashed
And shook the earth to its rims.

'They are gunpits', he gasped,
'Our men are at the guns.
Water—water—O water
For one of England's dying sons.'

'We cannot give you water,
Were all England in your breath,'
'Water!—water!—O water!'
He moaned and swooned to death.

A typescript with ink emendations, probably by R, shows exclamation marks after the words *water* that have been carefully erased in line 7, but not in line 11. CW omitted them in both lines, presumably for consistency, but I think R intended the crescendo effect.

IN WAR

Fret the nonchalant noon
With your spleen
Or your gay brow,
For the motion of your spirit
5 Ever moves with these.

When day shall be too quiet,
Deaf to you
And your dumb smile,
Untuned air shall lap the stillness
10 In the old space for your voice—

The voice that once could mirror
Remote depths
Of moving being,
Stirred by responsive voices near,
15 Suddenly stilled for ever.

No ghost darkens the places
Dark to One;
But my eyes dream,
And my heart is heavy to think
20 How it was heavy once.

In the old days when death
Stalked the world
For the flower of men,
And the rose of beauty faded
25 And pined in the great gloom,

One day we dug a grave:
We were vexed
With the sun's heat.
We scanned the hooded dead:
30 At noon we sat and talked.

How death had kissed their eyes
Three dread noons since,
How human art won
The dark soul to flicker
35 Till it was lost again:

And we whom chance kept whole—
But haggard,
Spent—were charged
To make a place for them who knew
40 No pain in any place.

The good priest came to pray;
Our ears half heard,
And half we thought
Of alien things, irrelevant;
45 And the heat and thirst were great.

The good priest read: 'I heard . . .'
Dimly my brain
Held words and lost . . .
Sudden my blood ran cold . . .
50 God! God! it could not be.

He read my brother's name;
I sank—
I clutched the priest.
They did not tell me it was he
55 Was killed three days ago.

What are the great sceptred dooms
To us, caught
In the wild wave?
We break ourselves on them,
60 My brother, our hearts and years.

1917

The above text follows CW, which in turn follows PIR verbatim, which suggests that Bottomley had sight of some MS in 1922 which had disappeared by 1937. It is not in the BL, and the only holograph known to me is in Rosenberg's hand on the fly-leaf of his copy of *Moses*. It consists of the first 2 verses only, gives *thy* for *your* in lines 2, 3 and 4, and omits *old* in line 10. It is followed by a further 4 lines, in indelible pencil, which may or may not have been intended to form part of this poem. They read:

Learn not such music here
The grave's door
Shall hear that music
Of the eternal taciturn.

CW printed them as fragment III.

THE IMMORTALS

I killed them, but they would not die.
Yea! all the day and all the night
For them I could not rest nor sleep,
Nor guard from them nor hide in flight.

5 Then in my agony I turned
And made my hands red in their gore.
In vain—for faster than I slew
They rose more cruel than before.

I killed and killed with slaughter mad;
10 I killed till all my strength was gone.
And still they rose to torture me,
For Devils only die in fun.

I used to think the Devil hid
In women's smiles and wine's carouse.
15 I called him Satan, Balzebub.
But now I call him, dirty louse.

1917

l. 12: CW gives *for fun*, but two holographs—one indubitably in R's hand
—both show *in fun*. They also differ from CW in having a comma after
him in the last line, which gives it more punch.

LOUSE HUNTING

Nudes—stark and glistening,
Yelling in lurid glee. Grinning faces
And raging limbs
Whirl over the floor one fire.
5 For a shirt verminously busy
Yon soldier tore from his throat, with oaths
Godhead might shrink at, but not the lice.
And soon the shirt was aflare
Over the candle he'd lit while we lay.

10 Then we all sprang up and stript
To hunt the verminous brood.
Soon like a demons' pantomime
The place was raging.
See the silhouettes agape,
15 See the gibbering shadows
Mixed with the battled arms on the wall.
See gargantuan hooked fingers
Pluck in supreme flesh
To smutch supreme littleness.
20 See the merry limbs in hot **Highland** fling
Because some wizard vermin
Charmed from the quiet this **revel**
When our ears were half lulled
By the dark music
25 Blown from Sleep's trumpet.

1917

Owing to the difficulty of deciphering R's **pencil** holograph of this poem,
there are several discrepancies between **the** printed versions of 1922 and
1937, e.g. PIR has *plunge* for *place* in line 13, *baffled* for *battled* in line 16,
and *that* for *hot* in line 20. R originally had: *Dug in Supreme flesh/For the
mortifying littleness* in lines 18-19, but corrected the second of these to the
CW reading followed above, and probably also intended to substitute
pluck for *dug*.

RETURNING, WE HEAR THE LARKS

Sombre the night is.
And though we have our lives, we know
What sinister threat lurks there.

Dragging these anguished limbs, we only know
5 This poison-blasted track opens on our camp—
On a little safe sleep.

But hark! joy—joy—strange joy.
Lo! heights of night ringing with unseen larks.
Music showering our upturned list'ning faces.

10 Death could drop from the dark
As easily as song—
But song only dropped,
Like a blind man's dreams on the sand
By dangerous tides,
15 Like a girl's dark hair for she dreams no ruin lies there,
Or her kisses where a serpent hides.

1917

l. 1: R originally wrote *sombre the night hangs.*
l. 9: Both PIR and CW have 'showering' *on* 'our upturned' . . . which R
also had originally; but in what is virtually a fair-copy of the poem, in
pencil holograph, he crossed out *on* and it does not appear in a subsequent
TS.

DEAD MAN'S DUMP

The plunging limbers over the shattered track
Racketed with their rusty freight,
Stuck out like many crowns of thorns,
And the rusty stakes like sceptres old
5 To stay the flood of brutish men
Upon our brothers dear.

The wheels lurched over sprawled dead
But pained them not, though their bones crunched,
Their shut mouths made no moan,
10 They lie there huddled, friend and foeman,
Man born of man, and born of woman,
And shells go crying over them
From night till night and now.

109

Earth has waited for them
15 All the time of their growth
Fretting for their decay:
Now she has them at last!
In the strength of their strength
Suspended—stopped and held.

20 What fierce imaginings their dark souls lit
Earth! have they gone into you?
Somewhere they must have gone,
And flung on your hard back
Is their souls' sack,
25 Emptied of God-ancestralled essences.
Who hurled them out? Who hurled?

None saw their spirits' shadow shake the grass,
Or stood aside for the half used life to pass
Out of those doomed nostrils and the doomed mouth,
30 When the swift iron burning bee
Drained the wild honey of their youth.

What of us, who flung on the shrieking pyre,
Walk, our usual thoughts untouched,
Our lucky limbs as on ichor fed,
35 Immortal seeming ever?
Perhaps when the flames beat loud on us,
A fear may choke in our veins
And the startled blood may stop.

The air is loud with death,
40 The dark air spurts with fire
The explosions ceaseless are.
Timelessly now, some minutes past,
These dead strode time with vigorous life,
Till the shrapnel called 'an end!'
45 But not to all. In bleeding pangs
Some borne on stretchers dreamed of home,
Dear things, war-blotted from their hearts.

A man's brains splattered on
A stretcher-bearer's face;
50 His shook shoulders slipped their load,
But when they bent to look again
The drowning soul was sunk too deep
For human tenderness.

They left this dead with the older dead,
55 Stretched at the cross roads.

Burnt black by strange decay,
Their sinister faces lie
The lid over each eye,
The grass and coloured clay
60 More motion have than they,
Joined to the great sunk silences.

Here is one not long dead;
His dark hearing caught our far wheels,
And the choked soul stretched weak hands
65 To reach the living word the far wheels said,
The blood-dazed intelligence beating for light,
Crying through the suspense of the far torturing wheels
Swift for the end to break,
Or the wheels to break,
70 Cried as the tide of the world broke over his sight.

Will they come? Will they ever come?
Even as the mixed hoofs of the mules,
The quivering-bellied mules,
And the rushing wheels all mixed
75 With his tortured upturned sight,
So we crashed round the bend,
We heard his weak scream,
We heard his very last sound,
And our wheels grazed his dead face.

1917

There are 3 TSS and 2 holograph fragments extant of 'Dead Man's Dump',
deservedly R's most renowned poem. TS1, the earliest of the 3 versions
of the complete poem, has *clenched mouths* in line 9, and the following 4 lines
after line 19:

> *Now let the seasons know*
> *There are some less to feed of them*
> *That winter need not hoard her snow,*
> *Nor Autumn her fruits and grain.*

Additionally, the last line of the penultimate stanza has *over his sight*
corrected in ink to *over his brains*—an alteration which R wisely rescinded
in TS2.

TS2, which is headed 'Dead Man's Dump' in pencil in R's hand (one of
the holographs is entitled 'The Young Dead') has the above 4 lines
deleted and, also in R's hand, *Emptied of God-ancestralled essences* for line 25
in place of:

> *Emptied of all that made it more than the world*
> *In its small fleshly compass.*

TS3 is presumably the latest version, since in addition to the T2 corrections
R changed *clenched* to *shut* in line 9 and, significantly, omitted the original
9th stanza entirely. So did Bottomley in PIR, but CW restored it. As T3

is signed and dated 'Isaac Rosenberg, May 14 1917, B.E.F. France' I have taken it as his final version, and as reflecting his wish not to break the stretcher-bearer sequence at this point by a distracting (and rather confused) apostrophe to the earth. The stanza in question reads:

> *Maniac Earth! howling and flying, your bowel*
> *Seared by the jagged fire, the iron love*
> *The impetuous storm of savage love.*
> *Dark Earth! dark heaven, swinging in chemic smoke*
> *What dead are born when you kiss each soundless soul*
> *With lightning and thunder from your mined heart,*
> *Which man's self dug, and his blind fingers loosed.*

Both holographs, and all 3 TSS, agree in having no punctuation at the end of line 20 and a question mark after line 21, which I have followed.

DAUGHTERS OF WAR

Space beats the ruddy freedom of their limbs—
Their naked dances with man's spirit naked
By the root side of the tree of life,
(The underside of things
5 And shut from earth's profoundest eyes).

I saw in prophetic gleams
These mighty daughters in their dances
Beckon each soul aghast from its crimson corpse
To mix in their glittering dances.
10 I heard the mighty daughters' giant sighs
In sleepless passion for the sons of valour,
And envy of the days of flesh
Barring their love with mortal boughs across—
The mortal boughs—the mortal tree of life.
15 The old bark burnt with iron wars
They blow to a live flame
To char the young green days
And reach the occult soul; they have no softer lure
No softer lure than the savage ways of death.

20 We were satisfied of our lords the moon and the sun
To take our wage of sleep and bread and warmth—
These maidens came—these strong ever-living Amazons,
And in an easy might their wrists
Of night's sway and noon's sway the sceptres brake,
25 Clouding the wild—the soft lustres of our eyes.

7. (a) The Road. Oil. 1911 $10\frac{1}{2}'' \times 14\frac{1}{4}''$

7. (b) Trees. Oil. 1912 $10\frac{1}{2}'' \times 13\frac{3}{4}''$

8. Hark, Hark, the Lark. Charcoal and monochrome wash. 1912 $14'' \times 13\frac{1}{4}''$

Clouding the wild lustres, the clinging tender lights;
Driving the darkness into the flame of day,
With the Amazonian wind of them
Over our corroding faces
30 That must be broken—broken for evermore
So the soul can leap out
Into their huge embraces.
Though there are human faces
Best sculptures of Deity,
35 And sinews lusted after
By the Archangels tall,
Even these must leap to the love heat of these maidens
From the flame of terrene days
Leaving grey ashes to the wind—to the wind.

40 One (whose great lifted face,
Where wisdom's strength and beauty's strength
And the thewed strength of large beasts
Moved and merged, gloomed and lit)
Was speaking, surely, as the earth-men's earth fell away;
45 Whose new hearing drunk the sound
Where pictures, lutes, and mountains mixed
With the loosed spirit of a thought.
Essenced to language, thus—

'My sisters force their males
50 From the doomed earth, from the doomed glee
And hankering of hearts.
Frail hands gleam up through the human quagmire and lips of
    ash
Seem to wail, as in sad faded paintings
Far sunken and strange.
55 My sisters have their males
Clean of the dust of old days
That clings about those white hands
And yearns in those voices sad.

But these shall not see them,
60 Or think of them in any days or years,
They are my sisters' lovers in other days and years.'

1917

There are no less than 7 extant TSS of this, one of R's longest and most
ambitious poems. They differ widely in content, varying in length from
47 to 61 lines. There is also a pencil hol. which R sent Bottomley.

T1 and T2 have *new bared* for *naked* in line 2, and after line 3 go straight
on to lines 15-17 above. The next two lines are also not included.

T3 has a different opening, ink-written in R's hand, and attached to the rest of the TS by a single thread. After the first 2 lines it continues:

> *Here, by the root side of the tree of life,*
> *Side, shut from earth's profoundest eyes,*
> *Their shining dances claim the astonied soul*
> *Even as its human voice expires in the boughs.*

Thereafter it follows T1 and T2, apart from substituting *Moved and merged, gloomed and lit* for *Transfiguring lit* in line 4 of stanza 5 above, and adding the additional line *Which worked like language of wavering dream* to that stanza.

T4 and T5 follow T3 right up to line 52, where they substitute *Frail hands gleam up* for *Frail hearts stick up*, a distinct improvement.

T6 and 7, presumably the last revisions, have the further revised opening lines that CW printed, followed here, and substitutes *Essenced to language, thus* for the additional line added to stanza 5 mentioned above. T7 also has a pencilled marginal note in R's hand indicating a break after line 19, which is not in T6 or CW. This, as well as a number of punctuational variants throughout, have been followed rather than PIR or CW in this context.

SOLDIER: TWENTIETH CENTURY

I love you, great new Titan!
Am I not you?
Napoleon and Caesar
Out of you grew.

5 Out of unthinkable torture,
Eyes kissed by death,
Won back to the world again,
Lost and won in a breath,

Cruel men are made immortal.
10 Out of your pain born.
They have stolen the sun's power
With their feet on your shoulders worn.

Let them shrink from your girth,
That has outgrown the pallid days,
15 When you slept like Circe's swine,
Or a word in the brain's ways.

1917

l. 5: R first wrote *out of your pain*, but evidently decided to forego the rhyme in favour of the more emphatic phrase.

l. 13: This originally read *Let the world shrink* etc.

The punctuation of the third verse differs in PIR and CW, neither of which follows R's usage in a very clearly written holograph of the poem. As the construction of the lines is —perhaps intentionally—ambiguous, I have thought it best to follow R's text exactly.

GIRL TO SOLDIER ON LEAVE

I love you—Titan lover,
My own storm-days' Titan.
Greater than the son of Zeus,
I know who I would choose.

5 Titan—my splendid rebel—
The old Prometheus
Wanes like a ghost before your power—
His pangs were joys to yours.

Pallid days arid and wan
10 Tied your soul fast.
Babel cities' smoky tops
Pressed upon your growth

Weary gyves. What were you,
But a word in the brain's ways,
15 Or the sleep of Circe's swine?
One gyve holds you yet.

It held you hiddenly on the Somme
Tied from my heart at home.
O must it loosen now? I wish
20 You were bound with the old old gyves.

Love! you love me—your eyes
Have looked through death at mine.
You have tempted a grave too much.
I let you—I repine.

1917

There is a fair-copy pencil holograph and a TS of this poem, which agree
in having *who* for the more grammatical *whom* which PIR and CW printed
in line 4. Both sources likewise show a clear comma at the end of line 13,
which has therefore also been restored.

THE BURNING OF THE TEMPLE

Fierce wrath of Solomon
Where sleepest thou? O see
The fabric which thou won
Earth and ocean to give thee—
O look at the red skies.

Or hath the sun plunged down?
What is this molten gold—
These thundering fires blown
Through heaven—where the smoke rolled?
Again the great king dies.

His dreams go out in smoke,
His days he let not pass
And sculptured here are broke
Are charred as the burnt grass
Gone as his mouth's last sighs.

1918

THE DESTRUCTION OF JERUSALEM
BY THE BABYLONIAN HORDES

They left their Babylon bare
Of all its tall men.
Of all its proud horses;
They made for Lebanon.

5 And shadowy sowers went
Before their spears to sow
The fruit whose taste is ash
For Judah's soul to know.

They who bowed to the Bull god
10 Whose wings roofed Babylon,
In endless hosts darkened
The bright-heavened Lebanon.

They washed their grime in pools
Where laughing girls forgot
15 The wiles they used for Solomon.
Sweet laughter! remembered not.

Sweet laughter charred in the flame
That clutched the cloud and earth
While Solomon's towers crashed between
20 The gird of Babylon's mirth.

1918

In PIR the exclamation mark and full stop in the last line of verse 4 are
interchanged, and the final line of the poem reads: *To a gird of Babylon's
mirth.* Neither of these variants appears in the 4 extant typescripts, or in
CW.

'THROUGH THESE PALE COLD DAYS'

Through these pale cold days
What dark faces burn
Out of three thousand years,
And their wild eyes yearn,

While underneath their brows
Like waifs their spirits grope
For the pools of Hebron again—
For Lebanon's summer slope.

They leave these blond still days
In dust behind their tread
They see with living eyes
How long they have been dead.

1918

The last poem R wrote, which he enclosed in a letter to Marsh dated March 28th 1918 (see p. 272). By the time it arrived, Rosenberg himself had been killed in action.

FRAGMENTS OF POEMS

I

TO WILHELM II[1]

It is cruel Emperor
The stars are too high.
For your reach Emperor
Far out they lie.
5 It is cruel for you Emperor
The sea has a stone,
England—they call it England,
That cannot shine in your crown.

Cruel the seas are deep,
10 Cruel for you Emperor
That all men are not in blind sleep,
And free hearts burn, Emperor.
It is cruel when a wronged world turns
And draws the claws of the beast
15 Cruel, cruel for you Emperor
Who would be most is least.

[1] This was sent in a letter, probably to R's sister Annie, with the note:
'The other side is doggerel I've just written'.

II

Power that impels,
Pulse of the void working to my vain grappling fingers,
Like a grave star drawing our gazes forlorn
Will kiss the sister star that is my soul,
So I a visible star, would penetrate the vast,
The unimaginable chasms and abysses
To reach the fountain star that hides the soul of thee.

The poet's dead soul whose flung word lights the world,
The struck music that panic whirls the world—
The hills decay and pass to blossoms of fire;
In their slow dust God kneads his changing forms.
Sculptor of infinite dreams, we thank our dreamer.

The above text follows CW, which may have been based on a version now
lost, or is possibly a conflation of two barely decipherable pencil holo-
graphs in the blank pages of 'New Numbers', a magazine published in
Gloucestershire which contained work by Abercrombie, John Drinkwater,
W. W. Gibson and Rupert Brooke. One of these versions has, for line 2,
Pulse of the void to our vain grappling fingers.

III

ART

O amber anger thrust
Out of a madman's lust
For a baulked perfection,
Sad lithe towering—
5 Eternal dereliction.

Barbaric tenderness
Burns swart for sorrowless
Roses in storm advance,
Abysmal as they swing
10 Through a tumult of trance.

l. 10: CW has *a tumult of deep trance*, but R seems clearly to have deleted
the extra foot. Cf. *Moses*, Sc. II, l. 4.

Another version, with 4 verses, reads:

This maenad anger thrust
Out of a madman's lust
For a baulked perfection,
This lithe towering
5 Of life to dereliction.

Barbaric tenderness
Swart and blithe as the stress
Of storm on rose adance,
Abysmal to swing
10 In your tumult of trance.

l. 10: An earlier draft has *In your wizard trance*, which suits the rhythm
better.

The riding pomp of the years,
Vigours our eyes and ears
When from your arm
Silence is flung from a sling
15 To sound song's alarm.

The streaming rigours of our blood
Where silence is a derelict;
Life's derelict, poesy,
Saith Life's no derelict of hers
20 Her sinews are and bone, saith she.

l. 12: CW has *vigorous*, but in both holographs R clearly wrote *vigours*,
which he presumably intended as a transitive verb.

Yet another version reads:

Amber of anger thrust
Out of a madman's lust
For a baulked perfection
Spices lithe towering
From an island's dereliction.

All amber dust and wine
Upon our fingers shine
Like under water hid
No net to air can bring
Though it trembles on the lid.

The riding pomp of the years
Vigours our eyes and ears
When your magic arm
Leaping from silence
Sounds song's alarm.

There are echoes of *Moses* in the above fragments, which may just possibly
have been intended for incorporation in that play, e.g. compare ll. 1-3 and
9-10 of the first version with *Moses*, Sc. II, ll. 248-50 and 202-3 respectively.

IV

Ah, if your lips might stir,
With one mood's breath behind,
To the touch of a certain mood
As easily as it alters
To all swift moods but this!
But you are afraid to smile
And bewitch yourself to a place
Where though your moods might alter
One mood would come in vain.

l. 2 originally read *With my mood's wind behind.*

V

You gave me leave to love you
In my own way I will.
Your leave you gave in your way.

In shy delight of loving,
The ways we two had met
Those ways we still must wander
There is one thing to forget.

We must forget ourselves, sweet,
Too much we feel the kiss,
Forget the bliss of loving,
And strive for God love's bliss.

1914

R was, understandably, unhappy about the last line of this fragment, which might otherwise be regarded as a complete poem. He considered *For love's eternal bliss* but rejected it, presumably as being both repetitive and trite, but failed to resolve the complex ambiguity of the existing line.

VI

My desires are as the sea
Whose white tongues fawn on the breast
Of sand and turn it again to sea,
Back to itself that prest.
My desires feed on me.

VII

Where the rock's heart is hidden from the sea
The unwearied sea whose white tongues fawn upon its breast
The rock's heart hidden from the unwearying sea

Whose white tongues fawn upon its dumb { wet cheeks / cold breasts / cold cheeks

It knows the hunger
O as the rock's heart is her heart
And my thoughts fawn and my eyes cover her
O wonderful sea—it is little rock

Her eyes, { that are the heavens / deep heavens } whose depths reach not to me.

1914

This fragment was written by R on the fly-leaf of a book of William Plomer's, at Camp Bay, South Africa. (*Berg Collection.*)

VIII

He was mad,
Brain drenched by luxury of pulsing blood,
While to his heart's throat his cold spirit pressed.
And ever rippled waves of golden curls,
Rose hue made of his thoughts a coloured fire.

1914

IX

The trees suffer the wind
And the sunbeams leap in their mail.
The shadows slide from leaf to leaf
And sudden and brief
Resounds like an avalanche
The throats of these things frail.

1914

l. 2: CW printed *on their mail*, which at first sight seems a helpful emendation; but when R sent the poem in a letter to Marda Vanne, the well-known S. African actress, he clearly wrote *in their mail*, and I believe intended to suggest the play of sunlight *within* the glittering leaves. He also, again I think deliberately, because he was trying to capture the effect of a sudden gust of wind, used none of the four slowing-down commas that CW has.

X

Heart, is there hope—or is there ordeal still in thy stars' horoscope?
Come, the keen years, the fierce years, laughing and cruel,
Heap on your trouble.

1914

XI

The brooding stones and the dissolving hills,
The summer's leafy luxury,
The winter shrewd,
And all thy changing robes, thy myriad forms.

XII

The monster wind prowls in the writhen trees,
The wind dives in the writhen trees,
They strain in angered leash their green,
They are only strong in ease.

Soft, forward, inarticulate,
Warm, wayward, drooping, or aburst,
Rushing, it tires, slacks to abate.

The wind wakes in the writhen trees

1914

XIII

In a concentrated thought a sudden noise startles.
Sensual motions of nerves
Vibrate from hushed sky curves,
Helpless, obscene and cruel.
My fires must drain that jewel
Of all its virgin rays.
Crunched in one black amaze
My life inert goes out,
Dissolves voluptuously.

XIV

O spear-girt face too far
Save for the sorcery that makes soft
Those points, or turns them inward on herself.
I cannot cleave through that inviolate tract
That virginal . . .

XV

Love, hide thy face—why in thy land
This garden blooms we understand
A little—not at all—but men
Live not who are not drunk sometime
With power of its scents that climb
Their tōwers of soul, and melt and sting
The thoughted throng unburnishing,
The spiritual shining.

Rapid the flames and swords, the chains
Flash and are flung, we burn, we writhe,
The blood is emptied from our veins
And wine streams through, fiercely and blithe,
The royal flesh whose panting legions . . .

1914

XVI

Poets have snared you in sweet word,
Such cage, immortal singing bird
Each soul finds you while tread your eyes
Its intricate infinities.
Bounding infinity in a mood
Whose habit is your roseate hood,
To ecstasy—to ecstasy
More sweet than Paradise can be,
Where every thought and pulse and vein
Melts into joy—till sense is fain
To cease lest . . .

XVII

Her grape green eyes have stained in weird
Lustrous fantasies the urn
Of one mood and ever they burn,
And the heart stands there to learn.

They are old carvings so long heard
In oldest struggle of man's brain
One of restlessness to gain,
Death dim—fair hair in vain.

l. 5: BL holograph has *pictures* for *carvings,* and in l. 7: has *One greed God's jealousy to gain.*

XVIII

Pale mother night, suckling thy brood of stars,
My fire, too, yearns for thy giant love,
But they are calm, and mine is frenzy fire.

XIX

In all Love's heady valour and bold pains
Is the wide storehouse for your female gains

XX

SENSUAL

Or where absence, silence is,
Of fleshly strings whose strains are Paradise
And pavin ecstasies
For the untravelled ardours leashed in eyes.

Youth's fearless wings are spread.
O Cynic life! fine mirrors are your walls.
O voice and lip unwed,
Hands beckon but my own wild shadow calls.

Is not love loveliness,
Truth beauty and all natural harmony
Unstriving happiness,
The mystic centre of all unity?

Life mirrors love and truth
Even as our love and truth within be deep.
His own self dazzles youth

1914

XXI

Beautiful is the day,
Sighs the beloved night.
Why do you fly away
When I come with my stars bright?
Your gaudy disarray

1914

l. 5: Cf. the last line of Fragment XLVIII (p. 135).

An earlier but rather more complete draft read:

Beautiful is the day
Of the beloved night
Between his breast there play
Dark forms waving bright
In stars' vague disarray
The hills have taken flight.

XXII

Wood and forest, drink
Of the blue delight,
Only of its brink.
But to my mind and sight
Drink from brink to brink.

XXIII

I know all men are withered with yearning—
O forest flame, guarded with swords that are burning,
O eyes that sea-like our madness entombs,
Gold hair whose rich metal enlocks us in terror

XXIV

I have heard the Gods
In their high conference
As I lay outside the world
Quiet in sleep

XXV

In the large manner and luxury
Of a giant who guests
In a little world of mortals,
He condescends a space
His ears to incline,
But as though list'ning were a trouble.
Who knows! but it were a hazard
To break speech on this matter,
To bid conference with a doctor!
Mayhap cod-liver-oil
Thrice in the day taken
Medicinal might be.

The above text follows CW and an ink holograph in BL, apart from the omission of commas at the end of lines 10 and 11, which CW inserted.

XXVI

Even as a letter burns and curls
And the mind and heart in the writing blackens,
Words that wane as the wind unfurls—
Obliteration never slackens.
Fate who wrote it and addressed it here,
Life who read it, loved it, called it dear,
Peace who slumbered, Love who tore it through.

XXVII

The thronging glories ringing round our birth,
The angels worshipping, th' adoring kings,
The inspired presence,
Surely the songs, the worship, and the burden
Of light washes beneath the lidded slumber
Of the shut soul.

1914

l. 3 originally read: *Enroofed nativity with a marvel of gold* and
l. 4: *Surely the songs are heard, the worship known.*

XXVIII

Nature, indeed, the plot you spin's so stale,
And each man's story is so like another,
I should advise—it's such a boring tale,
Suppress all copies and begin some other.

XXIX

From your sunny clime
Dream of earthly time
And the chill mist,
Wonder at earth's wreck
And the sorrow-strewn deck,
By death unkist.

Sailing as for joy,
Happy girl and boy,
In these waters grim
See their faces pale,
The broken sail,
For an idle whim.
God's dream, God's whim.

CW has *By friend death unkist* in line 6, and *Watch their faces* in line 10, but R's corrections to these lines are reasonably clear and seem intended.

XXX

Now think how high a mountain is,
Joy, could this tall oak's branches kiss
Its shoulder, less its brow, how blest?
If I lie low the skies are drest
With its broidered branches stretched across
Into the sky-scorned mountain's loss,
The sky, it gibbers to forever.
Nought is too low to make so high
As hope, if we stand right, and sever
Waste, the essential to descry.

l. 5: R originally wrote *fingered branches*.

XXXI

Violet is the maddest color I know
And opal is the color of dreams,
But a girl is the color of snow,
The violet like noon haze she seems
And of opal the lights on her brow . . .

For a note on R's frequent spelling of *colour* see p. 96.

XXXII

Drowsed in beauty
Of her face
Waking fancies
Strive to chase.

XXXIII

In the moon's dark fantasy
Here is a woman weeping,
Having the night for a palace.
And here in a house of stone
Harlots feast and revel.

1914

XXXIV

All pleasures fly,
O clinging lights
And wavering glory
Adieu you sigh,
Half-told your story,
To you we die.

l. 1: CW has *All pleasures die* but in a BL holograph R corrected *die* to *fly*, presumably to avoid a repetition in the last line.

XXXV

And like the artist who creates
From dying things what never dies . . .

XXXVI

For one thrilled instant am I you, O skies.
It passes, I am hunted, and the air
Lives with revengeful momentary fires.
O wilderness of heaven,
5 Whose profound spaces like some God's blank eyes
Roll in a milky terror, move and move,
While our fears make vague shuddering imprints there
And character such chained-up forms of sorrow

That a breath can unloose; in its white depths
10 Dream unnamed gulfs of sudden traps for men.
For all men's thoughts go up and form one soul
With unimagined might of evil scheming,
Wrought by the texture of selfish desires,
Of puny plotting, and inspired dreaming.

15 Or if a thought like spray by sudden moon
Is lit, that holy amorous instant knows
Transplanted time to make twin time in space,
My new born thought touch aeon-dusted thoughts.
From softly lidded lights, from breaking gleams,
20 Into a rainbow radiance, some pale light springs,
And the dim Sun stands midwife to this child.

l. 12: R originally wrote *unimagined powers*

XXXVII

THE SEARCH

Dawn like a flushed rose petal fleck'd with gold
Quickened youth's glow. Upon my barb I leap'd
While the blank desert's stretchèd leaguers slept,
And loosed his bridle of flame from idling cold.

XXXVIII

Be the hope or the fear,
Be the smile or the tear,
In the strife of a life
On Time's rolling river
That rolls on forever.

XXXIX

WILD UNDERTONES

I wash my soul in colours, in a million undertones,
And then my soul shines out—and you read—a poem.

XL

I have pressed my teeth in the heart of May,
I have dabbled my lips in the honey of June,
And the sun shot keen and the grass laughed gay
And the earth was buoyed on the tide of noon.

XLI

What songs do fill the pauses of our day
When action tires and motion begs to stay
And life can give to life a little heed?
Then when life only seems to pause
A life divine from heaven she draws,
From labour's earthly trammels freed.

XLII

In dimpled depths of smiling innocence,
In dimpled labyrinths of innocence,
My sunless sorrow made its rosy grave
In laughing liquid eyes that Time had wardened.
Fifteen skyey years,—my sad soul looked,
My sad soul looked and all its sadness vanished.

The pencil holograph of this fragment has no punctuation, apart from the comma followed by a dash in line 5, which were almost certainly inserted by R since they are in coloured crayon. He may well therefore have intended the last two lines to be read without pause. But for ease of reading I have followed the punctuation in CW.

XLIII

'WHAT MAY BE, WHAT HATH BEEN, AND WHAT IS NOW?'

I said, I have been having some fits of despondency lately; this is what they generally end in, some Byronic sublimity of plaintive caterwauling:

What may be, what hath been, and what is now?
God. God! if thou art pity, look on me;
God! if thou art forgiveness, turn and see
The dark within, the anguish on my brow!
O! wherefore am I stricken in grief thus low?
For no wrong done, or right undone to thee?
For, if that thou has made me, what must be
Thou hast made too. How canst thou be thy foe
To retribute what thou thyself hast done?
A little pity, or if that be vain,
If tears are dumb since there to hear are none,
If that the years mean lingering hours of pain,
If rest alone through death's gate is but won,

XLIV

The grasses tremble and quiver
Now at the set of day
The host of colours come
In gorgeous disarray

l. 4: R kept returning to this image, cf. the last lines of 'Frail hours that love to dance' and 'Beautiful is the day'.

XLV

SUMMER IN WINTER

SIX THOUGHTS

Before the winter's over
I know a way
The summer to recover,
The August and the May.

5 Before the month of blossoms
And sunny days,
I know that which unbosoms
Whate'er the summer says.

Ah! would you net the season?
10 And chain the sun?
For you will flowers do treason?
And how is treason done?

While still the land lies gleaming
And bare and dumb,
15 And love asleep is dreaming
Of the warm nights to come,

Catch these sweet thoughts in shadow,
Bring them to light,
At once the fragrant meadow
20 Will flash on sense and sight.

Six names of six sweet maidens,
Six honey flowers,
Name, and each name unladens
Its load of summer hours.

25 Ruth, joyous as a July
Song-throbbing noon,
And rosy as a newly
Flushed eager rose in June.

The August's dreamy languor
30 Is Maisy sweet.
Drowsed summer when she's sang her
Rich songs and rests her feet.

The stately smile and gracious
Of an April wood
[lacuna]
35 Is tall and fair Gertrude.

And like a clear May morning
When birds call clear
And quickly to each other,
Is little Lily dear.

40 And ripe as buxom Autumn
When she holds hands
With August, fruit enwroughten,
Fair sumptuous Ethel stands.

Sweet gleams of dawn and twilight,
45 Sunshine in shade,
Is Lena calm as starlight.
Now the six thoughts are said.

XLVI

L— AND M—

Once on a time in a land so fair
That the air you breathed was as wine,
And everything that you looked on there
Made you at once divine,

5 There lived two maidens, little and sweet,
Whose dear names I may not tell
Because they would call me blab and cheat,
Which would be terrible.

The eldest whom I will just call L,
10 Was most ladylike and smart,
And of M the youngest, she had ways that—well,
One had to guard one's heart.

And in this land, as of course you'd guess,
They did not live all alone,
15 And all the blessings that God could bless
These two could call their own.

A mother, so wise and good and kind,
A father as young as they
In heart, who while he formed their mind,
20 He did not mind their play.

They were taught music, and painting, and all
Of culture's thousand pothers,
To dance **and** to ply the bat and ball,
And also feel for others.

25 But sad to say, most sad it should be,
They were not always good;
Although they looked so fairily,
They oft did what no fairy would.

When they were set to drawing flowers
30 Then Lily in pique would say,
'I hate drawing, especially flowers,
Let's throw the flowers away'.

And Maisy, that buxom rosy Miss,
Would set the teacher riddles,
35 And his brain with 'Can you solve this and this?'
Buzzed as if with a hundred fiddles.

XLVII

Amber eyes with ever such little red fires,
Face as vague and white as a swan in shadow.

1914-1915

XLVIII

Frail hours that love to dance
To hear yon princely sun,
His golden countenance
Scatters you pale and wan,
Scatters your ghostly love
That was the breath of a dream,
Scatters light from above
Till day flows like a stream.

134

The stars fade in the sky
Taking our dreams away,
Day's banners flame on high
In gaudy disarray.

1914-1915

XLIX

There are sweet chains that bind
And gains that are strange loss.
Your ruddy freedom falters
And pales at hint of these.
You change, bewilder and gleam
In a labyrinth of light,
But one change calls dark and dumbly
To you and calls in vain.

1914-1915

The only holograph of this fragment has no punctuation whatever, apart from the final full stop. The above follows the punctuation in CW, which seems to me correct.
l. 3: cf the first line of 'Daughters of War' (p. 112).
l. 6: A pencil note in the margin which reads *And [? are] filled with ephemeral light* suggests that R wanted to amend this line.

L

'I live for you', says Ted to Jane
'And if you died, so I'd die too.'
'I'm sure you would' said working Jane
'You live for me—to live for you.'

LI

[?Tom] is so reserved and quiet
Before he married was so blatant
                    He finds his Prue
Will talk enough for two.

LII

Over the chasm they rolled together
Chasm that lay in tumult of trance
Blue is the sky and calm the Spring weather
Careless of two who have ended their dance.

A BL script shows that R changed *was* to *is* in l. 3, and *clear* to *calm*. The quatrain is then followed by some unfinished lines and alternative versions of the above lines.

135

LIII

EVENING

My roses lioter, lips to press
Of emerald winds
Fall'n from sky chasms of sunset stress . . .
Amongst their petals grope
Displacing hands, and vapoured heliotrope.

1915

BL has 2 pencil holographs, the second of them clearly a fair-copy.
Both give the first line as above, but continue:

> *Fallen from sky chasms of sunset stress,*
> *Of emerald winds, and heliotrope*
> *Displacing hands that grope.*

CW printed a second verse, of four lines, but as these are identical with
the first four lines of *Moses*, Sc. II, I have omitted them here.

LIV

[The following poem was written for a Christmas card that Rosenberg drew
for his Division in 1917. It is now in the British Library.]

British women! in your wombs you plotted
This monstrous girth of glory, this marvellous glory.
Not for mere love delights God meant the profound hour
When an Englishman was planned.
Responsible hour! wherein God wrote anew
His guarantee of the world's surety
Of honour, light and sweetness, all forgot
Since men first marred the writ of Mary's Son.

1917

For an earlier, very different, version see R's letter to Rodker (p. 251).

PLAYS
AND FRAGMENTS OF PLAYS

MOSES

PERSONS

MOSES, *an Egyptian Prince*
ABINOAH, *an Overseer*
TWO HEBREWS
KOELUE, *Abinoah's Daughter*
MESSENGER

SCENE I. *Outside a college in Thebes. Egyptian students pass by.*
MOSES *alone in meditation.*

[*Enter* MESSENGER]

MESSENGER (*handing papyrus*) Pharaoh's desires.

MOSES (*reads*) To our beloved son, greeting. Add to our
thoughts of you, if possible to add, but a little, and you
are more than old heroes. Not to bemean your genius, who
5   might cry 'Was that all!'. We pile barriers everywhere.
We give you idiots for tools, tree stumps for swords, skin
sacks for souls. The sixteenth pyramid remains to be built.
We give you the last draft of slaves. Move! Forget not the
edict. PHARAOH.

10 MOSES (*to* MESSENGER) What is the edict?

MESSENGER. The royal paunch of Pharaoh dangled worriedly,
Not knowing where the wrong. Viands once giant-like
Came to him thin and thinner. What rats gnawed?
Horror! The swarm of slaves. The satraps swore
15   Their wives' bones hurt them when they lay abed
That before were soft and plump. The people howled
They'd boil the slaves three days to get their fat,
Ending the famine. A haggard council held
Decrees the two hind molars, those two staunchest
20   Busy labourers in the belly's service, to be drawn
From out each slave's greased mouth, which soon,
From incapacity, would lose the habit
Of eating.

MOSES. Well, should their bones stick out to find the air,
25   I'll make a use of them for pleasantness—
Droll demonstrations of anatomy.

MESSENGER. And when you've ended find 'twas one on sharks.

[MOSES *signs to* MESSENGER *to go. Exit* MESSENGER]

MOSES. Fine! Fine!
See in my brain
30   What madmen have rushed through,

138

And like a tornado
Torn up the tight roots
Of some dead universe.
The old clay is broken
35   For a power to soak in and knit
It all into tougher tissues
To hold life,
Pricking my nerves till the brain might crack,
It boils to my finger-tips,
40   Till my hands ache to grip
The hammer—the lone hammer
That breaks lives into a road
Through which my genius drives.
Pharaoh well peruked and oiled,
45   And your admirable pyramids,
And your interminable procession
Of crowded kings,
You are my little fishing rods
Wherewith I catch the fish
50   To suit my hungry belly.

I am rough now, and new, and will have no tailor.
Startlingly,
As a mountain side
Wakes aware of its other side,
55   When from a cave a leopard comes,
On its heels the same red sand,
Springing with acquainted air,
Sprang an intelligence
Coloured as a whim of mine,
60   Showed to my dull outer eyes
The living eyes underneath.
Did I not shrivel up and take the place of air,
Secret as those eyes were,
And those strong eyes call up a giant frame?
65   And I am that now.

Pharaoh is sleek and deep;
And where his love for me is set, under
The deeps, on its floor, or in the shallow ways,
Though I have been as a diver—never yet

l. 64: Neither the published play nor the TS from which it was set shows
a question mark at the end of this line, the former having a semi-colon
and the latter a comma. But both Bottomley and Harding opted for a
query, which is surely right.
l. 68: All original sources have *on its floor*, which PIR and CW changed
to *their floor*, which is grammatical but not what R wrote.

70   Could I find . . . I have a way, a touchstone!
        A small misdemeanour, touch of rebelliousness;
        To prick the vein of father, monitor, foe,
        Will tell which of these his kingship is.
        If I shut my eyes to the edict,
75   And leave the pincers to rust,
        And the slaves' teeth as God made them,
        Then hide from the summoning tribunal,
        Pharaoh will speak, and I'll seize that word to act.
        Should the word be a foe's, I can use it well,
80   As a poison to soak into Egypt's bowels,
        A wraith from old Nile will cry
        'For his mercy they break his back'
        And I shall have a great following for this,
        The rude touched heart of the mauled sweaty horde,
85   Their rough tongues fawn at my hands, their red streaked
            eyes
        Glisten with sacrifice. Well! Pharaoh bids me act.
        Hah! I'm all a-bristle. Lord! his eyes would go wide
        If he knew the road my rampant dreams would race.
        I am too much awake now—restless, so restless.
90   Behind white mists invisibly
        My thoughts stood like a mountain.
        But Power, watching as a man,
        Saw no mountain there,
        Only the mixing mist and sky,
95   And the flat earth.
        What shoulder pushed through those mists
        Of gay fantastic pastimes
        And startled hills of sleep?

              [*He looks in the mirror*]

        Oh! apparition of me!
100   Ruddy flesh soon hueless!
        Fade and show to my eyes
        The lasting bare body.
        Soul sack fall away
        And show what you hold.
105   Sing! Let me hear you sing.
            A voice sings
        Upon my lips like a cloud
        To burst on the peaks of light,
        Sit cowled, impossible things
        To tie my hands at their prime and height.

l. 86: R originally wrote *Glitter with sacrifice*, which PIR and CW followed;
but in his personal copy of *Moses* R changed *Glitter* to *Glisten*.

l. 109: An earlier version read *To tie my hands at noon's height.*

110 Power! break through their shroud.
    Pierce them so thoroughly,
    Thoroughly enter me,
    Know me for one dead.
    Break the shadowy thread,
115 The cowering spirit's bond
    Writ by illusions blonde.

    Ah! let the morning pale
    Throb with a wilder pulse.
    No delicate flame shall quail
120 With terror at your convulse.
    Thin branches whip the white skies
    To lips and spaces of song
    That chant a mood to my eyes—
    Ah! sleep can be overlong.

125 Moses. Voices thunder, voices of deeds not done.
    Lo! on the air is scrawled in abysmal light
    Old myths never known, and yet already foregone,
    And songs more lost, more secret than desert light.
    Martyrdoms of uncreated things,
130 Virgin silences waiting a breaking voice—
    As in a womb they cry, in a cage beat vain wings
    Under life, over life,—is their unbeing my choice?

    Dull wine of torpor—the unsoldered spirit lies limp,
    Ah! if she would run into a mould
135 Some new idea unwalled
    To human by-ways, an apocalyptic camp
    Of utterest and ulterior dreaming,
    Understood only in its gleaming,
    To flash stark naked the whole girth of the world.

140 I am sick of priests and forms,
    This rigid dry-boned refinement.

l. 116: I have restored the final 'e' to 'blonde', omitted in PIR and CW
though present in all the original sources, to preserve the association with
lace.
l. 121: A draft in BL has *Thin branches whiten the skies*, and a fragmentary
TS has *cross the white skies*.
l. 141: After *refinement* BL has:

> *What priest can master one in the schools*
> *The deep brain-hearted philosopher,*
> *The old humanity cries for a saviour.*

As ladies' perfumes are
Obnoxious to stern natures,
This miasma of a rotting god
145   Is to me.
Who has made of the forest a park?
Who has changed the wolf to a dog?
And put the horse in harness?
And man's mind in a groove?

150   I heard the one spirit cry in them,
'Break this metamorphosis,
Disenchant my lying body,
Only putrefaction is free,
And I, Freedom, am not.
155   Moses! touch us, thou!'

There shall not be a void or calm
But a fury fill the veins of time
Whose limbs had begun to rot.

Who had flattered my stupid torpor
160   With an easy and mimic energy,
And drained my veins with a paltry marvel
More monstrous than battle,
For the soul ached and went out dead in pleasure.

Is not this song still sung in the streets of me?
165   A naked African
Walked in the sun
Singing—singing
Of his wild love.

I slew the tiger
170   With your young strength
(My tawny panther)
Rolled round my life.

Three sheep, your breasts,
And my head between,
175   Grazing together
On a smooth slope.

l. 144: R used this image again in the final line of the poem 'God' (see page 94).
l. 165: BL1 has two ink holographs of this song, separate from the drafts of *Moses*, both entitled 'Savage Song'.

Ah! Koelue!

Had you embalmed your beauty, so
It could not backward go,
180 Or change in any way,
What were the use, if on my eyes
The embalming spices were not laid
To keep us fixed,
Two amorous sculptures passioned endlessly?
185 What were the use, if my sight grew,
And its far branches were cloud hung,
You, small at the roots, like grass.
While the new lips my spirit would kiss
Were not red lips of flesh,
190 But the huge kiss of power.
Where yesterday soft hair through my fingers fell
A shaggy mane would entwine,
And no slim form work fire to my thighs.
But human Life's inarticulate mass
195 Throb the pulse of a thing
Whose mountain flanks awry
Beg my mastery—mine!
Ah! I will ride the dizzy beast of the world
My road—my way.

SCENE II: *Evening before Thebes. The Pyramids are being built. Swarms of Hebrews labouring. Priests and Taskmasters. Two Hebrews are furtively talking.* KOELUE *passes by singing.*

200 KOELUE.   The vague viols of evening
                   Call all the flower clans
                   To some abysmal swinging
                   And tumult of deep trance;
                   He may hear, flower of my singing,
205   And come hither winging.
     OLD HEBREW (*gazing after her in a muffled frenzy*)
         Hateful harlot. Boils cover your small cruel face.
         O! fine champion Moses. O! so good to us,
         O! grand begetter on her of a whip and a torturer.
         Her father, born to us, since you kissed her.
210   Our champion, O! so good to us.
     YOUNG HEBREW. For shame! Our brothers' twisted blood-
             smeared gums
         Tell, we only, have more room for wreck curtailed,

l. 212: The commas round 'we only', which do not appear in PIR or CW and at first sight seem improbable, were inserted in pencil (presumably by R) in the TS given to the printer, and appear in the printed text. I surmise that R wanted them for emphasis.

143

For you, having no teeth to draw, it is no mercy
Perhaps, but they might mangle your gums;
215   Or touch a nerve somewhere. He barred it now.
And that is all his thanks, he, too, in peril.
Be still, old man, wait a little.
OLD HEBREW.   Wait!
All day some slow dark quadruped beats
220   To pulp our springiness.
All day some hoofed animal treads our veins,
Leisurely—leisurely our energies flow out.
All agonies created from the first day
Have wandered hungry searching the world for us,
225   Or they would perish like disused Behemoth.
Is our Messiah one to unleash these agonies
As Moses does, who gives us an Abinoah?
YOUNG HEBREW. Yesterday as I lay nigh dead with toil
Underneath the hurtling crane oiled with our blood,
230   Thinking to end all and let the crane crush me,
He came by and bore me into the shade.
O what a furnace roaring in his blood
Thawed my congealed sinews and tingled my own
Raging through me like a strong cordial.
235   He spoke! since yesterday
Am I not larger grown?
I've seen men hugely shapen in soul
Of such unhuman shaggy male turbulence
They tower in foam miles from our neck-strained sight.
240   And to their shop only heroes come.
But all were cripples to this speed
Constrained to the stables of flesh.
I say there is a famine in ripe harvest
When hungry giants come as guests.
245   Come knead the hills and ocean into food.
There is none for him.
The streaming vigours of his blood erupting
From his halt tongue is like an anger thrust
Out of a madman's piteous craving for
250   A monstrous baulked perfection.
OLD HEBREW. He is a prince, an animal

l. 227: A BL version has the following additional line: *Is he not their foster
child weaned with their tiger milk.*
ll. 239-240: BL1 has the following variant:

> *Out of all measure that we see them not
> Lodgings of towered barbaric tenderness*

l. 248: PIR and CW changed *is* to *are* but I have reinstated the singular
tense that R used.

144

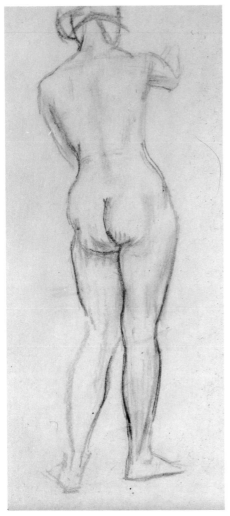

9. Three Nude Drawings. Black Chalk.
c.1912

10. (a) Head of a Woman in Profile looking left. Sanguine. 1912
$7\frac{1}{8}'' \times 6\frac{1}{8}''$

10. (b) Head of a Woman in Profile looking right. ? Chalk. 1914 Whereabouts and dimensions unknown

Not of our kind, who perhaps has heard
Vague rumours of our world, to his mind
An unpleasant miasma.
255 [Young] Hebrew. Is not Miriam his sister, Jochabed his
      mother?
In the womb he looked round and saw
From furthermost stretches our wrong.
From the palaces and schools
Our pain has pierced dead generations
260 Back to his blood's thin source.
As we lie chained by Egyptian men
He lay in nets of their women,
And now rejoice, he has broken their meshes.
O! his desires are fleets of treasure
265 He has squandered in treacherous seas
Sailing mistrust to find frank ports.
He fears our fear and tampers mildly
For our assent to let him save us.
When he walks amid our toil
270 With some master mason
His tense brows critical
Of the loose enginery.
Hints famed devices flat, his rod
Scratching new schemes on the sand.
275 But read hard the scrawled lines there,
Limned turrets and darkness, chinks of light,
Half beasts snorting into the light,
A phantasmagoria, wild escapade,
To our hearts' clue; just a daring plan
280 To the honest mason. What swathed meanings peer
From his workaday council, washed to and from
Your understanding till you doubt
That a word was said.
But a terror wakes and forces your eyes
285 Into his covertly, to search his searching.
Startled to life starved hopes slink out
Cowering, incredulous.
  Old Hebrew (*to himself*) His youth is flattered at Moses' kind
  speech to him.

(*To the* Young Hebrew)

l. 260: After this line BL3 has:

> *He has the deep schools drained of their brain ore*
> *Now worked of their ore*
> *And his desires are fleets of sunbright treasure*
> *Sailing mistrust to find the frank eyed ports.*

l. 262: Originally read *So has he lain chained by their women.*

290 I am broken and grey, have seen much in my time,
And all this gay grotesque of childish man
Long passed. Half blind—half deaf, I only grumble
I am not blind or deaf enough for peace.
I have seen splendid young fools cheat themselves
295 Into a prophet's frenzy; I have seen
So many crazed shadows puffed away,
And conscious cheats with such an ache for fame
They'd make a bonfire of themselves to be
Mouthed in the squares, broad in the public eye.
300 And whose backs break, whose lives are mauled, after
It all falls flat? His tender airs chill me
As thoughts of sleep to a man tiptoed night-long
Roped round his neck, for sleep means death to him.
Oh! he is kind to us.
305 Your safe teeth chatter when they hear a step.
He left them yours because his cunning way
Would brag the wrong against his humane act
By Pharaoh; so gain more favour than he lost.
  Young Hebrew. Help him not then, and push your safety
            away.
310 I for my part will be his backward eye,
His hands when they are shut. Ah! Abinoah!
Like a bad smell from the soul of Moses dipt
In the mire of lust, he hangs round him.
And if his slit-like eyes could tear right out
315 The pleasure Moses on his daughter had,
She'd be as virgin as ere she came nestling
Into that fierce unmanageable blood,
Flying from her loathed father. O, that slave
Has hammered from the anvil of her beauty
320 A steel to break his manacles. Hard for us,
Moses has made him overseer. O, his slits
Pry—pry . . . for what? . . . to sell to Imra . . .

[Abinoah *is seen approaching*]

l. 300: BL2 has Old Hebrew (to young)

> *This prince loves pleasure,*
> *Pleasures in his mastery* [,]
> *Ferocious and unsafe and shot with terror*
> *To a fool's trust. His wild flesh is his ruling* [,]
> *His women blab.*
> *Here's Abinoah follows him about.*

l. 302: In the TS used by the printer this line ends *to a man who stands nightlong,* but both in a proof and the published text it had become the much more vivid *tiptoed night-long.*

Sh! the thin-lipped abomination!
Zigzagging haschish tours in a fine style.
325 It were delightful labour making bricks,
And know they would kiss friendly with his head.
ABINOAH (*who has been taking haschish, and has one obsession,*
    hatred of Jews) Dirt draggled mongrels, circumcised slaves.
You puddle with your lousy gibberish
The holy air, Pharoah's own tributary.
330 Filthy manure for Pharaoh's flourishing.
I'll circumcise and make holy your tongues,
And stop one outlet to your profanation.

[*To the* OLD HEBREW]

I've never seen one beg so for a blow,
Too soft am I to resist such entreaty.

[*Beats him*]

335 Your howling holds the earnest energies
You cheat from Pharoah when you make his bricks.

AN AGED MINSTREL [*sings from a distance*]
          Taut is the air and tied the trees,
          The leaves lie as on a hand.
          God's unthinkable imagination
340   Invents new tortures for nature.

          And when the air is soft and the leaves
          Feel free and push and tremble,
          Will they not remember and say
          How wonderful to have lived?

[*The* OLD HEBREW *is agitated and murmurs*]

345 Messiah, Messiah . . . that voice . . .
O, he has beaten my sight out . . . I see
Like a rain about a devouring fire . . .

[*The* MINSTREL *sings*]

Ye who best God awhile,—O, hear, your wealth
Is but His cunning to make death more hard.
350 Your iron sinews take more pain in breaking.
And he has made the market for your beauty
Too poor to buy although you die to sell.

l. 326: PIR and CW have *Knowing they would kiss* . . ., but both R's
proof copy of the play and his bound copy of *Moses*, in which he made
several corrections, have *And know they would kiss* . . .
l. 345: After the Minstrel's song BL1 has: OLD HEBREW: *Here comes one*
will ask you a question.
ll. 351-2: Cf. the poem entitled 'God' on p. 94, lines 14-15.

147

OLD HEBREW. I am crazed with whips . . . I hear a Messiah.
YOUNG HEBREW. The venerable man will question this.
355 ABINOAH [*overhearing*] I'll beat you more, and he'll question
    The scratchiness of your whining; or may be,
    Thence may be born deep argument
    With reasons from philosophy
    That this blow, taking longer, yet was but one,
360   Or perhaps two; or that you felt this one—
    Arguing from the difference in your whine—
    Exactly, or not, like the other.
MINSTREL. You labour hard to give pain.
ABINOAH [*still beating*] My pain is . . . not . . . to labour so.
365 MINSTREL. What is this greybeard worth to you now,
    All his dried-up blood crumbled to dust?

   [*Motions* ABINOAH *to desist, but not in time to prevent the old man
      fainting into the hands of the* YOUNG HEBREW]

ABINOAH. Harper, are you envious of the old fool?
    Go! hug the rat who stole your last crumbs,
    And gnawed the hole in your life which made Time
      wonder
370   Who it was saved labour for him the next score of years.
    We allowed them life for their labour—they haggled.
    Food they must have—and (god of laughter!) even ease;
    But mud and lice and Jews are very busy
    Breeding plagues in ease.

     [*The* MINSTREL *pulls his beard and robe off*)

375 ABINOAH. Moses!
MOSES. You drunken rascal!
ABINOAH. A drunken rascal! Isis! hear the Prince.
    Drunken with duty, and he calls me rascal.
MOSES. You may think it your duty to get drunk;
380   But get yourself bronze claws before
    You would be impudent.
ABINOAH. When a man's drunk he'll kiss a horse or king,
    He's so affectionate. Under your words

ll. 357-59: BL1 has the following variant:
    Thence might be born some brainy argument
    Riched with deep reasons from philosophy
    That this blow . . . being longer, yet was but one . . .
l. 371: BL1 and a TS here continue:
    We buy their labour with a lease of life
    And they would haggle, want ease
    What do the locusts with their stinking ease?
    The mud, the lice, are busy breeding plagues
    In ease.

There is strong wine to make me drunk; you think,
385 The lines of all your face say, 'Her father, Koelue's father.'
MOSES. This is too droll and extraordinary.
I dreamt I was a prince, a queer droll dream,
Where a certain slave of mine, a thing, a toad,
Shifting his belly, showed a diamond
390 Where he had lain. And a blind dumb messenger
Bore syllabled messages soaked right through with glee.
I paid the toad—the blind man; afterwards
They spread a stench and snarling. O, droll dream!
I think you merely mean to flatter me
395 You subtle knave, that, more than prince, I'm *man*,
And worth to listen to your bawdy breath.
ABINOAH. Yet my breath was worth your mixing with.
MOSES. A boy at college flattered so by a girl
Will give her what she asks for.
400 ABINOAH. Osiris! burning Osiris!
Of thee desirable, for thee, her hair . . .

[*He looks inanely at* MOSES, *saying to himself*]

Prince Imra vowed his honey-hives and vineyards.
Isis! to let a Jew have her for nothing.

[*He sings under his breath*]

Night by night in a little house
405 A man and woman meet.
They look like each other,
They are sister and brother;
And night by night at that same hour
A king calls for his son in vain.
410 MOSES [*to himself*] So, sister Miriam, it is known then.
Slave, you die.
[*Aloud*] O, you ambiguous stench.
You'll be more interesting as a mummy
I have no doubt.
415 ABINOAH. I'm drunk, yes—drenched with the thought
Of a certain thing. [*Aside*] I'll sleep sounder to-night
Than all the nights I've followed him about.
Worrying each slight clue, each monosyllable
To give the word to Imra. The prince is near,
420 And Moses' eyes shall blink before next hour
To a hundred javelins. I'll tease him till they come.

l. 401: A BL draft has *My girl, my Koelue to be a plaything thus* for this line.
l. 402: The same draft has *Prince Imra wished her for a* 100 *shekels*.
l. 412: BL3 has:
> *O you ambiguous and unnecessary stench*
> *You mud bank of the nile.*

  [Aloud] On Koelue's tears I swam to you, in a mist
  Of her sighs I hung round you,
  As in some hallucination I've been walking
425 A white waste world, we two only in it.
  MOSES. Doubtless the instinct baulked to bully the girl,
  Making large gapings in your haschish dreams,
  Led you to me, in whom she was thoroughly lost.
  Pah! you sicken me.

     [He is silent awhile, then turns away]

430 ABINOAH. Prince Imra is Pharaoh's choice now, and Koelue's.

     *[*MOSES *turns back menacingly]*

  MOSES. Silence, you beast!

    [He changes his tone to a winning softness]

  I hate these family quarrels: it is so
  Like fratricide. I am a rebel, well?
  Soft! You are not, and we are knit so close
435 It would be shame for a son to be so honoured
  And the father still unknown. Come, Koelue's (so *my*) father,
  I'll tell my plans. You'll beg to be rebel, then.
  Look round on the night,
  Old as the first, bleak, even her wish is done,
440 She has never seen, (though dreamt perhaps of the sun),
  Yet only dawn divides; could a miracle
  Destroy the dawn, night would be mixed with light,
  No night or light would be, but a new thing.
  So with these slaves, who perhaps have dreamt of freedom,
445 Egypt was in the way; I'll strike it out
  With my ways curious and unusual.
  I have a trouble in my mind for largeness,
  Rough-hearted, shaggy, which your grave ardours lack.
  Here is the quarry quiet for me to hew,
450 Here are the springs, primeval elements,
  The roots' hid secrecy, old source of race,
  Unreasoned reason of the savage instinct.
  I'd shape one impulse through the contraries
  Of vain ambitious men, selfish and callous,
455 And frail life drifters, reticent, delicate.
  Litheness thread bulk; a nation's harmony.
  These are not lame, nor bent awry, but placeless
  With the rust and stagnant. All that's low I'll charm;
  Barbaric love sweeten to tenderness.

l. 447: BL3 originally had *And can all Thebes deepest teach me more* which
R changed to the line printed here, but followed it with *A purity in the
rough hearted manner* instead of line 448 above.

460   Cunning run into wisdom, craft turn to skill.
        Their meanness threaded right and sensibly
        Change to a prudence, envied and not sneered.
        Their hugeness be a driving wedge to a thing,
        Ineffable and useable, as near
465   Solidity as human life can be.
        So grandly fashion these rude elements
        Into some newer nature, a consciousness
        Like naked light seizing the all-eyed soul,
        Oppressing with its gorgeous tyranny
470   Until they take it thus—or die.

[*While speaking, he places his hand on the unsuspecting Egyptian's head and gently pulls his hair back (caressingly), until his chin is above his forehead, and holds him so till he is suffocated. In the darkness ahead is seen the glimmer of javelins and spears. It is Prince Imra's cohorts come to arrest* MOSES]

l. 466: A BL draft reads *Thus these rude elements would I grandly fashion.*

LONGER VARIANTS IN BL MANUSCRIPTS

l. 176: After the song, BL1 inserts these lines:

Can I rest in you who grow less and less.
I who enlarge and wax suiting an inward mould—
A pent infinity driving my nature's force
To gird the rim of all power, to draw the rib from man.
And create a shapelier doom and more princely hope.
These arms must rim the world, these arms where you have
    lain.

l. 205: After Koelue's song, BL1 inserts:

OLD HEBREW. Abinoah's daughter. No reason have we to love
    her.
This is all Moses has done for us.
First he ruins her, then makes her spiteful father
Our overseer.
YOUNG HEBREW. The night must grow to make the morning
    possible
We must wait.
OLD HEBREW. Wait!

l. 250: After this line BL1 inserts:

OLD HEBREW. He is a prince pampered in palaces
    And such division in his splendid sphere
    Rolls that from ours; what can he know of ours?

l. 271: After *His tense brows critical*, BL1 has:

> As purposing some loose machinic laws
> To perfect[,] or builded base to touch
> With wisdom bettering it.
> Sleek ambush! for covert under such council
> Peer muffled meanings, inner mirrored words.
> Like doubtful sounds scarce heard; terror in you
> Forces your eyes into his[,] covertly
> To search his searching. Startled to life
> And still incredible dead hopes slink out.
> Seeking a shape of trust they feared they saw.

OLD HEBREW [*His youth is flattered at* Moses' *kind speech to him.*]
> And he looms grand to his enthusiasm
> It may be as you say. But I who am grey
> Have seen so often conscious impostors
> Or such who have imposed upon themselves
> Have seen many heroic rebels—lost,
> Why does Abinoah follow him about?
> And if his slit-like . . .

l. 385: After this line, BL1 inserts:

> Remember that your rod is in your hands
> But what you are, in mine. Because[,] crabbed tree[,]
> You grew a ruddy spiced apple for me
> Because you're like some blind deaf messenger
> That bore a shining message for my ear
> I put the rod in your hands for that service
> Now you are impudent and scratch at me
> Perhaps you merely mean to flatter one,
> You subtle knave—that more than prince I'm man,
> And worth to listen to all braggart breath.

ABINOAH. Yet my breath was worth fouling with your lust.

A TS has for lines 2-3 of the above variant:
> *Because you're dung*
> *Out of which grew a lordly rose for me.*

And for lines 8-9 has:

> *What wrong by these o'errides obsequiousness*
> *To sting you to forget—or subtly meant*
> *This flattery . . .*

l. 403: After *a Jew have her for nothing*, BL1 inserts this long passage:
ABINOAH. [*His vindictiveness is getting the better of himself helped by*
   the haschish]
> I know
> A story of an ark by rushes placed

Cunningly to attract where naked girls
Sang to a barren princess and the Nile
Flowed by as clean as Egypt's royal blood.
A quick-wit Jewish girl stood by laughing
While each accused the other of the bastard.
My girl is Egypt on whose body for lust you practised
The part your alien hate would play in earnest
On Egypt's spirit and soul.
See[;] as I strike from this slave music[,] music
That mixes with the pure darkness which it fouls.
MOSES. O you ambiguous and unnecessary stench.
    You'll be more interesting as a mummy
    I have no doubt.
ABINOAH. I am not afraid. Even were you Pharaoh's son
    Princes walk on slippery paths
    And all suspect your brooding quiet
    Your boisterous college triumphs,
    All know your lust to domineer[,] and this strange lull
    As in some hallucination I have shadowed you
    Without wish or will
    Doubtless the old instinct to bully my girl
    Making a[? gaping] in my haschish dreams
    Or perhaps the wish to drain in some strange way
    Pride urging—
    The smirch you made the good you drew in you
    I found you plotting your own dreadful ruin.
MOSES. You have marvellous skill to move me.
ABINOAH. She was my child.
MOSES. Your dog you mean. You beater of girls and old men.
    Why do I vindicate myself to you?
    You blind rod in the throned hands of kings.
    Can I give to the blind eyes of your brain
    Clear light? Your pigmy spirit denies
    Stature above it, in its narrow mould
    Pens the infinite, and in its denseness muds
    All sunlike actions and original.
    Your private anger would turn to my hurt[,]
    Neath justice colour my unusual means,
    Training on sense to knead the world of the spirit.
    I would be skilled in arts of government,
    And shape one impulse through the contraries
    Of vain ambitious men[,] selfish and callous,
    And frail life-drifting natures, reticent,
    Litheness through bulk, nation's grand harmony.
    Here are the springs, primeval elements;
    The roots' hid secrecy, old source of race.
    Unreasoned reason of the savage instinct.
    I have a trouble in my mind for largeness.

A purity in the rough hearted manner
Which the grave ardours the Egyptian wants.
My brainful fingers will charm these wild herbs
Unto a rich deliverance, brave juices.
Barbaric love to bring forth tenderness[,]
Cunning, to nurture wisdom, wise desires
Meanness enlarged to prudence
And hugeness be a driving wedge to truth.
Thus these rude elements would I grandly fashion.

An untitled holograph in BL has this quatrain, corrected by R as indicated in the second version.

Surprise that stops sharp breath and things to touch
Giving a shape quite other to the eye[,]
Form that refutes all sway, chaos that coincides
Freedom manacled to passion overmuch.

Chaos that coincides, form that refutes all sway
Shapes to the eye quite other to the touch
All twisted things continue to our clay
Like other limbs and hair disspreaded overmuch.

Another untitled BL holograph has the following fragments, which clearly belong to *Moses*:

These wishes that hide themselves even from ourselves
See a meaning and an end
Peering through his simple speech
As he walks amid our toil.
Talking mildly of our labours.

The savour of our blood has worked into
His very springs of being[,] his blood's old source[,]
Our pain has gnawed a fibre from strange roots
And shown the old sap to the grafted stem.

In addition to the BL materials there exist 3 TSS of earlier versions of the play, consisting of roughly 150 lines only. TS1, clearly the earliest of them, is entitled MOSES: AN EGYPTIAN PRINCE, and opens with the following lines:

1st HEBREW. What's he, the father of this venture?
2nd HEBREW. I have seen men hugely and large proportioned
In spirit, of such noble indignation
Accoutred to no credence of the times,
Lodgings of swift barbaric tendencies,
Wherein the towers of babel found a top,
Whose ears were prest against Jehovah's mouth,
But all were cripples to this mettled speed
Constrained to the stables of proud flesh.

R eventually abandoned these lines in favour of ll. 237-242

TS1 also has, after line 399, the following variant:

ABINOAH. No love but hatred of Egypt made you
   Steal love that should be Egypt's;
   [then follow the 4 lines from BL1 beginning *I know a story of an ark*]
   You hate the Egyptians and would ruin Pharaoh
   As my poor girl. This slave you hate me beat
   Is more my Father than is Pharaoh yours.
   I beat all with that thought.
MOSES. A prince and a philosopher still is man
   Do not tempt me.
   [TS2 has: *I will smudge your life out like a bug's* in place of the above 2 lines.]
ABINOAH. Why should I fear? If you were Pharaoh's son
   You have in mind should make you fear, not me.
   Your frequent hooded whispers amongst these,
   And loose words dropt and quick looks backward cast
   The strained aspect and disimulation
   These are your own accusers.

TS2, much corrected by R both in pencil and ink, has the following alternative opening:

1st HEBREW. But he, the father of this venture
   Against our masters, in their foster child.
   His flesh is wild, and we will suffer for it.

It then continues, 17 lines later, with the following passage:

2nd HEBREW. Nine months he drew the dreaming years to him
   As dark in antenatal womb he lay
   Papped with the life of Abram's prophecy.
   We trodden careless under
   The riding pomp of heavy handed years,
   Have pierced him with our pain a tunneled way
   Back to the springs of being, his blood's old source.
   He has the deep schools now worked of their ore
   And his desires are laden ships of treasure
   Ideas and mountained intellect he would use
   To buy the safety of our nailed God.
   Deeply politic, sounding our feared assent
   To his hopes of our shrivelled hopes, he walks
   As purposing some skilled machinic laws . . .

TS3 follows TS2 and the printed text in the main, but improves ll. 11-13 of the above TS2 variant with:

He has the deep schools drained of their brain ore,
And his desires are fleets of sunbright treasure
Sailing mistrust to find the frank eyed ports.

THE UNICORN

For nearly a year before his death Rosenberg had been working intermittently, as opportunity offered, on a play called 'The Unicorn'. It was never finished, and the sections and fragments of it that exist (some of them undecipherable in places) belong to several different conceptions of the play. First came 'The Amulet' which Rosenberg finished and sent home for typing. A pencil holograph of it exists, as well as a typescript, which shows that Rosenberg made substantial revisions to the early draft. The more important of these are indicated in the footnotes.

THE AMULET

LILITH. SAUL. AMAK. NUBIAN.[1]

LILITH *sits under pomegranate trees watching* AMAK *playing with his father's helm and spear. A light smoke is ascending from the chimney of the hut, and through the doorway a naked Nubian man[2] is seen stirring the embers.* SAUL *sleeps.*

> LILITH. Amak, you'll break your father's sleep,
>   Come here and tell me what those spices are
>   This strange man bakes our cakes with.
>   It makes the brain wild. Be still, Amak.
> 5 I'll give you the strange man your father brought
>   And he will run with you upon his back to-day.
>   Come from your father or you'll get no cakes;
>   He's been a long journey.
>   Bring me the pictured book he brought for you.
> 10 What! Already cut to pieces?
>   Put away that horn from your father's ear
>   And stay that horrid noise; come, Amak.
>
>   (AMAK *runs to his mother with a jade amulet, shouting*)
>
> AMAK. Look mother what I've found.
>
>   (*He runs back again, making great shouts*)
>
> LILITH. It dances with my blood. When my eyes caught it first
> 15 I was like lost and yearned, and yearned and yearned,
>   And strained like iron to stay my head from falling
>   Upon that beggar's breast where the jade stone hung.
>   Perhaps the spirit of Saul's young love lies here
>   Strayed far and brought back by this stranger [?means]

l. 7: CW has *no cake*, but this does not accord with line 3 or the original sources.
l. 19: The last two words are virtually undecipherable, but seem more like *stranger means* than *stranger near* as in CW.

[1] The holograph version has 'Beggar' for 'Nubian' throughout.
[2] R originally wrote *a half-clad man.*

20   Saul said his discourse was more than deep Heaven.
       For the storm trapped him ere he left the town
       Loaded with our week's victuals. The slime clung
       And licked and clawed and chewed the clogged dragging
           wheels
       Till they sunk nigh to the axle. Saul sodden and vexed
25   Like fury smote the mules' mouths, pulling but sweat
       From his drowned hair and theirs, while the thunder knocked
       And all the air yawned water, falling water,
       And the light cart was water, like a wrecked raft,
       And all seemed like a forest under the ocean.
30   Sudden the lightning flashed upon a figure
       Moving as a man moves in the slipping mud
       But singing not as a man sings, through the storm,
       Which could not drown his sounds. Saul bawled 'Hi! Hi!'
       And the man loomed, naked vast, and gripped the wheels.
35   Saul fiercely dug from under. He tugged the wheels,
       The mules foamed, straining, straining,
       Sudden they went.
       Saul and the man leaped in, Saul miserably sodden
       Marvelled at the large cheer in a naked glistening man.
40   And soon fell in with that contented mood.
       That when our hut's light broke on his new mind
       He could not credit it. Too soon it seemed.
       The strange man's talk was witchery.
       I pray his baking be as magical.
45   The cakes should be nigh burnt.

           (*She calls the* NUBIAN. *He answers from within*)

NUBIAN. They are laid by to cool, housewife.
LILITH. Bring me the sherbet from the ledge and the fast-dried
     figs.

           (*The* NUBIAN *brings sherbet and figs and a bowl of ice and*
            lays them down)
           (*She looks curiously at him. He is an immense man with*
            squat, mule-skinned features: his jet-black curled beard,
            crisp hair, glistening nude limbs, appear to her like some
            heathen idol of ancient stories)

           (*She thinks to herself*)

---

l. 24: The holograph clearly has *nigh*, which the TS mis-typed as *night*.
CW, understandably, corrected this to *right*, compounding the typist's
error.
l. 31: R originally wrote *slipping slime*.
l. 47 seq.: There is no reference to figs in the holograph, and none of the
lines beginning *She looks curiously at him* down to *Moses and Buddha he met*
(l. 61) occurs in that version.

Out of the lightning
In a dizzying cloven wink
50 This apparition stood up,
Of stricken trunk or beast spirit
Stirred by Saul's blasphemies.
So Saul's heart feared aghast.
But lo, he touched the mischance and life ran straight.
55 Was it the storm-spirit, storm's pilot,
With all the heaving debris of Noah's sunken days
Dragged on his loins;
Law's spirit wandering to us
Through Nature's anarchy,
60 Wandering towards us when the Titans yet were young?
Perhaps Moses and Buddha he met.

(*She speaks aloud*)

The shadow of these pomegranate boughs
Is sweet and restful. Sit and ease your feet. Eat of these figs,
You have journeyed long.
65 NUBIAN. All my life, housewife.
LILITH. You have seen men and women,
Soaked yourself in powers and old glories,
In broken days and tears and in some glee,
And touched cold hands—
70 Hands shut in pitiless trance when the feast is high,
I think there is more sorrow in the world
Than man can bear.
NUBIAN. None can exceed their limit, lady.
You either bear or break.
75 LILITH. Can one choose to break? To bear,
To wearily bear is misery.
Beauty is this corroding malady.
NUBIAN. Beauty is a great paradox—
Music's secret soul creeping about the senses

l. 63: The holograph has *Lie down and ease your feet.*
l. 70: CW has *trances*, but this cannot be right. And after this line one fragment has:

> *Have you willed good and been repulsed?*
> *An evil spirit walks the world.*

l. 79: After *Beauty is a great paradox*—the holograph has:

> *Mutable moods*
> *In man, discrown or deify her.*
> *The market for your beauty is*
> *Too poor to buy although you die to sell*
> *You give yourselves away and are held cheap.*

80 To wrestle with man's coarser nature.
It is hard when beauty loses.
LILITH. I think beauty is a bad bargain made of life.
Men's iron sinews hew them room in the world
And use deceits to gain them trophies.
85 Ah! when our beauty fails us did we not use
Deceits, where were our room in the world?
Only our room in the world?
Are not the songs and devices of men
Moulds they have made after my scarlet mouth,
90 Of cunning words and haughty contours of bronze
And viols and gathered air?
They without song have sung me
Boldly and shamelessly.
I am no wanton, no harlot.
95 I have been pleased and smiled my pleasure,
I am a wife with a woman's natural ways.
Yet through the shadow of the pomegranates
Filters a poison day by day,
And to a malady turns
100 The blonde, the ample music of my heart.
Inward to eat my heart
My thoughts are worms that suck my softness all away.
I watch the dumb eyeless hours
Drop their tears, then shapeless moaning drop.
105 Unfathomable is my mouth's dream
Do not men say?
So secret are my far eyes,
Weaving for iron men profound subtleties.

Sorceress they name me,
110 And my eyes harden, and they say
'How may those eyes know love
If God made her without a heart?

'Her tears, her moaning,
Her sad profound gaze,

l. 88: After this line, one holograph fragment and a corrected TS of it,
have the following 4 lines:

> *Yet we, the world's security,*
> *Soul of the eterne force whose body is man,*
> *Whose pores must suck our light, (blood of his kins),*
> *And the world's users leave it all at the last.*

ll. 95-6: The holograph has *Mine are a woman's natural ways* in lieu of these
two lines.
l. 100: CW here, as elsewhere, changed R's spelling of *blonde* to *blond*.

115 The dishevelled lustres of her hair
Moon-storm like', they say,
'These are her subtleties,' men say.
My husband sleeps,
The ghosts of my virgin days do not trouble him.
120 His sleep can be over-long,
For there is that in my embers
Pride and blushes of fire, the outraged blood,
His sleep makes me remember.

Sleep! hairy hunter, sleep!
125 You are not hungry more
Having fed on my deliciousness.
Your sleep is not adultery to me,
For you were wed to a girl
And I am a woman.
130 My lonely days are not whips to my honour.

(*She dries her tears with her hair, then fingers the amulet at
her throat*)

Yours, friend.
NUBIAN (*eagerly*) My amulet! My amulet!
(*He speaks gravely*) Small comfort is counsel to broken lives,
But tolerance is medicinal.
135 In all our textures are loosed
Pulses straining against strictness
Because an easy issue lies therefrom.
(Could they but slink past the hands holding whips
To hunt them from the human pale
140 Where is the accident to cover; Spite fears bias.)
I am justified at my heart's plea;
He is justified also.

For the eyes of vanity are sleepless—are suspicious;
Are mad with imaginings
145 Of secret stabs in words, in looks, in gestures.
Man is a chimera's eremite,
That lures him from the good kindness of days
Which only asks his willingness.

There is a crazed shadow from no golden body
150 That poisons at the core
What smiles may stray.
It mixes with all God-ancestralled essences
And twists the brain and heart.

ll. 120-23 inclusive are omitted in the holograph.
ll. 133-48 inclusive do not appear in the holograph.

11. (a) A Cape Coloured
Woman. Oil. 1914
16″ × 12″

11. (b) A Cape Coloured
Man. Oil. 1914
16″ × 12″

12. The Artist's Father. Pencil. c.1913 $9\frac{1}{2}'' \times 8''$

This shadow sits in the texture of Saul's being,
155 Mauling your love and beauty with its lies;
I hold a power like light to shrivel it.
There, in your throat's hollow—that green jade.

(*He snatches at it as she lets it fall. He grows white and troubled, and walks to where* AMAK *is playing, and sees minutely strewn pieces of paper.*)

(*He mutters*) Lost—Lost.

The child has torn the scroll in it
160 And half is away. It cannot be spelt now.
LILITH. God, restore me his love.
Ah! Well!

(*She rises*)

I will go now prepare our evening meal
And waken my husband, my lover once.
165 NUBIAN (*musing*) The lightning of the heavens
Lifts an apocalypse.
The dumb night's lips are seared and wide,
The world is reeling with sound.
Was I deaf before, mute, tied?
170 What shakes here from lustre-seeded pomegranates
Not in the great world,
More vast and terrible.
What is this ecstasy in form,
This lightning
175 That found the lightning in my blood,
Searing my spirit's lips aghast and naked.
I am flung in the abyss of days
And the void is filled with rushing sound
From pent eternities.
180 I am strewn as the cypher is strewn.
A woman—a soft woman!

l. 155: A holograph fragment has after this line:

> *Sometimes it shapes like God, it takes God's shape,*
> *Who rests in its flattery then. Your wealth*
> *Is but a cunning to make death more hard*
> *Your iron sinews take more pain in breaking.*

cf. *Moses*, ll. 348-50

l. 160: After this line the holograph has 2 inserted lines which read:

> *The mould of it is in an ancient world*
> *Unhaunted by illusions. Far and not far . . .*

l. 170 The holograph has *lustral seeded.*
ll. 180-96 inclusive are not in the holograph.

Our girls have hair
Like heights of night ringing with never-seen larks,
Or blindness dim with dreams.
185 Here is a yellow tiger gay that blinds your night.
Mane—Mane—Mane!
Your honey spilt round that small dazzling face
Shakes me to golden tremors.
I have no life at all,
190 Only thin golden tremors.
Light tender beast!
Your fragile gleaming wrists
Have shook the scaled glaciers from under me,
And bored into my craft
195 That is now with the old dreamy Adam
With other things of dust.
LILITH. You lazy hound. See my poor child.

> (*He turns to see* LILITH *drop the bowl and cakes and run to* AMAK *who is crying, half stifled under* SAUL'S *huge shield*)
>
> (SAUL *opens his eyes*)

l. 183: cf. l. 8 of 'Returning, We Hear the Larks' (see p. 109).

l. 188: CW has *shaken*, which is marginally more grammatical, but does not appear in either of the prime sources.

Soon after he had sent away 'The Amulet' Rosenberg wrote to Marsh: 'I hope you have not yet got my poem, "The Amulet", I've asked my sister to send you. If you get it, please don't read it, because it's the merest sketch and the best is yet to come. If I am able to carry on with it, I'll send you it in a more presentable fashion. I believe I have a good idea at bottom. It's a kind of "Rape of the Sabine Women" idea: some strange race of wanderers have settled in some wild place and are perishing out for lack of women. The prince of these explores some country near where the women are most fair. But the natives will not hear of foreign marriages; and he plots another Rape of the Sabines, but is trapped in the act.' The theme of lament at the prospect of extinction appears in the following poem, which exists only as a fragment without dramatic context.

THE TOWER OF SKULLS

MOURNERS

These layers of piled-up skulls,
These layers of gleaming horror—stark horror!
Ah me! Through my thin hands they touch my eyes.

Everywhere, everywhere is a pregnant birth,
5 And here in death's land is a pregnant birth.
Your own crying is less mortal
Than the amazing soul in your body.

Your own crying yon parrot takes up
And from your empty skulls cries it afterwards.

10 Thou whose dark activities unenchanted
Days from gyrating days, suspending them
To thrust them far from sight, from the gyrating days
Which have gone widening on and left us here,
Cast derelicts lost for ever.

15 When aged flesh looks down on tender brood;
For he knows between his thin ribs' walls
The giant universe, the interminable
Panorama—synods, myths and creeds,
He knows his dust is fire and seed.

The following fragment was evidently an early attempt to deal with the theme of the emotion of Tel, prince of the decaying race, when he first sees a woman.

SCENE I. *Tel on his Unicorn. He sees a girl and boy in the field. He leaves the Unicorn.*

TEL'S SONG

Small dazzling face!
I shut you in my soul;
How can I perish now?

But thence a strange decay—
5 Your fragile gleaming wrists
Waver my days and shake my life
To golden tremours. I have no life at all,
Only thin golden tremours
That shudder over the abyss of days
Which hedged my spirit, my spirit your prison walls
10 That shrunk like phantasms with your vivid beauty.

Towering and widenening till
The sad moonless place
Throngs with a million torches
And spears and flaming wings.

ll. 7-8 PIR and CW printed *tremors*, but a TS corrected by R has the medieval spelling, which I have therefore kept.

At one time Rosenberg planned to have the story of the decaying race told in a myth which was to be read by Lilith, the wife of Saul. 'Saul and Lilith', says Rosenberg in a letter to Marsh, 'are ordinary folk into whose ordinary lives the Unicorn bursts. It is to be a play of terror—terror of hidden things and the fear of the supernatural.' The following scene belongs to this conception of the play, and also develops a theme neglected in the last complete draft—the evival of Saul's love under the stress of his terror.

THE UNICORN

SAUL. DEALER. LILITH. TEL. AMAK.

The Unicorn

SCENE. *A Market.*

SAUL *leaning against his cart in converse with* DEALER.

SAUL. I saw it plain. I could have touched it.
DEALER. Against Lot's Pool you say? Strange as [the myth]
    Of barren men, strange beasts, I lent your wife.
    (Our wines are strong, the pool vapours queer shapes
5   And the cart's jolting made him doze and mix,
    Phantasing from the story.)
    The victuals are all tied secure. Now haste,
    Before the storm breaks. The sequel of the myth
    I'll seek and bring your wife. My greetings to her.
10 SAUL. The myth? Ah yes.
    Here was the usual road, the usual sky,
    The same brown surging flanks, the well thewed legs
    Jogging between my thoughts, the long queer ears
    That seemed to hear a calling from the town.
15   Here was Lot's Pool, bare of the shining boys
    I looked for, fishing; but it was mealtime then,
    As I remember by a hut I passed,

ll. 5-6: The holographs of this version are very tattered and obscure at this point. CW printed:

> *And the cart's jolting made him doze and dream,*
> *Fantasy from the strong.*

But R clearly changed *dream* to *mix*, and followed this with *phantasing from the* ?'story' or 'strong'. I have opted for the former as making better sense, and because I suspect that R, writing hastily, reversed the 'o' and 'r' in 'story'.

ll. 15-16: Cf. ll. 11-12 of 'Midsummer Frost' (see p. 85).

Then . . . I was nigh jerked from the cart
At the dead stop—like a wind it flew by—
20   The haughty contours of a swift white horse
And on its brows a tree, a branching [tree].
My blood froze up . . . Wait . . . listen!
DEALER. What shrieks? who run? why flee you, friend?
So white and mute? I'll run with you.
25 SAUL. Hide me, hide me. There, there, its horns . . .

[*The Unicorn rushes by*]

SAUL. Is it gone? I shake, I shake.

[SAUL *slowly clambers into his cart, dazed*]

SAUL. Go on, go on, go from this cursed [place].
It is no use if things are ordered so.
The streets are bare and strange, all seems detached.
30   What if I died last night, and I that ride
Is what the old place will not relinquish yet
Because Lilith now wrings her vain hands at last
By my cold form, a little colder yet,
And holds my soul back, saying, 'It cannot be.
35   Look look, I know his eyeballs tried to move.'

[Lacuna]

. . . this white terror is that virgin will
Of all my unused love. To die, to die
Before I laid my great love bare, so hidden
While she asked tenderness for alien things
40   Apart from my mood, or my mood despised.
I yearned for some outlet for my towering love.
My taciturn ways, cold, laconic
Like this metallic sky, scintillant.
No, no, I feel the wet drops.
45   How black, profoundest midnight,
There is no road or sky, yet on the brink
Noon glitters, I ride eyeless
And the rain beats and beats like endless hoofs.

*The trapping of Tel, the chief of the decaying race, was evidently abandoned,
but some fragments refer to the trapping of the Unicorn and apparently to its
escape.*

TEL.   . . . Beauty,
50   Music's secret soul creeping about man's senses,
Gleaming and fading unknowable and known.

165

Man yearns and woman yearns and yearning is
Beauty and music, faith, and hope and dreams,
Religion, love, endeavour, stability
55   Of man's whole universe.
  LILITH. Most secret, hidden, is my own music from me.
    Where is Saul gone?
    I hear him in the cellar with Amak.
  AMAK (*off*) Father, the chain is rusty.
60   Is it to chain the Unicorn?
  TEL. Be wary, heart; I fear it is for me.

[*The door is burst open and the* TRADER *rushes breathless in*]

TRADER. Hide, hide! The Unicorn! The riders!
    Our women are all taken—

l.55: At one stage this line read *On which the world is built.*

*The Unicorn itself took the place of a woman for Tel. Something of its more
general significance appears in the following rough fragment.*

  LILITH. The mateless soul haunts all the elements, it wails
    In the wasting wind of obliteration.
    Surely
    The white beast is the figure of man's soul,
    Blind, passing and repassing the thing it needs
    That utters no sound, for it knows not the thing's will,
    Evil or good.
  TEL. Ah Umusol, my eyes love, you have feared them
    But you have brought me hither.
    But you are barren, and man will not willingly suffer obliteration.
    This woman is for me—
    What Titans will those heaving breasts suckle . . .

*It was from these and other early conceptions, fragmentary and often con-
flicting with each other, that Rosenberg produced the complete draft which he
had hoped to use as a basis for further work on the play. His first attempt at
such a draft was sent to Gordon Bottomley to read; and, when that was
returned to him in camp in France, he set to work on the following remodelling,
of which also he sent a typescript to Gordon Bottomley a few days before he
was killed—so few that he never learnt of its safe arrival in England.*

THE UNICORN

SAUL. LILITH. TEL. ENOCH.

Umusol . . . The Unicorn

SCENE. *A track through a woody place. Against the hedge is a half sunk
wagon in a quagmire. The mules stand shivering.* SAUL *sits with his head
between his knees. Thunder and lightning.*

SAUL.   Ah! miserable! miserable!
    Is it gone . . . oooooh! that wild might of wind
    Still howling in my ears . . . the glittering beast.
    If I look up and see it over me
5   I will shrink up . . . I cower, I quail,
    I am a shivering grass in a chill wind.
    This is no mortal terror . . . spectres wail,
    Stricken trunks' and beasts' spirits wail across to mine
    And whirl me, strew me, pass and repass me.
10   Let me look up; break this unnatural fear.
    Ah God! Ah God! what black thing towers towards me
    Wailing . . .

[*A young man on horseback sweeps past crying in a despairing voice
'Dora, Dora'*]

SAUL. Is there no end? Murderers are suffered to die.
    What have I done; these ghosts that seek their loves
15   The fearful unicorn has devoured, pass me
    As if I was the road to it.
    It has breathed on me, and I must reek of it.
    Twice have I seen this flaring thing,
    My life stormed in the wind of this.
20   And always wailing, wails and floats away,
    The shrieks of women and the wail of men.
    How chilled my spirit is, how clutched with terror,
    Lilith, my Lilith
    Like my hands in the membranes of my brain
25   To pluck your blond hair out.

I'll run to you . . . I totter . . . A wavering wall
Against me is the air; what pulls me back?

God! in that dizzying flash, I saw just now
Phantoms and nomads
30   And balls of fire pursuing
A panting streaming maenad.
What ghosts be these so white and mute.
Stay . . . Stay . . . Ah miserable . . .
That crash . . . thunder . . . no . . .
35   O God it falls on me.
My brain gives way; look, look . . .

[*The Unicorn flashes by, lit by lightning and a voice calls 'Umusol'.*
SAUL *sinks moaning and shivering against a tree*]

Ooowe . . . Oooowe . . . I sink.
A breath will lift me up and scatter me.
My name was wailed and all my tissues
40   Untwined and fell apart.

Sick . . . Sick . . . I will lie down and die. How can I die?
Kind lightning, sweetest lightning, cleave me through
Lift up these shreds of being and mix me with
This wind, this darkness.
45   I'll strive once more. See how the wheels are sunk
Right to the axle . . . Ah impotent puny me . . .
Vain. Futile.
Hi hi hi hi, is there no man about.
Who would be wandering in a storm like this?—
50   Hark . . . was that a human voice?
Sh . . . when that crash ceases.
Like laughter . . . like laughter,
Sure that was laughter . . . just the laughter of ours.
Hi hi hi hi hi hi . . .
55   My voice fears me.
God cover my eyes.

*The Unicorn rushes by and when he looks up again, his hair stands
up. A naked black giant stands there and signs for* SAUL's *hand.
Mechanically as in a trance,* SAUL *gives his hand and together they
heave and lift the wheels. The mules suddenly start;* SAUL *is lifted into
the cart and the black drives. The exertion has revived* SAUL *who is
thinking of the warm humanlike grasp of the hand in his.*

l. 53: After this line one holograph fragment has the following three
lines, as well as two further lines that are not comprehensible:

I wish that beast would come[,] *and stop this terrible suspense*[,]
It passes as though blind and tracking me and brings
Some mischance, hint of doom . . .

168

SAUL. Why quails my heart? God riding with
A mortal would absorb him.
He touched my hand, here is my hand the same.
60   Sure I am whirled in some dark fantasy—
A dizzying cloven wink, the beast, the black,
And I ride now . . . ride, ride, the way I know
That rushing terror . . . I shudder yet.
The haughty contours of a swift white horse
65   And on its brows a tree, a branching tree,
And on its back a golden girl bound fast.
It glittered by
And all the phantoms wailing.
Then sudden, here I ride.
70   His monstrous posture, why his neck's turn
Were our thews' adventures; some Amazon's son doubtless
From the dark countries. Can it be
The storm spirit, storm's pilot
With all the heaving debris of Noah's sunken days
75   Dragged on his loins.
What have I lived and agonised today, today.
It seems long centuries since I went to the town
For our week's victuals, I saw the beast
And rode into the town a shaken ghost,
80   Not Saul at all, but something that was Saul,
And saw folk wailing; and men that could not weep.
And my heart utterance was Lilith,
Whose face seemed cast in faded centuries
While the blind beast was rushing back towards her,
85   Sweeping past me, leaving me so with the years.
Mere human travail never broke my spirit
Only my throat to impatient blasphemics.
But God's unthinkable imagination
Invents new tortures for nature
90   Whose wisdom falters here.
No used experience can make aware
The imminent unknowable.
Sudden destruction
Till the stricken soul wails in anguish
95   Torn here and there.
Man could see and live never believed.
I ride . . . I ride . . . thunder crowned
In the shelter of a glis'ning chanting giant.
What flaring chant the storm's undertones,
100   Full of wild yearning,

ll. 81-2: One holograph has:

      And saw folk wailing, and my heart
      uttered Lilith.

169

And makes me think of Lilith
And that swift beast, it went that way.
My house my blood all lean to its weird flight.
But Lilith will be sleeping . . . ah miss my Lilith.
105   Swifter my mules swifter
Destroy the space . . . transport me instantly
For my soul yearns and fears.
    TEL. How his voice fears . . . If I strove utterance
What fear would be in mine.
110   I saw her . . . I fled . . . he brings me back.
Umusol . . . a golden mane shall mingle with your horns
Before the storm shall cease.
    SAUL. Yonder, my house is yonder.
I feared to see it vanished
115   On the ground from Lilith.
    TEL. The powered storm means such devastation.
    (I dread to enter, yet my soul hungers so intense).

[SAUL *springs from the cart and hurries into the room where* LILITH *si
white and terror stricken, wringing her hands*]

LILITH. Pity me. Where is Saul . . .
Do not touch me.
120 SAUL. Lilith dear, look up, it is me.
    LILITH. Saul, oh Saul, do not go away.
Who is that?

             [SAUL *kisses her*]

SAUL. How frightened you are.
See where I sunk in the mire, the mud . . .
125   His was the healing hand.
Lilith your viol
To force this gloom away even while I dry
In the inner chamber.
I am dank and tired.
130 LILITH. Saul do not leave me,
I dread to look up and see again
Two balls of fire casement glaring . . .
    SAUL. This is some fantasy: play music till I come.

ll. 118-120: A pencil holograph reads:

> *Pity me. O where is Saul . . .*
> *O is that beast gone.*
> SAUL. *Dear Lilith, look up in my eyes, it is only me.*

l. 123: After this line one holograph inserts:

> *My friend is vast and naked*
> *You should feel safer. Use him graciously, play music*
> *To drive this gloom away.*

[TEL *crouches in the shadow and she turns to take the viol down*]

LILITH. The roots of a torn universe are wrenched,
135   See the bent trees like masts of derelicts in ocean
    That beats upon this house this ark.
  TEL. Unearthly accents float amid the howling storm.
    Her mouth moves . . . is it thence . . .
    Secret Mother of my orphan spirit
140   Who art thou?
  LILITH. I think he speaks, this howling storm sheets out all so.
    I'll play and ease my heavy heart.
  TEL. Was that the lightning?
    Those fragile gleaming wrists untangle me,
145   Those looks tread out my soul.
    Somewhere I know those looks, I lost it somewhere.

[LILITH *draws nearer and sings softly*]

LILITH. Beauty is music's secret soul,
    Creeping about man's senses.
    He cannot hold it, or know it ever,
150   But yearns and yearns to hold it once.
    Ah! when he yearns not shall he not wither?
    For music then will have no place
    In the world's ear, but mix in windless darkness.
  TEL. Am I gone blind?
155   I swim in a white haze.
    What shakes my life to golden tremors . . .?
    I have no life at all . . . I am a crazed shadow
    From a golden body
    That melts my iron flesh, I flow from it.
160   I know the haze, the light,
    I am a shuddering pulse
    Hung over the abyss. I shall look up
    Even if I fall, fall, fall, fall forever,
    I faint, tremble.
165 LILITH. Still the rain beats and beats.

[TEL *looks up furtively, then prostrates himself*]

ll. 135: CW printed *nests of derelicts* but this was surely a misreading.

l. 154 *et seq.*: The holograph which the 1937 editors seem to have followed
in the main, departs from CW here to read:

> *Am I gone blind?—What abyss—*
> *What is this frozen unquiet forest[?]*
> *An influence flows . . .*
> *I am dissolved. I gulp greatness.*

TEL. Ah woe, ah woe. [*He sobs*]
LILITH. Has lightning turned his brain?
　　Is this a maniac? Saul, Saul.
　TEL. Hear me, hear me.
170　Do I speak, or think I speak,
　　I am so faint . . . Wait,
　　Let my dazed blood resolve itself to words.
　　Where have I strayed . . . incomprehensible . . .
　　Yet here . . . somewhere
175　An instant flashes a large face of dusk
　　Like heights of night ringing with unseen larks
　　Or blindness dim with dreams.
　　I hear a low voice . . . a crooning . . .
　　Some whisperings, and shadows vast,
180　A crying through the forest—wailing
　　　　　　　　　behind impassable places
　　Whose air was never warmed by a woman's lips
　　Bestial man-shapes ride dark impulses
　　Through roots in the bleak blood, then hide
185　In shuddering light from their self loathing.
　　They fade in arid light—
　　Beings unnatured by their craving for they know
　　Obliteration's spectre. They are few.
　　They wail their souls for continuity
190　And bow their heads and knock their breasts before
　　The many mummies whose wail in dust is more
　　Than these who cry, their brothers who loiter yet.
　　Great beasts' and small beasts' eyes have place
　　As eyes of women to their hopeless eyes
195　That hunt in bleakness for the dread might,
　　The incarnate female soul of generation.
　　The daughters of any clime are not imagined
　　Even of their occult ears, senses profound,
　　For their corporeal ears and baby senses
200　Were borne from gentle voices and gentle forms

l. 166 *et seq.* the same holograph here reads:

> TEL. *That was some charm . . . not words*
> *Words could not draw my life out . . .*
> *My soul ebbs out delicious agonies*
> *Intense pleasure and sharp pain.*

l. 196: Some holographs have *the occult female soul,* but *incarnate* is a pre-ferable adjective since *occult* occurs again two lines later.

l. 200: CW has '*for* gentle voices' in lieu of *from,* but this does not seem to make such good sense, and the principal holograph unquestionably gives *from.*

By men misused flying from misuse
Who gave them suck even from their narrow breasts
Only for this, that they should wither
That they should be as an uttered sound in the wind.

[*He sees* SAUL's *glittering eyes in the dark doorway. It rouses him*]

205 By now my men have raided the city,
    I heard a far shrieking.
  LILITH. This is most piteous, most fearful,
    I fear him, his hungry eyes
    Burn into me, like those balls of fire.
210 TEL. There is a tower of skulls,
    Where birds make nests
    And staring beasts stand by with many flocks
    And man looks on with hopeless eyes . . .
  LILITH. O horrible, I hear Saul rattle those chains in the cellar.
215 TEL. What clanking chains?
    When a man's brains crack with longing
    We chain him to some slender beast to breed.
  LILITH. Tell me, tell me, who took my cousin Dora,
    Oh God those balls of fire . . .
220 Are you men? . . . tell me.
  TEL. Marvellous creature.
    Night tender beast.
    Has the storm passed into me,
    What ecstasy, what lightning
225 Has touched the lightning in my blood.
    Voluptuous
    Crude vast terrible hunger overpowers . . .
    A gap . . . a yawning . . .
    My blood knocks . . . inarticulate to make you understand,
230 To shut you in itself
    Uncontrollable. [*He stretches his arms out*]
    Small dazzling face I shut you in my soul—

[*She shrieks.* SAUL *appears, looking about dazed, holding an iron chain; while the door is burst open and* ENOCH *bursts in. He springs on* TEL]

ENOCH. Where is my Dora, where?
    Pity, rider of the Unicorn.
235 TEL. Yonder.

[*Through the casement they see riding under the rainbow a black naked host on various animals, the Unicorn leading. A woman is clasped on every one, some are frantic, others white or unconscious, some nestle laughing.* ENOCH *with madness in his eyes leaps through the casement and disappears with a splash in the well.* SAUL *leaps after him shouting* 'The Unicorn'. TEL *places the unconscious* LILITH *on the Unicorn and they all ride away*]

LONGER UNPUBLISHED VARIANTS OF 'THE AMULET' AND 'THE UNICORN'

Somewhere after l. 10 of the earlier version of 'The Unicorn' the following passage occurred in an early draft:

> . . . Of my obscurest brain, how clear and white,
> I think I walked the town today—today
> Surely today in the bright noon, or centuries dim[,]
> And I loved Lilith centuries buried long
> And Amak ask[ed] old questions, long how long[.]
> Here is Lot's Pool—half way now.
> Sh . . . what was that[?] Vapours—ah vapours
> There lightning . . . fool fool you are [? about] a girl.
> Can I be Saul whom the Iron heroes [? sung]
> When Lonely Lilith gave herself to me
> For that fierce triumph that shook the [? heavens]
> I wish I were well home and covered with Lilith
> Her blonde hair in my brain, a look . . .
> Her looks—kind skies soak in . . .

The only clue to the placing of this fragment is the statement in the preamble to 'Tel's Song' that 'He sees a boy and girl in the field'.

> I passed a girl and boy in the fields
> Fantastic fragile gleaming was his wrist that wrote the world's
>   security.
> Gaza who nursed me told of a girl and boy
> He was the boy, my mother was the girl,
> Another boy, my father[,] stole her: told of the . . . breasts,

Conjecturally the following fragment would have been fitted in somewhere after l. 25 and before the 'Lacuna' in the earlier version of 'The Unicorn'.

> Is it gone? I shake, I shake. I can scarce climb
> Into the cart. Go on, go on; no, hark—
> What was that, kind gods, that sighing sound.
> . . . only the wind.
> What crashed just now—a stone dropped on my heart—
>   . . . I will turn back
> And cover me in the thick buried vaults . . .
> I know it seeks me, treads the world for me,
> I am all unstrung, I am not Saul at all.
> Instinct apprehends, yet dreads surprise
> It comes so swift, when that intensest fear
> Lulls in suspense. It is no mortal terror[,] for the soul quails.

Between ll.36 and 49 of the final draft a holograph fragment has:

What ails the mules[?] Back, back

[*They shoot into a quagmire, and lit by the lightning the Unicorn races by. A voice calls 'Umusol, Umusol'*]

SAUL. Terrible creature, strong, strong, come back.
   It called me, it called me
      This is miserable
   I will lie down and say goodnight[.]
   Dear storm, shatter me, kind lightning cleave me, cleave me.
   Has earth sunk under the ocean; . . .
      I'll wrench your axle
   Out of the slime—no use . . . is there no soul about
   Hi hi hi hi hi
   What wayfarer would chose a night like this?

In place of ll.91 et seq. of the final draft a holograph fragment has:

   No used experience can dull
   Man's sensitiveness in this
   His wary instincts startle[,] ever dreading
   What obsesses and terrorises
   Till the stricken soul wails in anguish
   For God enlists colourless [? emissaries] that hide
   In woods, in gestures and in common things
   And put on visibility at will.

and between ll.98-104 another holograph has:

         What if an angel sent from God
   To chain the wandering beast, escaped from bonds,
   And made this day so full of terror for me . . .
   God what a day. I thought I had known anguish
   But Lilith will be sleeping. I'll speak to him.
   'Friend, which way fled the beast? Saw you?'
TEL. The road we travel.
SAUL. My house my blood all lean to its weird flight
   O Lilith will you be sleeping? (O miss my Lilith)
   She'll be distraught. Swifter my mules, swifter
   Shrivel the space. My house lies yonder, yonder.

Following l. 122 one fragment has:

SAUL. That your fears were false is because of him.
   See this mud—I would be sinking still.
   I must unload the cart. The slave was not ready.
   Then I will sleep till supper.

And following l. 138 the same holograph has:

TEL. Dead mother of my orphan spirit
Who art thou?
Her mouth moves, her gaze is on me
Treading my soul, treading my life out.
I would fly but cannot.
LILITH. He seems as lost.
The Unicorn is tearing through his brain.

This long dialogue between Lilith and Tel would have belonged somewhere between ll. 139 and 146 of the final draft.

LILITH. How my heart fears. Saul[,] O saul
His eyes are mad to spring on me[.]
TEL. He unloads now (Did I speak. O mother of
My orphan spirit—who art thou?
Her mouth moves, her gaze is on me
Treading my soul. . . . I would fly)
LILITH. He seems as lost. The myth said they were wild[—]
There is such gentle beauty in his tones.
He fears the safety of the world—the loosed unicorn
Is tearing through his brain.
LILITH. Today has been a day out of old histories
For a magician's spelling.
Have you deep stories in your land,
Are there who read strange portents[?]
TEL. We live deep stories, insatiable dreams,
(This is unbearable, the impulse to seize
And strain her to me! I must not look on her
We have soaked ourselves in pain.

An unidentified fragment reads:

TEL. They know, they know, your husband calls
LILITH. Husband did you call[?] He sleeps, waking
He calls me not—how thus in sleep? Today
A common terror brought back old tenderness,
Sometimes I acquiesce with my life cowed,
Sometimes the tigress in my blood leaps, is audible,
For he slays me with a passive knife.

ADAM

[The following is a fragment of a play called 'Adam', or 'Adam and Lilith', which Rosenberg abandoned in favour of 'The Unicorn'. Chronologically it came just before the latter play, and it includes a theme that reappears in parts of that.]

Spirit of Dissolution. Lilith.

SPIRIT. Crazed shadow from your golden body
  Lilith, Lilith, I am.
  I am a tremor in space
  Caught in your beauty's grasp.
  My tentacles that bore so secretly
  Into the health of the world, go suddenly lax.
  When my pulses pale to your beauty's music
  At night in your bed chamber
  Cruel your glimmering mirror shakes,
  As my thoughts, my pulses, pass
  Hungry to you, to roam your vivid beauty.
  Do you not hear their moan
  Beside those four lips darkened in glee,
  Shapeless in voluntary glee,
  Two where mine should be
  Of his your master Adam,
  Whose common bread you are
  Now he is hungry no more?
  Lilith—be kind.
LILITH. If you are stronger than Adam.
SPIRIT. For your sake only, girl,
  I have been cruel to my instinct
  And the venom in my hand.
  For your sake, and the mutable winds of love.
LILITH. I am beautiful.
SPIRIT. Ask Adam.
LILITH. He is a widower since I died to him.
SPIRIT. I am a ghost and you are, we will wed then.
LILITH. I was a lover without a lover.
SPIRIT. Let him be king without a kingdom,
  Let me destroy a city, his people.

LETTERS
AND EXTRACTS FROM LETTERS

[1910 ?]   159 Oxford Street,
                                                      Mile End, E.

I hope I am not taking too great a presumption by intruding in this
matter on your valuable time. If the poems do not merit any part of the
time you may do me the honour to bestow on them, then the presumption
is the more unpardonable; but though I myself am diffident about them,
one has, I suppose, whether one has reason or not, a sort of half-faith;
and it is this half-faith—misplaced or not—that has led me to this course.
If you think them worth criticism, (which is more than I expect,) on that
depends whether this half-faith is to be made an entire one or none at all.
I don't know whether it's justifiable, and I do not mention it to abate one
jot of your candour, but only in extenuation of my presumption, to
remind you that this is not the first time I have wearied you with my
specimens of desperate attempts to murder and mutilate King's English
beyond all shape of recognition; for about five years ago, when I had
just been apprenticed to Carl Hentschel's as a Photo Etcher, I had the
hardihood to send you some verses which you were kind enough to think
were 'promising', and told me I would hear from you again. Of course,
it isn't likely you will remember the occasion, amid your multifarious
duties of your valuable life but to me it was an event; and I only mention
it to show that I have some sort of right to bother you with these; it
being in a way your own kind criticism of the poem five years ago that
encouraged me to continue in these,

                        Yours humbly,
                              ISAAC ROSENBERG

To Miss Seaton,[1] [before 1911]

It is horrible to think that all these hours, when my days are full of
vigour and my hands and soul craving for self-expression, I am bound,
chained to this fiendish mangling-machine, without hope and almost
desire of deliverance, and the days of youth go by . . . I have tried to
make some sort of self-adjustment to circumstances by saying, 'It is all
experience'; but, good God! it is *all* experience, and nothing else . . . I
really would like to take up painting seriously; I think I might do something at that; but poetry—I despair of ever writing excellent poetry. I
can't look at things in the simple, large way that great poets do. My

---

[1] Miss Winifreda Seaton was a middle-aged schoolmistress whom R met in
Amschewitz's studio some time in 1910. She encouraged him with advice, criticism of his poems, and by recommending books for him to read. It was she who
introduced him to Donne and the metaphysicals, and he showed his appreciation
of her friendship by continuing to correspond with her, and to send her his
poems, right up to the time of his death.

mind is so cramped and dulled and fevered, there is no consistency of purpose, no oneness of aim; the very fibres are torn apart, and application deadened by the fiendish persistence of the coil of circumstance.

[1911]

Congratulate me! I've cleared out of the ——— shop, I hope for good and all. I'm free—free to do anything, hang myself or anything except work . . . I'm very optimistic, now that I don't know what to do, and everything seems topsy-turvy.

* * *

I am out of work. I doubt if I feel the better for it, much as the work was distasteful, though I expect it's the hankering thought of the consequences, pecuniary, etc., that bothers me . . . All one's thoughts seem to revolve round to one point—death. It is horrible, especially at night, 'in the silence of the midnight'; it seems to clutch at your thought—you can't breathe. Oh, I think, work, work, any work, only to stop one thinking.

* * *

One conceives one's lot (I suppose it's the same with all people, no matter what their condition) to be terribly tragic. You are the victim of a horrible conspiracy; everything is unfair. The gods have either forgotten you or made you a sort of scapegoat to bear all the punishment. I believe, however hard one's lot is, one ought to try and accommodate oneself to the conditions; and except in a case of purely physical pain, I think it can be done. Why not make the very utmost of our lives? . . . I'm a practical economist in this respect. I endeavour to waste nothing . . . Waste words! Not to talk is to waste words . . .

To most people life is a musical instrument on which they are unable to play: but in the musician's hands it becomes a living thing . . . The artist can see beauty everywhere, anywhere . . .

* * *

You mustn't forget the circumstances I have been brought up in, the little education I have had. Nobody ever told me what to read, or ever put poetry in my way. I don't think I knew what real poetry was till I read Keats a couple of years ago. True, I galloped through Byron when I was about fourteen, but I fancy I read him more for the story than for the poetry. I used to try to imitate him. Anyway, if I didn't quite take to Donne at first, you understand why. Poetical appreciation is only newly bursting on me. I always enjoyed Shelley and Keats. The 'Hyperion' ravished me . . .

Whenever I read anything in a great man's life that pulls him down to me, my heart always pleads for him, and my mind pictures extenuating circumstances.

* * *

181

Have you ever picked up a book that looks like a Bible on the outside, but is full of poetry or comic within? My Hood is like that, and, I am afraid, so am I. Whenever I feel inclined to laugh, my visage assumes the longitude and gravity of a church spire.

*   *   *

I can't say I have ever experienced the power of one spirit over another except in books, of course, at least in any intense way that you mean. Unless you mean the interest one awakes in us, and we long to know more, and none other. I suppose we are all influenced by everybody we come in contact with, in a subconscious way, if not direct, and everything that happens to us is experience; but only the few know it. Most people can only see and hear the noisy sunsets, mountains and waterfalls; but the delicate greys and hues, the star in the puddle[1], the quiet sailing cloud, is nothing to them. Of course, I only mean this metaphorically, as distinguishing between obvious experiences and the almost imperceptible. I still have no work to do. I think, if nothing turns up here, I will go to Africa. I could not endure to live upon my people; and up till now I have been giving them from what I had managed to save up when I was at work. It is nearly run out now, and if I am to do nothing, I would rather do it somewhere else. Besides, I feel so cramped up here, I can do no drawing, reading, or anything . . .

Create our own experience! We can, but we don't. Very often it's only the trouble of a word, and who knows what we miss through not having spoken? It's the man with impudence who has more experience than anybody. He not only varies his own, but makes other people's his own.

*   *   *

Do I like music, and what music I like best? I know nothing whatever about music. Once I heard Schubert's 'Unfinished Symphony' at the band; and—well, I was in heaven. It was a blur of sounds—sweet, fading and blending. It seemed to draw the sky down, the whole spirit out of me; it was articulate feeling. The inexpressible in poetry, in painting, was there expressed. But I have not heard much, and the sensation that gave me I never had again. I should like very much to be one of the initiated.

*   *   *

Some more confidences. I've discovered I'm a very bad talker: I find it difficult to make myself intelligible at times; I can't remember the exact word I want, and I think I leave the impression of being a rambling idiot.

*   *   *

The thoroughness is astounding. No slipshod, tricky slickness, trusting to chance effects, but a subtle suggestiveness, and accident that is the consequence of intention.

[1] Cf. the last line of 'Song' (p. 56).

182

Thanks so much for the Donne. I had just been reading Ben Jonson again, and from his poem to Donne he must have thought him a giant. I have read some of the Donne; I have certainly never come across anything so choke-full of profound meaningful ideas. It would have been very difficult for him to express something commonplace, if he had to.

* * *

I forgot to ask you to return my poetry, as I mean to work on some. I agree the emotions are not worth expressing, but I thought the things had some force, and an idea or so I rather liked. Of course, I know poetry is a far finer thing than that, but I don't think the failure was due to the subject—I had nothing to say about it, that's all. Crashaw, I think, is sometimes very sexual in his religious poems, but it is always new and beautiful. I believe we are apt to fix a standard (of subject) in poetry. We acknowledge the poetry in subjects not generally taken as material, but I think we all (at least I do) prefer the poetical subject— 'Kubla Khan', 'The Mistress of Vision', 'Dream-Tryst'[1]; Poe, Verlaine. Here feeling is separated from intellect; our senses are not interfered with by what we know of facts: we know infinity through melody.

* * *

[*1912 or earlier*]

159 Oxford St
Mile End E

DEAR MISS SEATON

I'm sure I don't know what to say, or how to say it; my brains, as Sterne says, are as dry as a squeezed orange; but I've got your letter to answer; and my conscience wouldn't let me sleep if I didn't do that. Not that I don't enjoy writing to you, (writing to and hearing from you is a real treat) but even enjoyment is a laggard at times with the end in view, and must be spurred by conscience. 'Gee up' says conscience, cracking his whip. 'Where?' cries enjoyment with dancing heart but empty head. 'To Mademoiselle Seaton, of course, you noodle!' 'But how?, I dont know the road; besides my feet are heavy though my heart is light'[.] 'That matters not', says conscience, 'Up, and look for it; be sharp about it too', and here, giving a cut with the whip, enjoyment comes galloping delighted but astounded at the wide prospect of white fields of blank paper; and here I am groping for what to say, and beating the bush for ideas that won't come. Now, you know the state of mind I'm in, or rather the mindless state I'm in, you'll know how to take what I say. In your last letter you deprecated your powers as critic. I most emphatically disagree with your verdict, and absolutely deny your right to judge yourself. Before a less prejudiced court you are found guilty of that most heinous crime of modesty. You are convicted (the jury are all agreed) of having vilely slandered your critical abilities; of having perjured yourself by forswearing and denying the 'gifts the gods gave you'. But

[1] By Francis Thompson

183

I'm not going to flatter or say anything, (though I could hardly flatter); I'm sure if anyone's got anything in one it will out, in spite of everything, though it may take time. I wish you had a little more faith in yourself.

Here is an answer to what you say about too much has been written on books. It is by Rossetti. I suppose you've read it. It is called 'the choice'.

> 'Think thou and act: tomorrow thou shalt die.
> Outstretched in the sun's warmth upon the shore
> Thou say'st "Man's measured path is all gone o'er:
> Man clomb until he touched the truth; and I,
> Even I am he whom it was destined for".
> How should this be? Art thou then so much more
> Than they who sowed, that thou should'st reap thereby?
> 'Nay come up hither. From this wave-washed mound
> Unto the furthest flood-brim look with me:
> Then reach on with thy thought till it be drowned.
> Miles and miles distant though the last line be
> And though thy soul sail leagues and leagues beyond,
> Still leagues beyond those leagues there is more sea.'

Is'nt it magnificent. What space, what suggestion of immensity.

I suppose Flint's poems[1] gave me pleasure because of their newness to me. They don't seem to be ambitious, they seem to me just experiments in versification except some, which are more natural; and I think those are the ones I like best. I like of the first lot, 'The hearts hunger', for the energy intensity and simplicity with which it expresses that strange longing for an indefinite ideal; the haunting desire for that which is beyond the reach of hands. I like the one called 'Exultation', very much. The image in the last stanza; of the—

> 'birds, unrooted flowers of space,
> Shaking to heaven a silver chime of bells',

I think is fine.

I don't think the measure he generally uses allows the poems to stamp itself on the mind, I've got a particularly bad memory, I seldom remember the words of any poem I read; but the tone of the poem, the leading idea, nearly always fix their impression. I didn't find that with these poems; but Dr Eder[2] told me he was very young, about 22; and I expect he'll do something yet.

Last Sunday, I got up early, and feeling very energetic, I locked

---

[1] F. S. Flint was a poet associated with the Imagist group in the period 1910-1930. His poetry was published by The Poetry Bookshop, which also published the 'Georgian' anthologies, but he does not feature in them. His dry, factual, ironic mode evidently did not appeal to Marsh.

[2] Dr Eder, a cousin of Israel Zangwill, with whom he lived, was a practising psychiatrist and pioneer Freudian in England. R met him early in 1911, probably in Amschewitz's studio.

myself in till about two o'clock and worked on a painting to 'La Belle dame Sans Merci', 'I set her on my pacing steed', you know the rest, I should like you to see it. I didn't quite get what I wanted, but—so-so. It was the first bit of painting I've done for months.

Here is a sonnet I wrote to Mr Amschewitz;[1] he hasn't seen it yet.

Well, enjoyment must come to a full stop here, breathless. Conscience growls out a sort of inarticulate monosyllable of—is it satisfaction or disgust?—but I construe the former, and—well, that is all, while enjoyment can just manage to gasp out

I am

Yours sincerely

I ROSENBERG

Does this sound as if I'm glad to come to a stop. No!—I mean the enjoyment stops with the letter, and I'm sorry I can't think of any more —no doubt luckily for you.

[*1912, ?March*]   159 Oxford St
                                                            Mile End E

DEAR MISS LÖWY,

I feel very elated at Mr Picciotto[2] liking my poems, as I was very anxious to know. Nothing is rarer than good poetry—and nothing more discouraging than the writing of poetry. One might write for pleasure but I doubt[,] if there is no stronger motive[,] whether one would be incited to ambitious work. Circumstances and other considerations have prevented me from applying myself assiduously, and also diffidence—so you can imagine what a rare pleasure it is to me when people appreciate my efforts. As to the prose I sent him, it was an early thing I did some years ago—I had no other by me when I sent. You did not say whether the poem I sent you would do for the publication. Since I sent it I found in my copy the typist had been trying to improve on parts, which, when I noticed, sent me into ecstasies—and also, the two or three verses about the parents and brother should be left out. I expect though, there's plenty of time and I may hit off something better. So your commis[s]ion bothers you. Thats a calamity indeed. All I can suggest is that you should bother it, and bother it, until you bother it into shape. I have been doing practically nothing—except leading a lordly life—not getting up till tea time and then cursing myself for letting the daylight go. Its getting terribly on my conscience. I shan't torture you with my adventures in the land of Nod, or accounts of the wonderful dream castles I have built and unbuilt by myriads,—also not quite so substantial architecturally as those of Mr Joseph's building.

---

[1] See the poem 'To J. H. Amschewitz' on p. 43.
[2] Cyril Picciotto K. C., whose wife was a first cousin of Ruth Löwy.

The other night I met Michael Sherbrooke, the actor I told you of.[1] He took me home with him and almost made me delirious with delight at some of his marvellous recitations. His power is almost incredible—I have never seen anything like it and could hardly conceive anything so. He gave the Raven. The melancholy insistence—the perpetual recurring note of despair—the gradual tightening to the climax—which is almost unbearable—and then the unutterable broken pathos of the last verse— has so tremendous a grip on you—and so supreme is the acting—one almost faints. I wish you heard it—I should like you to.

If Mr Picciotto would like to see me I should not like to go unprepared —I mean, would it be inquisitive on my part to ask you for information— you needn't give me all his autobiography, his genealogy &c. I might know more than he knows, then, about himself—and that would be unfair,—but I have a dread of meeting people who know I write, as they expect me to talk and I am a horrible bad talker. I am in absolute agonies in company and it needs a sympathetic listener like yourself to put me at ease,—I have been tempted into a letter and I need very little tempting—so you must excuse this egotism—if a letter isn't that its nothing.

The Pre-Raphaelite show at the Tate closes very shortly[2]—when you get back I wish you could come with me—and exchange impressions. We would both learn. I think the Rossetti drawings would be a revelation to you.

Yours sincerely

I. ROSENBERG

[Latter part of a letter, presumably to Miss Seaton]

Whitechapel Gallery. The paintings are in the upper gallery. Some wonderful Reynolds and Hogarths. There is Hogarth's Peg Woffington the sweetest the most charming, most exquisite portrait of a woman I've ever seen. A Rossetti drawing—fine and a lot of good things. It's open Sunday as well. You could easily manage to go in the afternoon.

I read the Ivan Turgeneff. Panshin is very good—and the aunt does live. It is very sad; I almost think books like that are immoral; in this sense that one leaves them with a discouraging sense of the futility of life; a sort of numbing effect. I like to read something joyous—bouyant, a clarion call to life, an inspirer to endeavour, something that tells one life is worth living, and not death only is worth having. You can keep 'The man of feeling', if you want it, I've got it again somewhere at home, I think.

---

[1] See footnote to letter to Mrs Cohen on p. 196.

[2] This was an Exhibition of works by the English Pre-Raphaelite painters lent to the Tate Gallery by Birmingham Corporation. It ran from December 1911 to March 1912.

I've got a letter from Dr Eder. Of course his criticism does not refer to the lastest things I showed you; but I know he's right. Here it is, word for word

DEAR MR ROSENBERG

Do you want your verse[s] back now. I have been keeping them to show to a friend—but he is not back yet in England. Much I like very much. You are young, and your verse shows that much. My own counsel would be not to think of publishing yet awhile (I never thought [to] publish). You have the artist's feeling for expression and for words. I should say you have not yet developed your own technique. That is not meant as a fault—[to] the contrary. But there is a fault. And that is, you have so far not given utterance to your own personality and it is all too reminiscent. I think you want courage to strike out into a line of your own. I should not write thus to anyone whom I did not respect for what he had done. We have all done a little versifying in our green days and hence these counsels.

EDER

I am sending these poems in type so you can read easier but I'll let you have copies if you like.

Yours sincerely
I. ROSENBERG

[*Postmarked July 15, 1912*] 32 Carlingford Rd
Hampstead

DEAR MISS WRIGHT [1]

I am so glad you and your sister like my poems—and I should so like to be able to agree with you about their merits. I would have sent them to you long ago but I always had an idea of going up to the Birkbeck which somehow never came off. I should be delighted to be able to come round some evening—in the day my times are rather muddled and I don't think it would be safe to make an appointment—

I am just going to paint a fairly big picture for the school competition[2] 'Joy'. If you could find time ever to come and see how it was getting on and give suggestions I should be so pleased.

Yours sincerely
ISAAC ROSENBERG

[1] When R started evening classes at the Birkbeck School of Art in 1908 one of his teachers was a Miss Alice Wright. She not only assisted him in his painting but also encouraged and criticized his poetry. She and her sister befriended R at a crucial period of his life, and introduced him to the work of two poets who profoundly influenced his own work—Shelley and Blake.

[2] This was the Slade Summer Competition, to be executed during the Long Vacation and submitted at the beginning of the Autumn Term.

[Fragment of a letter to Ruth Löwy, 1912, probably July]   *[No address]*

I hope you have a good time when you are away—live in the garden of Joy so that when you get back you will know what sort of expression to wear when I put you in my 'garden of Joy'. If you find you can spare a line when you are away I should be so glad to hear.

Yours sincerely
ISAAC ROSENBERG

[Postmarked August 6, 1912]   32 Carlingford Rd
Hampstead

DEAR MISS WRIGHT

Thank you for the post card. I don't think I shall be able to come either Wed or Thur—as Wed I have to see the dentist and Thur I believe I am getting a model in my studio—If no one turns up here I may come as I like the idea very much. I have been frantically busy—I have the working fever this week. I have started my picture again, having taken a violent dislike to my first design—it is absolutely another thing now, though the literary idea is the same. My colour conception is a wonderful scheme of rose silver and gold—just now it is all pink yellow and blue—but I have great hopes in it.

My appointment with the dentist is not till 12, so I may be able to come at 10 and leave early.

Yours sincerely
ISAAC ROSENBERG

[Postmarked August 10, 1912]   32 Carlingford Rd
Hampstead

Friday

DEAR MISS WRIGHT

I have not seen the pearl by day but it looks gorgeous by night—it is just that iride[sce]nce—that shimmering quality I want to make the whole scheme of my picture—and that will help me tremendously—Thank you so much—I had Miss Grimshaw this afternoon and we both worked hard—She is a very good sitter—though her figure was much too scraggy for my purpose—I practically finished the drapery, and the upper part I will do from some more titanic model if I can get the type—

I forgot when you were here to ask you to put your names in the Shelley you gave me—I think a present is no present without the—I mean a book is no present without it has the names of the giver—I would appreciate it very much. I owe some of the most wonderful sensations I have ever experienced to that book—the speech by Beatrice about death[1]—I think it is quite the most intense passage in the whole of literature—the literature I know.

Yours sincerely
ISAAC ROSENBERG

[1] See *The Cenci*, Act V, Sc. IV, ll. 48-74.

32 Carlingford Road
Hampstead

Thursday

DEAR MISS LÖWY,

Thanks for letter—I did not think your holiday was going to be over so soon, but as long as you have rested and been happy the time has done its duty. The weather here is terrible, I suppose the sun has gone somewhere for his holidays and has forgotten to leave a substitute to attend to his business,—my God—the elements are having a lark—the wind plays shuttlecock with the trees—and all the work I've been doing is chasing my hat through the streets—writing doleful ditties—and wondering when the deuce the rain is going to stop. I have seriously thought—knowing the wickedness of the times—(with suffragettes throwing hatchets at kings—and poets compelling people to read their poems,) that God has sent another deluge—and have been looking about for a carpenter to build me an ark. I started my picture all again and have been working day and night at it since Friday and feel very tired. It is a gorgeous scheme of rose pearl and gold—a dream picture. My landlady asked me if it was a dream—a splendid proof of the dream-like quality it has. Everything now depends on the models (if I can afford any) and the types I get for them. Fine types are so rare and when you see them circumstances make it impossible to use them. There was a girl with just the head I wanted came to our place the other day—but her father said he didn't like the idea of her sitting—I don't know what the man imagined I was going to do. But I think I know someone who may do—and then there are two more—one, you promised to sit for—though it seems wrong of me to ask you to waste your time so—but I don't think it'll take long—and perhaps I may be of use to you for small things in yours. But I can't get anyone for my chief head Joy—I think I will leave it until I come across someone. You must buck up if you want to do anything—there is about 7 weeks I think and as soon as you get back—I should get in the big canvas and go ahead—you'll find when you transfer your sketch down and get models that it will come. I feel mine though it looks vague now—improves with each touch—though I haven't use[d] models yet.

I hope Lena is enjoying herself.

Could you come round Monday and get over the sitting—or if you liked I could come round to you and do it[,] though that would be a bit awkward as I may want to paint direct on the picture. If you haven't ordered your canvas you could do so on the way.

Yours sincerely,
I. ROSENBERG

You will continue your holiday in going on with your picture

[*Postmarked September 5, 1912*]   32 Carlingford Rd
                                                          Hampstead

DEAR MISS WRIGHT

    I have been very busy on my picture and have not been able to come round. Besides, I thought I may not find you in unless I made an appointment which is rather difficult for me just now as I never know when I am to be busy or not. It is very good of you to interest yourself so—in a few weeks perhaps you will come round and see my picture—I have no more copies of my poems here—but I fancy my printer has some and I will see this week—if I get any I shall send them. Boss and Dickson came to see me a short while back and liked my picture. Ought I to have shown up their bad taste so?

Yours sincerely
I. ROSENBERG

Regards to your sister

[*Postmarked September 16, 1912*]   159 Oxford St
                                                          Mile End E

DEAR MISS WRIGHT

    I was far from expecting the pleasure that awaited me when I got home last night in your letter and your sister's poems. I read them while having supper, and, I can assure you, I have seldom enjoyed a supper more, a proof that the ordinary material facts of life can be made more pleasurable with the assistance of some intellectual garnish. They seem to me very beautiful, though I cannot quite agree with the pessimistic tone of the mirror poem. When Milton writes on his blindness, how dignified he is! how grand, how healthy! What begins in a mere physical moan, concludes in a grand triumphant spiritual expression, of more than resignation, of conquest. But I think the concluding idea very beautiful. I like the sonnets very much, an uncommon artistic expression of the artist's common lament. But this pettifogging, mercantile, money-loving age is deaf, dead as their dead idol gold, and dead as that to all higher enobling influences.

    After seeing these, the poems, I wonder how I could ever have shown mine; still, you must understand I showed mine not so much out of vanity, as, on the contrary, out of a conciousness of their poverty, to have their defects pointed out.

    I should be much obliged for a criticism.

Yours,
I. ROSENBERG

[*Probably September 26, 1912*]   32 Carlingford Rd
                                                          Hampstead

DEAR MISS WRIGHT

    I cannot come round either Wed or Thur—but Friday if you do not write to the contrary—I can come—about 5. My picture is undergoing a transforming process, it is as it were—in the frying pan—not quite raw—nor yet quite done—I think in another week I shall be quite decided on the arrangement—then I hope it will be plain sailing. I managed to find another copy of my poems which I enclose.

Yours sincerely
ISAAC ROSENBERG

[1912 ?September]   159 Oxford St
                                                     Mile End E.

DEAR MISS SEATON

I saw Miss Cook and she told me what has fired me to write this letter—that you think I don't want to do the drawing I promised of you. Or at least she hinted so. I thought it was plain that the conditions were awkward—no convenient place to do it—but Mr Amschewitz has kindly promised to lend his studio for the purpose Sat—as he will not be in. If you cared to come there, I should be delighted to do the drawing. I don't suppose you have aged much since I saw you although it seems ages ago; because I don't seem to be in sympathy with old heads, I am seldom successful. You must be prepared to sit about 2 hours as I draw slowly—of course resting when you like. I wrote you a letter some time ago which perhaps you never received. I have a habit of forgetting to address my letters which often has disastrous results. When I heard about you then you were ill and had been away to the country. I hope you are allright now and dont work too hard. I am studying at the Slade, the finest school for drawing in England. I do nothing but draw—draw— You've heard of Professor Tonks[1]—he's one of the teachers. A most remarkable man. He talks wonderfully. So voluble and ready—crammed with ideas—most illuminating and suggestive—and witty. I am still keen on writing. I sent some poems to the English Review. I heard nothing for several months and then I got them back—with a letter from Austin Harrison[2] saying he kept them so long because he liked two of them (I sent 3) very much, and he asked me to send more. I have done so this week—I have not heard yet. I have been writing some prose, I will bring with me.

Hope you will come

Yours sincerely
I ROSENBERG

[1] Henry Tonks (1862-1937) became assistant to Professor Frederick Brown at the Slade School in the last decade of the 19th century, and succeeded to his Chair in 1918—a post which he occupied for the next 12 years. A brilliant if rather formidable teacher of drawing, he also had a remarkable gift for initiating students into the appreciation of pictures.

[2] Austin Harrison (1873-1928), author and journalist, became Editor of *The English Review* in 1910. His particular interest at that time was Germany, about which he published 3 books during the next decade. He also regularly contributed to the political and literary periodicals of the day.

[*No date*]   [*No address*]

DEAR MISS WRIGHT

I am so sorry about not being able to fix up to come round. Monday evening I joined some classes, and Sunday I am having a friend at my place—could we leave it to the Sunday after. Trust you find the school agrees with you again. Remember me to your sister.

Yours sincerely
I ROSENBERG

To Laurence Binyon[1] [*1912*]

I must thank you very much for your encouraging reply to my poetical efforts . . . As you are kind enough to ask about myself, I am sending a sort of autobiography I wrote about a year ago . . . You will see from that that my circumstances have not been very favourable for artistic production; but generally I am optimistic, I suppose because I am young and do not properly realize the difficulties. I am now attending the Slade, being sent there by some wealthy Jews who are kindly interested in me, and, of course, I spend most of my time drawing. I find writing interferes with drawing a good deal, and is far more exhausting.

[*No date. Presumably Sept-Oct 1912*]   32 Carlingford Rd
                                                         Hampstead
DEAR MRS COHEN

I am sorry if there was any confusion about paying the Slade fees. I still have the cheque and was waiting for the other 5 shillings so as to pay it all. I thought I could pay it out of this week's money but I have had extra expenses—mending boots and other little necessities, which made it awkward. I must thank you for returning my letter as it gives me a chance of doing that which you said ought to be done—of throwing it in the fire. I am very sorry that you noticed it as of course I did not, or I shouldn't have sent it. I said what I had to say, and had done with it, it must have been quite an accident its smudging. I don't think any other letters of mine are in that state. No stranger could receive such a letter of mine as I never write to strangers.

I sent a letter before I received this asking you to see the picture. I am not at the Slade—Tuesdays Thursdays—the picture has to go in by next Monday. I suppose you will let me know.

Yours sincerely
I ROSENBERG

[1] Laurence Binyon (1869-1943) poet and art critic. Became Keeper of Prints and Drawings in the British Museum in 1932, and was Professor of Poetry at Harvard University from 1933-34. He took an active interest in R's poetry, corresponded with him about it over the next 5 or 6 years, and wrote the admirable Introductory Memoir to the 1922 volume of R's poems.

32 Carlingford Rd
                                            Hampstead

DEAR MRS COHEN

I am very sorry I have disappointed you. If you tell me what was expected of me I shall at least have the satisfaction of knowing by how much I have erred. You were disappointed in my picture for its unfinished state—I have no wish to defend myself—or I might ask what you mean by finish:—and you are convinced I could have done better. I thank you for the compliment but I do not think it deserved—I did my best.

You did ask me whether I had been working hard, and I was so taken back at the question that I couldn't think what to say. If you did not think the work done sufficient evidence, what had I to say? I have no idea what you expected to see. I cannot conceive who gave you the idea that I had such big notions of myself, are you sure the people you enquired of know me, and meant me. You say people I have lately come in contact with. I have hardly seen anyone during the holidays—and I certainly have not been ashamed of my opinions, not about myself, but others—when I have; and if one does say anything in an excited unguarded moment—perhaps an expression of what one would like to be—it is distorted and interpreted as conceit—when in honesty it should be overlooked. I am not very inquisitive naturally, but I think it concerns me to know what you mean by poses and mannerisms—and whose advice do I not take who are in a position to give—and what more healthy style of work do you wish me to adopt?

I feel very grateful for your interest in me—going to the Slade has shown possibilities—has taught me to see more accurately.—but one especial thing it has shown me—Art is not a plaything, it is blood and tears, it must grow up with one; and I believe I have begun too late.

I suppose I go on as I am till Xmas. Till then I will look about. I should like all the money advanced on me considered as a loan—but which you must not expect back for some years as it takes some time settling down in art.

Yours sincerely
I ROSENBERG

The Slade pictures will be on view shortly, I will let you know more if you care to see them.

[*1912 ?October*]   32 Carlingford Road
                                            Hampstead

DEAR MISS LÖWY,

Thank you for sending the cards. If you see Mr Kohan will you thank him for me—I am always eager to hear Newbolt—I enjoyed his lecture on Milton very much.

I don't think the professor was at all fair to Bomberg.[1] He may have been perfectly right from his point of view, but not to enter into Bomberg's at all I don't think was just.

I have had a bit of a scuffle with Mrs Cohen lately. She was very disappointed at my picture and said she was sure I could have done better. I thanked her for the compliment and assured her it was quite undeserved—I did my best. She said that unless I get into a more healthy style of work she won't help me—and many other things that showed great invention. I told her she could do what she liked—God knows what she means by a more healthy style of work[.]—Do you feel ill when you see my work[?] I know some feel people faint looking at a Michel Angelo[.]—How are you getting on?

Yours sincerely
I. ROSENBERG

32 Carlingford Rd
Hampstead

[*No date, but must be October 1912*]

DEAR MISS WRIGHT

I forgot to mention in my last letter the result of the criticism[2]. The 'Nativity' took the prize as was expected. Mine got well praised—The Pro-[3] said it showed a hopeful future—had great charm etc but I wanted more study. I am sending a drawing and perhaps a painting to the New English as the Pro- advised me to. I am moving from here Monday so shall be busy Sunday but I shall try and be round at four. I have written other poems which I shall bring round. Trust you don't find the weather too cold.

Yours sincerely
ISAAC ROSENBERG

159 Oxford St
Mile End E

[1912 ?October]

DEAR MISS WRIGHT

I have been very unsettled since I saw you so I could not write as I promised. I moved to Hampstead Rd and only slept there a night when I

---

[1] David Bomberg (1890-1957) was the son of an immigrant Polish Jew. Like Gertler and Rosenberg he was a member of that remarkable group of talented East-end painters and writers known as 'the Whitechapel Boys', which also included Joseph Leftwich, John Rodker and Samuel Winsten. Bomberg was a contemporary of Rosenberg's at the Slade and became his close friend. A founder member of the London Group, he held more radical views about art than most of his friends, and was invited to exhibit at the Vorticist Exhibition in 1915. After serving with the Royal Engineers for the next 3 years, he travelled widely before starting to teach during the Second World War and founding the Borough Group.

[2] The annual judging of the Slade Summer Competition.

[3] Professor Tonks.

found I had to move again—on account of the train noises going on all night. I could not find another room so have gone back to my people. I have not been able to find prose things but if your friend will come to a decision I shall hunt up for them.

My drawing was accepted and bought, but not my painting. MacIvoy[1] told me it was liked very much, and hung half a dozen times but . . .

Yours sincerely
I ROSENBERG

[No date]   32 Carlingford Rd
                                                             Hampstead
DEAR MISS WRIGHT
    I am sorry not to have turned up Sat as I promised. Sat. is a very awkward day for me and the other days I am at the Slade or the N.G.[2]

Yours sincerely
I ROSENBERG

Here is a poem I wrote.[3]

[Probably December 1912]   159 Oxford St
                                                             Mile End E
DEAR MRS COHEN
    I saw Mr Lesser today and he is going to put my case before the committee[4] next meeting—that is, Friday a week. I told him that my reasons for applying were, firstly my reduced allowance, and that we couldn't agree, which made my position very awkward. I told him I was very vague as to what you expected me to do, or in which way you wished me to show my appreciation of what you had done,—and that I was accused of all sorts of things, and that I was put into a state of mind which made working very difficult.

    Perhaps I was wrong in not consulting you, and I suppose if I tell you there was no time to consult you, you will think I am trying to make myself out right. The fact of the matter was, I looked about for a room and couldn't find any. When I went home Sunday as usual, and mentioned my difficulty of sleeping, my mother made me sleep at home that night, which decided me to stay till I found a place. You can call me rude, ungentlemanly ungrateful etc—but you know it is only my honesty

---

[1] Presumably Ambrose McEvoy (1878-1927), landscape and portrait painter. Was at the Slade with Augustus John, exhibited at the New English from 1900 on, and became a founder-member of the National Portrait Society 1911. Served with Royal Naval Division 1916-18.

[2] The National Gallery.

[3] Two poems were enclosed: 'We are sad with a vague sweet sorrow' and 'Spring' (see pp. 17 and 57).

[4] Of the Jewish Educational Aid Society. Ernest Lesser was the Hon. Sec.

in not concealing what I think that leaves me open to this. You know I am not in a position to gain anything—I mean I can only be the loser by being so. Naturally I am concerned at being thought all this by people I respect, but as I, being ignorant of the existence of the qualities that go to make the opposite, can't be expected to agree with them, I certainly don't feel conscience stricken.

Quarreling is an unneccessary waste of energy, and the reason I broke with Mr Sherbrooke[1] was to prevent quarreling.

It was only when Mr Sherbrooke's goodness became unendurable that I broke with him. When I was at Hampstead I worked all day and walked about in the rain all the evening until I was wet through and tired out—that was the only amusement I got.

The isolation there so preyed on my spirits that I don't think I'd be far wrong if I attributed the unfinished state of my picture to the mental and physical looseness so caused.

I shall return the £2 you lent me for printing[,] out of the £4 I shall get for my drawing.

Yours sincerely
ISAAC ROSENBERG

[*No date*]   Slade School of Art
                                               University College, London
                                               Gower Street, W.C.

DEAR MISS WRIGHT
    You must forgive me for not having written before, but things are still very unsettled and all sorts of annoyances happened to interfere. I could not come on Sunday as Sundays I am especially busy. I enclose another poem.[2]

Yours sincerely
ISAAC ROSENBERG

[*No date*]   159 Oxford St

DEAR MISS WRIGHT
    I saw Miss Cook at the N.G. and she told me Mr Quick had seen my poems and wished to see my drawings.[3] I have not got a room yet so

---

[1] Michael Sherbrooke, an actor of Polish origin (his parents' name was originally Czevzik) was the son of an East End Rabbi. He made some reputation on the stage in Ibsen's plays, was a friend of J. H. Amschewitz, in whose studio R met him about 1911-12. For a time Sherbrooke helped and befriended R, giving recitals of R's poems, but eventually the older man's patronage became irksome, as this letter indicates. It was Sherbrooke who presented Amschewitz's portrait of R in 1909, which is reproduced on the back flap of this book's dust-wrapper, to the Jews College, London.

[2] 'O'er the Celestial Pathways' (see p. 29).

[3] I have not been able to identify either of these people.

its difficult to arrange about seeing them—in fact I've hardly got anything to show. I am very bothered—I think I've been saying that in all my letters to you—but I really am in a very serious situation. I have thrown over my patrons they were so unbearable, and as I can't do commercial work, and I have no other kind of work to show, it puts me in a fix. I only mention these private troubles to excuse my backwardness in answering your letter—

I trust you and your sister enjoy the holidays.

I have written other poems since[.] I send the last one[1] as I can't find the others just now.

Yours sincerely
ISAAC ROSENBERG

[*Postmarked December 27, 1912*] 159 Oxford St
Mile End E

DEAR MISS WRIGHT

Thank you for your letter. My affairs have cleared up a little, I have managed to get fixed up for some time at least satisfactorily. I shall not be able to turn up Sat, as I have work to do, but I think Thursday I could. By then I think I shall be living in Fitzroy St, I have come across a place there, but haven't quite made up my mind.

I haven't got the poems I promised but will try and remember on the the other side.[2]

Yours sincerely
ISAAC ROSENBERG

[*late December 1912*] 1 St Georges Sq
Chalk Farm

DEAR MR LESSER

I enclose another receipt dated last Monday when I received it. I saw Dr Davis but he couldn't do anything as he has nothing to do with eyes—but he gave me a card for the O[p]thalmic Hospital which I havn't been able to use yet because of the Xmas holidays. I shall go some day next week. Thanks for the information about my being a British Subject. I am getting along with my things for this competition[.][3]

Yours sincerely
ISAAC ROSENBERG

[1] 'The Poet,' I (see p. 20).
[2] Copy of 'Peace' (see p. 18).
[3] The first (British) Rome Prize, 1913. It was an annual 'open' competition, for which the prize was a stipend of £200 p.a., renewable for a total of 3 years, and carried with it the right to studio facilities in the British School at Rome. At that time, candidates had to be under 30 and British subjects; hence R's enquiry to Lesser referred to in the above letter.

DEAR MISS SEATON

Excuse me writing in pencil as my pen has gone wrong and I want to write just now. I have not been reading Donne much as I am drawing a lot, and when I'm not drawing my mind is generally occupied that way. A great deal of Donne seems a sort of mental gymnastics, the strain is very obvious, but he is certainly wonderful, 'The ecstacy' is very fine, but F. Thompson's 'Dream tryst'[1] to me is much finer. There is a small book of contemporary Belgian poetry like the German you lent me (which by the way I don't feel inclined to open) some Maeterlincks seem marvellous to me, and Verhaern[2] in the 'Sovran Rythm' knocks Donne into a cocked hat. I mean for genuine poetry, where the words lose their interest as words and only a living and beautiful idea remains. It is a grand conception,—Eve meeting Adam. Maeterlinck[3] has a superb little thing 'Orison'—a most trembling fragile moan of astonishing beauty. The Blakes at the Tate show that England has turned out one man second to none who has ever lived. The drawings are finer than his poems, much clearer, though I can't help thinking it was unfortunate that he did not live whan a better tradition of drawing ruled. His conventional manner of expressing those astounding conceptions is the fault of his time, not his.

Yours sincerely
ISAAC ROSENBERG

DEAR MR LESSER

I have failed in the Prix De Rome competition, but when I get the things back, I can do a little more to them and send them to Exhibitions. Since I did those things I have been unwell, and been coughing very badly for about two months. Last week I saw a doctor and though at first he thought it was serious and said I had a very bad chest, the next time he said it wasn't so bad but I needed to go away for a couple of weeks and be out in the open. I have been sleeping here while unwell. Do you think the Society would let me have some money to go away so that I would be fairly comfortable and I could go somewhere on the South Coast.

---

[1] See *The Works of Francis Thompson, Poems: Vol. 1, p. 167.*

[2] Emile Verhaeren (1855-1916), Belgian poet and dramatist, was a radically inclined writer who drew much of his inspiration from the sufferings of the poor at the turn of the century.

[3] Maurice Maeterlinck (1862-1949), Belgian poet and playwright, was much influenced by the Pre-Raphaelites and the French Symbolists, which no doubt accounts for R's sympathy with his work.

The 'Prix De Rome' things, successful and not, are on show at the Imperial Institute, South Kensington, from 10 till 4, all this week. No Slade people got it, though Prof Tonks thought they should have done so. He was disgusted with the decision.[1] I trust you will let me know soon.

Your's sincerely

ISAAC ROSENBERG

<table>
<tr><td>[1913 ?November]</td><td align="right">1, St George's Square
Regent's Park, N.W.</td></tr>
</table>

DEAR MR MARSH

Thanks for your criticisms which of course I agree with. If a poem doesn't sound real it has missed its end,—but I think you can understand one's fondness for an idea or a line prompting one to show poems that one knows are otherwise poor.

I have seen Bobbie—he has not been able to get his drawings yet, being busy at the workshop, but he expects to get them this week.

Yours sincerely

ISAAC ROSENBERG

<table>
<tr><td>[1913 ?December]</td><td align="right">87 Dempsey St
Stepney E</td></tr>
</table>

DEAR MARSH

Thanks very very much for the book.[2] I know so little of these men, and from that little[,] I know how much I miss by not knowing more. I think the Queen's song of Flecker,[3] delicious; and 'The end of the world' by Bottomley,[4] very fine imagination and original. That is all I have

---

[1] A strange mistake here somewhere, for the 1913 Rome Prize was in fact won by Colin Gill, a Slade student. Either Tonks had been misinformed about the winner, or R was repeating inaccurate Slade gossip.

[2] *Georgian Poetry 1911-1912*. This was the first of the five anthologies of contemporary poetry edited by Edward Marsh and published by Harold Monro of The Poetry Bookshop.

[3] James Elroy Flecker (1884-1915) was a leading poet of the 'Georgian' school, whose popularity increased steadily following the publication of his *Collected Poems* in 1916, and reached its zenith with the London production of his play *Hassan* in 1923. By the following year 10 impressions, totalling 10,500 copies, of his poems had been printed.

[4] 'The End of the World' by Gordon Bottomley (1874-1948), Georgian poet and dramatist, had appeared in *Chambers of Imagery*, 2nd Series. His work was greatly admired by R and he was one of the first to recognise and encourage R's own exceptional gifts. They corresponded at intervals to within a few weeks of R's death. Bottomley selected and edited *Poems by Isaac Rosenberg*, published in 1922, and collaborated with D. W. Harding in the preparation of the *Collected Works* in 1937. Many of R's original Mss, and some of his drawings, have been preserved through the good offices of Bottomley and his literary executors.

had time to read yet. What strikes me about these men [is] they are very much alive, and have personal vision—and what is so essential, can express themselves very simply. But writing about a poem is like singing about a song—or rather, as Donne says, fetching water to the sea, and in my case, very dirty water. You can talk about life, but you can only talk round literature; you will be talking about life, I think.

Yours sincerely
ISAAC ROSENBERG

[*Postcard to his mother, postmarked February 24, 1914*]   195 Wimbourne Rd

Winton Bournemouth
c/o Cohen

I forgot to put the address yesterday. I'm not lucky with the weather yet but the air is very good,—I don't cough much. The town here is like a big sanatorium. I'll send a card of the invalids' garden. Pine Woods a few minutes from here[.] I'm going there now[.]

ISAAC

[*No date, but must be Spring 1914*]   87 Dempsey St

Stepney E

DEAR MR LESSER

Do you think the E A S [1] would make me a grant of 12 or 15 pounds to go to S. Africa.

The doctor has told me my chest is weak and that I must live in the country and take care of myself. I cannot live here in the country just now, and it is now that it is so essential. I have a relation in Cape Town who could put me up until I sold things some way or other, and I believe I could get heaps of good subject matter.

The kaffirs would sit for practically nothing. In a year I'd have a lot of interesting stuff, to send to England. I am sending several things to Whitechapel show. The fare to S. Africa is £12. Could you let me know at once as I am convinced of the importance of not stopping here.

Your's sincerely
ISAAC ROSENBERG

To Miss Seaton, [Spring 1914]

So I've decided on Africa, the climate being very good, and I believe plenty to do ... I won't be quite lost in Africa ... I dislike London for the selfishness it instils into one, which is a reason of the

---

[1] The Jewish Educational Aid Society

peculiar feeling of isolation I believe most people have in London. I hardly know anybody whom I would regret leaving (except, of course, the natural ties of sentiment with one's own people); but whether it is that my nature distrusts people, or is intolerant, or whether my pride or my backwardness cools people, I have always been alone. Forgive this little excursion into the forbidden lands of egotism.

[*1914 ?May*]   87 Dempsey St
                                                   Stepney E

DEAR MR MARSH

I should feel very pleased and proud to have my drawing printed in your book.[1] I know someone who might be a subscriber and would like to know what the subscription is,—and I suppose a copy would be sent on. I am about to sail for Africa as I have been told my chest is not strong and I must live away from towns. If I get the chance I may work on a farm for a year or two as I am young enough to afford it. I might also this way get ideas for real things. One is so cramped up here and one must either do cubism or what I propose to do to avoid the rut etc. I could not resist mentioning this having this occasion to write to you. I hope you will let me know the subscription for my friend.

                                   Yours sincerely
                                   ISAAC ROSENBERG

Berg Collection

[*Postmarked May 15, 1914*]   87 Dempsey St
                                                   Stepney E

DEAR MARSH

I have been to the Emmigration Office and find there are no other restrictions beside those you wrote me. They would want some sort of guaranteee that my sister could keep me, but that depends on what the other side (in Africa) take for guarantee. I shouldn't think I need fear anything that way, as I'm sure my sister could put me up for some months during which I could turn out enough work to make some sort of stir. I have no tuberculosis as far as I know, but a weak chest.

It is very kind of you to go to all that bother—I hope it doesn't interfere with anything you have to do.

I am enclosing the lines I lately wrote, and those I showed you. I think the more recent read more musically. At present they have no connection with the first but that is the only way I can write, in scraps, and then join them together—I have the *one idea* in mind.

                                   Yours sincerely
                                   ISAAC ROSENBERG

[1] The reference is to a suggestion that Marsh might include a drawing of R's in an anthology representing the work of contemporary artists which he was planning. But it never materialized.

[*May 1914*]   87 Dempsey St
                                                Stepney E
DEAR MARSH
    I shall not be going for about 2 weeks, when I expect to be quite
ready. I should be delighted to see your pictures before I go,—I have
heard you have a fine collection. I can spare any evening you like and
will bring one or two drawings. I'm also having some things at the Whitechapel,[1] but they're very incomplete—I suppose you'll see them there.
The address I should like you to send the prospectus [to] is

                        Mrs Löwy
                        11 Ladbroke Terrace
                        Holland Park W.

                        Yours sincerely
                                ISAAC ROSENBERG

[*May 1914*]   87 Dempsey St
                                                Stepney E
DEAR MARSH
    Thank you very much—I am very eager to see your pictures. I will
be at the restaurant Fri, with some silly drawings.

                        Yours sincerely
                                ISAAC ROSENBERG

[*May-June 1914*]   87 Dempsey St
                                                Stepney E
DEAR MARSH
    This is my rest while packing. My things have to be on board by
Wed—and I only knew today—so you can imagine the rush I'm in. Your
criticism gave me great pleasure; not so much the criticism, as to feel
that you took those few lines up so thoroughly, and tried to get into them.
You dont know how encouraging that is. People talk about independence
and all that—but one always works with some sort of doubt, that is, if
one believes in the inspired 'suntreaders'. I believe that all poets who are
personal—see things genuinely, have their place. One needn't be a
Shakespeare. Yet I never meant to go as high as these—I know I've come
across things by people of far inferior vision, that were as important in
their results, to me.
    I am not going to refute your criticisms; in literature I have no judg-
ment—at least for style. If in reading a thought has expressed itself to
me, in beautiful words; my ignorance of grammar etc, makes me accept
that. I should think you are right mostly; and I may yet work away your

    [1] The Whitechapel Art Gallery, which held an annual exhibition in which
Bomberg, Gertler and Rosenberg, among others, showed their work. It held a
Memorial Exhibition for R in 1937, which was opened by Marsh.

chief objections. You are quite right in the way you read my poem,[1] but I thought I could use the 'July ghost' to mean the Summer, and also an ambassador of the summer, without interfering with the sense. The shell of thought is man; you realise a shell has an opening. Across this opening, the ardours—the sense of heat forms a web—this signifies a sense of summer—the web again becomes another metaphor—a July ghost. But of course I mean it for summer right through, I think your suggestion of taking out 'woven'[2] is very good. I enclose another thing which is part of this. I told you my idea—The whole thing is to be called the poet, and begins with the way external nature affects him, and goes on to human nature.

In packing my things I found a little painting of a boy that I dont think looks at all bad. I could show it to you if you cared to see it—

Yours sincerely
ISAAC ROSENBERG

c/o Mrs Horvitch
Hill House
43 De Villiers St
Cape Town

[*Early June 1914*]

DEAR MARSH
Thank you very much for your letter to your friend. I hope he will be in C T and that I'll be able to see him. I'm eagerly waiting for Sat. The above will be my address, but I'll write when I get there and know what sort of outlook it is.

Yours sincerely
ISAAC ROSENBERG

[*Letter Card from Capetown,*   43 De Villiers St
Postmarked June 20 or 30, 1914]   C T

DEAR MARSH
I've had a fearfully busy week—seeing people and preparing for work. I want to write a long letter I have lots to write about,—wait till next week. Stanley[3] has given me a small job—painting two babies. I'm just off to do them.

The place is gorgeous—just for an artist.

Yours sincerely
ISAAC ROSENBERG

[1] 'Midsummer Frost', see p. 85.

[2] From the line, 'How, like a sad thought buried in light woven words'.

[3] Sir Herbert Stanley, a member of the South African Government, to whom Marsh had given R an introduction.

43 Devilliers St
                                                                       Cape Town

Dear Marsh

I should like you to do me a favour if its not putting you to too much bother. I am in an infernal city by the sea. This city has men in it—and these men have souls in them—or at least have the passages to souls. Though they are millions of years behind time they have yet reached the stage of evolution that knows ears and eyes. But these passages are dreadfully clogged up; gold dust, diamond dust, stocks and shares, and heaven knows what other flinty muck. Well I've made up my mind to clear through all this rubbish. But I want your help. Now I'm going to give a series of lectures on modern art (I'm sending you the first, which I gave in great style. I was asked whether the futurist[s] exhibited at the Royal Academy.) But I want to make the lectures interesting and intelligible by reproductions or slides. Now I wonder whether you have reproductions which you could lend me till I returned or was finished with them. I want to talk about John,[1] Cézanne, Van Gogh, Innes,[2] the early Picasso (not the cubist one), Spencer,[3] Gertler,[4] Lamb.[5] Puvis De Chavannes, Degas. A book of reproductions of the P Impressionist[s] would do and I could get them transferred on slides. I hope this would

---

[1] Augustus John (1878-1961) studied at the Slade School 1894-98. A portrait painter whose sitters included many famous contemporaries, he was also an outstanding draughtsman and painter of figure subjects.

[2] J. D. Innes (1887-1914), a talented Welsh landscape painter, followed John to the Slade and later worked with him in France and N. Wales. He died of consumption aged only 27.

[3] Stanley Spencer (1891-1959) was a painter of figure subjects with a very individual religious inspiration. He, too, was a student at the Slade, where he overlapped briefly with R.

[4] Mark Gertler (1891-1939) was the son of impoverished Polish-Jewish immigrants. Born in Spitalfields, he lived for the greater part of his childhood and youth in Stepney, where he was a near neighbour of R, John Rodker, and other members of the Whitechapel Group. In 1908 he entered the Slade, helped by the Jewish Educational Aid Society, and studied there until 1912, thus overlapping with Bomberg and R. Like them he was dissatisfied with the conventional approach to art and soon came under the influence of the Post-Impressionists, whom he recommended to R. It was Gertler who introduced R to Marsh at the Café Royal in November 1913. An early member of the New English Art Club and the London Group, Gertler quickly made a name for himself, was taken up by Lady Ottoline Morrell and her circle, but had a protracted and unhappy love affair with Dora Carrington. After the war he continued to paint impressive figure subjects, portraits and still-lifes, but ill-health, domestic worries, the declining popularity of his work in the 1930's and consequent financial problems led to his suicide in June 1939.

[5] Henry Lamb (1883-1960), portrait painter, studied in Paris and worked in France, later Ireland, between 1907 and 1913, becoming a member of the Camden Town and the London Group. Originally a medical student, he served as an M.O. and also as an official War Artist 1916-18.

not put you to any great trouble but if you could manage to do it you dont know how you would help me. Epstien[1] . . .

Stanley gave me a little job to paint two babies, which helped me to pay my way for a bit. I expect to get pupils and kick up a row with my lectures. But nobody seems to have money here, and not an ounce of interest in Art. The climate's fine, but the Sun is a very changeable creature and I can't come to any sort of understanding with this golden beast. He pretends to keep quiet for half an hour and just as I think, now I've got it, the damnid thing has frisked about.

There's a lot of splended stuff to paint. We are walled in by the sharp upright mountain and the bay. Across the bay the piled up mountains of Africa look lovely and dangerous. It makes one think of savagery and earthquakes—the elemental lawlessness. You are lucky to be in comfortable London and its armchair culture.

I've painted a Kaffir, and am pottering about. I expect if I get pupils to get a room and shall be able to work better. Do write to me—think of me, a creature of the most exquisite civilization, planted in this barbarous land. Write me of Spencer, Lamb, Currie and the pack of them. I mean to write to Gertler myself, but so far I've not been able to get away from my own people here to write. They don't understand the artist's seclusion to concentrate, and I'm always interrupted. Write me of poetry and do send me that little thing of Binyon's in your album.

Yours sincerely
IsAAC RosENBERG

I'll send my lecture next week as they may be printing it in a local paper.[2]

'Hill House'
43 Devilliers St
Cape Town

[Postmarked Capetown, August 8, 1914]

DEAR MARSH

I enclose the lecture. By the time it reaches you I expect the world will be in convulsions and you'll be in the thick of it. I know my poor innocent essay stands no chance by the side of the bristling legions of war-scented documents on your desk; but know that I despise war and hate war, and hope that the Kaiser William will have his bottom smacked—a naughty aggressive schoolboy who will have *all* the plum pudding. Are we going to have Tennyson's 'Battle in the air', and the nations deluging the nations with blood from the air? Now is the time to go on an exploring expedition to the North Pole; to come back and find settled order again.

Yours sincerely
IsAAC RosENBERG

[1] In the original the single word 'Epstien' (for Epstein) follows immediately after 'help me'. Evidently R intended to add something about the sculptor, but changed his mind.

[2] It duly appeared in *South African Women in Council.*

'Hill House'
43 de Villiers St
Cape Town

DEAR MARSH

You are very kind to think of me. I see though from the papers your friend is not coming out but is going to hotter places than this. Its a fearful nuisance, this war. I think the safest place is at the front,—we'll starve or die of suspense, anywhere else.

I feel very much better in health; I keep a good deal in the open and walk a[?lot]. We have had very damp weather and wonderful storms and winds; houses blown over,—the very mountains shaken. We are expecting the fine weather, which I mean to see right through and then come back. I've been trying to get pupils to teach, but this war has killed all that. I painted a very interesting girl, which I'm rather pleased with. It's very quiet and modest and no fireworks. I may send it to the New English if I don't bring it back myself in time. Also a self portrait, very gay and cocky, which I think will go down very well.[1] I'm waiting for better weather to paint the kaffirs against characteristic landscapes. Also I've written poems, of which I'm sending the small ones. By the time you get this things will only have just begun I'm afraid; Europe will have just stepped into its bath of blood. I will be waiting with beautiful drying towels of painted canvas, and precious ointments to smear and heal the soul; and lovely music and poems. But I really hope to have a nice lot of pictures and poems by the time all is settled again; and Europe is repenting of her savageries.

I know Duncan Grant's dance and if the one you have is better, it must be very fine indeed. I've just written to Cokeham;[2] I hadn't his address so sent it to Cokeham on Thames. I hope he got it. His brother is very lucky. I also just wrote to Gertler. I really get no privacy here and can't write or even think. But this coming away has changed me marvellously, and makes me more confident and mature. Here's a chance to exercise any bloodthirsty and critical propensities.

[*The Female God, see p. 70*]

This is the last thing I've written but I've got more, which I may enclose in this letter. What's become of Currie?[3]

Yours sincerely
ISAAC ROSENBERG

Berg Collection

[1] Almost certainly the portrait of himself in a green hat, see Colour Plate XIV(a).

[2] Presumably a misspelling of Cookham, where Stanley Spencer lived and from which he took his Slade nickname. The reference to his brother Gilbert, also an artist, is obscure.

[3] John Currie was a gifted young painter, of Irish ancestry, who became Gertler's closest friend in the years 1912-14. Originally an engraver and ceramic

DEAR MOTHER—FATHER—AND EVERYBODY.

I have not read your letters this week as I've been staying out at a pretty suburb with a very pretty name, Rondebosch, and with very nice people. It was through my lecture and poems being printed. I went one day to see the lady who is the editor of the paper it was printed in, and there I met a Miss Molteno—who told me how delighted she was with my poems. She asked me to come to Rondebosch where she lives; and there she took me to see some beautiful places, and then asked me whether I'd like to be her guest there for a week or two. She is a sister of the speaker to the House of Parliament here. Her father was famous out here—Sir John Molteno, and she has crowds of relations. Anyway I'm here at Rondebosch having a happy time, you will be glad to hear—I'm anxious to know how you all are and will run down to town about the letters tomorrow, today being Sunday. I'm living like a toff here. Early in the morning coffee is brought to me in bed. My shoes (my only pair) are polished so brightly that the world is pleasantly deceived as to the tragedy that polish covers. I don't know whether there are snakes or wild animals in my room, but in the morning when I get up and look at the soles of my shoes, every morning I see another hole. I shan't make your mouths water by describing my wonderful breakfasts—the unimaginable lunches —delicious teas, and colossal dinners. You would say all fibs. I won't tell of the wonderful flowers that look into my window and the magnificent park that surrounds my room. Of the mountain climbing right to the sheerest top until the town the sea and fields were like little picture postcards lying on the pavement to one looking from the top of the Monument. In a few months I hope to be back in England—I should like to get there for the warm weather—about March or so.

ISAAC

[*Spring 1915*] 87 Dempsey St
Stepney E

DEAR MARSH

I hope you wont think it too forward of me to try and keep myself in your mind by writing to you, as you promised to buy something of me. I dont know which of mine you liked best but I could bring them all again when you have more time.

Yours sincerely
ISAAC ROSENBERG

---

artist, he took to painting and attended the Slade for a short time in 1910, later exhibiting at the N.E.A.C. and (with Gertler) at the Chenil Gallery. It was through Currie that Gertler got to know Sydney Schiff and Edward Marsh. Currie had a tempestuous love affair with a girl named Dolly Henry, which ended tragically when he shot her and then himself in October 1914. He was possibly already dead when Marsh received R's letter.

How's this for a joke?[1]

> You cleave to my bones,
> Prop and hold in a noose
> One of the lives God loans.
> Sinew of my sinews!
>
> What will the Lord say
> When I shall nowhere be found
> At the judgement day,
> My life within you being wound?

To Miss Seaton [Undated. ? Jan-Feb 1915]

Do you know Emerson's poems? I think they are wonderful. 'Each and All' I think is deep and beautiful. There is always a kind of beaminess, like a dancing of light in light, in his poems. I do think, though, that he depends too much on inspiration; and though they always have a solid texture of thought, they sometimes seem thin in colour or sensuousness.

To Miss Seaton [Undated. Probably March 1915]

I saw Olive Schreiner[2] last night. She's an extraordinary woman—full of life. I had a little picture for her from a dear friend of hers in Africa I stayed with while I was there. She was so pleased with my pictures of Kaffirs. Who is your best living English poet? I've found somebody miles and miles above everybody—a young man, Lascelles Abercrombie[3]—a mighty poet and brother to Browning.

[? Spring 1915]   87 Dempsey St
                                                              Stepney E
DEAR MISS SEATON
    Could you let me have the 'Georgian book' back, unless you have not finished with it. I want to show somebody some poems there. I do

---

[1] 'This' was the first tentative draft of 'The One Lost' (see p. 89). R sent Marsh a revised draft of these two verses a little later, and when it appeared in *Youth* he had made further alterations to them, and added two more stanzas.

[2] Olive Schreiner (1855-1920) the South African author of *The Story of an African Farm* which she published in 1883, under the pseudonym 'Ralph Iron'. It became a classic.

[3] Lascelles Abercrombie (1881-1938), poet and critic, was a friend of Marsh and in at the birth of the 'Georgian' movement in 1912. Later a distinguished academic, he was Professor of English Literature first at Leeds University and then at Bedford College, London. His early work was extravagantly admired by R.

IX. The Murder of Lorenzo. 1912   12″ × 9¾″. Whereabouts unknown.

X. Minnie Horvitch (the Artist's sister). 1914   16″ × 12″

XI. (a) The Artist's father. 1914   12″ × 13″

XI. (b) Wolf
Horvitch
(the Artist's
brother-in-law).
1914   16″ × 12″

XII. (a) Self Portrait in a Red Tie.
1914   16″ × 12″

XII. (b) Self Portrait in a Pink
Tie. 1914   18″ × 14″

XIII. Self Portrait in a Felt Hat, looking right. 1915   12″ × 9″

XIV. (a) Self Portrait in a Felt Hat.
looking left. 1914–15   12″ × 9″

XIV. (b) Self Portrait.
S. Africa, 1914   20″ ×

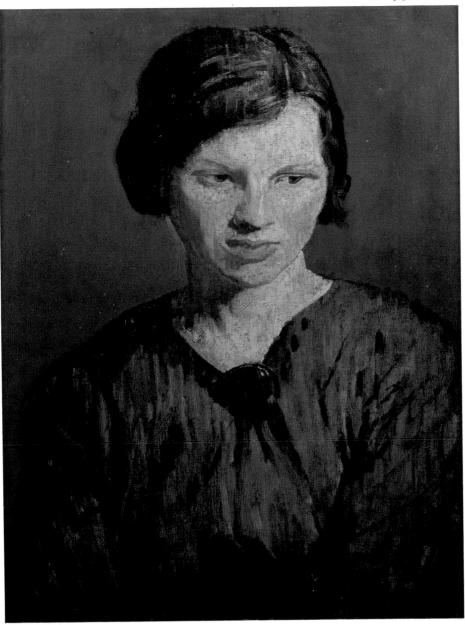

XV. Sonia Rodker. 1915   24″ × 18″

XVI. Clara Winsten (née Birnberg). 1917 $22\frac{1}{2}'' \times 18''$

not know whether I lent you Abercrombie's 'Olympians'[1] in *New Numbers*, will you tell me? The book you lent me of G Bottomley made me buy the second 'Chambers of Imagery'.[2] The fine things in this are simpler and more harmoniously complete than the first book. I like Bottomley more than any modern poet I have yet come across. I will lend you this book.

I have been writing better than usual, (I think) lately, but the things are slight—they all have the same atmosphere and I may be able to work them into one, if I can hit on an episode to connect them. When they're all together I'll show you them. Trust you're doing well.

Yours sincerely
ISAAC ROSENBERG

[*? Spring 1915*]   87 Dempsey St
                                                          Stepney E

Do write me exactly what you think of my play.

DEAR MISS SEATON

Thanks for copying those things for me. I do wish though you had copied that 'Marriage of convenience'—it is more interesting to me than these. I am sending you a thing I copied out years ago from one of our greatest poets and I think one of his best. It is very unlike his usual style, and it is is not by F. Thompson. I am showing you this because I think its a discovery of mine.[3] I don't like L. Douglas' sonnets very much.[4] Rossetti never published anything that wasn't good, but he must have written a good deal very much like those sonnets and burnt them. I like that line "And thy great oak of life a rotten tree". I will be able to give you your Goethe back when I see you. Its the most interesting autobiography I've ever read. It is as much like an autobiography of Shakespeare as one could be. He is the most comprehensive of writers since Shakespeare.

I met somebody yesterday who is a great friend of G Bottomley. He also thinks he is the best modern poet. He tells me B lives in Yorkshire[,] has only one lung and writes in great pain. He is a large giant of a fellow but mustn't exert himself much. He will lend me some of his plays. I have

---

[1] For Lascelles Abercrombie see p. 208 n3 and for *New Numbers* see p. 119, note to Fragment II.

[2] The first volume of Bottomley's *Chambers of Imagery* appeared in 1907, the second in 1912. Marsh included 2 poems from the latter in G. P. 1911-12.

[3] Probably Coleridge's 'Sole Positive of Night', a fair copy of which, in R's hand, is among his manuscripts.

[4] Lord Alfred Douglas (1870-1945).

never come across your London poem[1] before. Why do you ask me who wrote it? 'Truth should have no man's name'.

Yours sincerely

ISAAC ROSENBERG

87 Dempsey St

Stepney E

[*Spring 1915*]

DEAR MARSH

Thank you for the cheque. I love poetry—but just now the finest poem ever written would not move me as the writing on that cheque. I saw Olive Shreiner last night. She's an extraordinary woman. Full of go and makes every word live. I think I gave her real pleasure with my kaffir pictures and if I'd done more I'd have given her one.

If you do find time to read my poems, and I sent them because I think them worth reading, for God's Sake! don't say they're obscure. The idea in the poem I like best[2] I should think is very clear. That we can cheat our malignant fate who has devised a perfect evil for us, by pretending to have as much misery as we can bear, so that it witholds its greater evil, while under that guise of misery there is secret joy. Love—this joy—burns and grows within us trying to push out to that. Eternity without us which is God's heart. Joy-love, grows in time too vast to be hidden from God under the guise of gloom. Then we find another way of cheating God. Now through the very joy itself. For by this time we have grown into love, which is the rays of that Eternity of which God is the sun. We have become God Himself. Can God hate and do wrong to Himself?

I think myself the poem is very clear, but if by some foul accident it isn't, I wonder if you see that idea in it.

I'll bring the picture Wed[.] I want to get the hands and feet a bit more explained.

Yours sincerely

ISAAC ROSENBERG

[1] Part of a letter, with the poem referred to, reads:
'Who wrote this?

LONDON

Let but thy wicked men from out thee go,
And the fools that crowd thee so,—
Even thou, who dost thy millions boast,
A village less than Islington will grow,
A solitude almost.'

[2] The poem is clearly 'God Made Blind' from *Youth* (see p. 91).

[Spring 1915]   87 Dempsey St
                                                    Stepney E
DEAR MARSH

   I've done a lovely picture I'd like you to see. Its a girl who sat for
Da Vinci, and hasn't changed a hair, since, in a deep blue gown against
a dull crimson ground.[1] If you have time to see it I'd also like Gertler to
be there if he can.

   I don't know whether you've shown my things to Abercrombie yet—
if you haven't I'd like you to show these also I enclose,—one of them you
have is corrected here.

                                         Yours sincerely
                                            ISAAC ROSENBERG

[Spring 1915]   87 Dempsey St
                                                    Stepney E
DEAR MARSH

   I will bring the picture tomorrow. I think you will like to see it,
though if I had a little longer on it it would have been very fine indeed
but the model cleared off before I could absolutely finish. I've also been
working hard at my poems. I'm glad you haven't shown A. my things.
I've made that poem quite clear now I think. I've a scheme for a little
book called 'Youth', in three parts.

   1. Faith and fear.
   2. The cynic's lamp.
   3. Sunfire.

   In the first the idealistic youth believes and aspires towards purity.
The poems are: Aspiration. Song of Immortality (which by the way, is
absolutely Abercrombie's idea in the Hymn to Love,[2] and its one of my
first poems). Noon in the city. None know the Lord of the House. A
girl's thoughts. Wedded. Midsummer frost.

   In the second, The cynic's lamp, the youth has become hardened by
bitter experience and has no more vague aspirations, he is just sense.
The poems are: Love and lust. In Piccadilly. A mood. The cynic's path.
Tess.

   In the third, Change and sunfire, the spiritualizing takes place. He
has no more illusions, but life itself becomes transfigured through
Imagination, that is, real intimacy—love.

---

   [1] This almost certainly refers to the portrait of Sonia Rodker reproduced as
Colour Plate No. XV. In which case this, as well as the following two letters
which refer to *Youth*, must be dated 1915 and therefore follow R's visit to S.
Africa, rather than precede it as in CW.

   [2] One of the poems in *Emblems of Love*, published by John Lane in 1912. See
Abercrombie's *Collected Poems* 1930, p. 129.

   N.B. For ease of understanding, R's unconventional punctuation of paras 2,
3 and 4 has been regularized (see CW, pp. 292-3).

The poems are: April dawn. If I am fire. Break in by nearer ways. God made blind etc. Do you like the scheme?

Yours sincerely

ISAAC ROSENBERG

[*March-April 1915*]

87 Dempsey St

Stepney E

DEAR MARSH

Don't you think this is a nice little thing now

The one lost

I mingle with your bones.
You steal in subtle noose
This starry trust He loans,
And in your life I lose.

What will the Lender say
When I shall not be found,
Sought at the Judgement Day,
Lost—in your being bound?

I've given my things to the printer[1]—he's doing 16 pages for £2. 10. I know for certain I can get rid of ten. My notion in getting them printed is that I believe some of them are worth reading, and that like money kept from circulating, they would be useless to myself and others, kept to myself. I lose nothing by printing and may even make a little money. If you like you can have my three life drawings for the money if you think they're worth it. You don't know how happy you have made me by giving me this chance to print.

Yours sincerely

ISAAC ROSENBERG

[*1915, ?April*]

87 Dempsey St

Stepney E

DEAR MR SHIFF[2]

I am always glad to show people my work and if you ever feel inclined to come down and see it, let me know a little beforehand and it

---

[1] The poems that appeared in *Youth*. The printer was Israel Narodiczky, of 48 Mile End Road, an ardent Zionist with a fine mind and compassionate heart, who printed books and pamphlets, mainly in Hebrew and Yiddish, often at give-away prices for penurious writers. He numbered many highly distinguished Jewish authors and politicians among his friends (see Cohen, pp. 78-79, and 203n).

[2] R's frequent mis-spelling of Sydney Schiff's surname. Schiff was a cultured English Jew, who wrote and translated under the pen-name Stephen Hudson. They met some time in the spring of 1915 and corresponded intermittently up

will be all right. Buying pictures of me is the last thing in the world I expect people to do, in the best of times, so you needn't worry about that.

I believe I was introduced to you as a poet, and as poems are not quite so bulky and weighty, at least outwardly, as pictures, I am sending some.

Yours sincerely
ISAAC ROSENBERG

On second thoughts I will wait till I've printed some in a few weeks.

[*1915 ?May*] 87 Dempsey St
Stepney E

DEAR MR SCHIFF,
Thank you for your letter and for what you say. I have already sent my poems to the printer and you will have a copy in about 2 weeks. But I am sending poems I wrote before I was 20 and I leave you to pick out anything good in them.

Yours sincerely
ISAAC ROSENBERG

It is the only copy I have
I shall want it back

[*?1915*] 87 Dempsey St
Stepney E

DEAR MARSH
I'm doing a nice little thing for Meredith's 'Lark ascending'

Their faces raised
Puts on the light of children praised [1].

Everybody is in a sort of delirious ecstasy, and all, feeling in the same way, express the same feelings in different ways, according to their natures. I think you'll like it. I'll bring others, in case you don't. I can't refrain from sending my last poems which I think are much better and clearer than my others.

Yours sincerely
ISAAC ROSENBERG

---

till November 1917, possibly later. Schiff regularly helped Rosenberg after he enlisted, with money, artist's materials, and by sending him books and newspapers in France. Above all, like Marsh, Schiff encouraged R by criticizing his poems and introducing him to literary friends. His careful annotation of the dates on which he received R's letters has enabled many of them to be more accurately dated than would otherwise have been possible.

[1] The first line of the couplet to which R was clearly referring reads, in actual fact, *And every face to watch him raised*. The drawing in charcoal and wash entitled 'Hark, Hark the Lark', now in the possession of Joseph Cohen, corresponds closely with the above description (see Monochrome Plate 8) but is usually dated 1912, well before R first met Marsh.

[Apparently unfinished letter to Ezra Pound, 1915]

87 Dempsey St
Stepney E

DEAR MR POUND

Thank you very much for sending my things to America. As to your suggestion about the army I think the world has been terribly damaged by certain poets (in fact any poet) being sacrificed in this stupid business. There is certainly a strong temptation to join when you are making no money.

[1915 ?April]

87 Dempsey St
Stepney E

DEAR MARSH

I left a parcel of pictures for you to see, at the porter's lodge. Friday. I remember now I did not put your address on as I could not think of the number, so I am rather worried to know whether you got them. There may be somebody else of your name there. If you have, I suppose you have been too busy to see them—my fear that you might be was the reason I never wrote to you first to bother you for replies. I want to cart those things round London to try and sell as I am very low and I took them round to you first[,] thinking you might like something there. Do drop me a line to say you have them—I dont want them to get lost.

Yours sincerely
ISAAC ROSENBERG

[Late April 1915]

87 Dempsey St
Stepney .E

MY DEAR MARSH

I am so sorry—what else can I say?

But he himself [1] has said 'What is more safe than death?' For us is the hurt who feel about English literature, and for you who knew him and feel his irreparable loss.

Yours sincerely
ISAAC ROSENBERG

Berg Collection

[1] Rupert Brooke (1887-1915) poet and close friend of Marsh, had died of blood-poisoning on his way to the Dardanelles with the Naval Division on April 23rd, and was buried on the island of Skyros. R did not admire Brooke's 1914 sonnets (see his letter to Mrs Cohen on p. 237).

[April-May 1915]   87 Dempsey St
                                                             Stepney E

DEAR MARSH

I am very sorry to have had to disturb you at such a time with pictures. But when one's only choice is between horrible things you choose the least horrible. First I think of enlisting and trying to get my head blown off, then of getting some manual labour to do—anything—but it seems I'm not fit for anything. Then I took these things to you. You would forgive me if you knew how wretched I was. I am sorry I can give you no more comfort in your own trial[1] but I am going through it too.

Thank you for your cheque[;] it will do for paints and I will try and do something you'll like.

Yours sincerely

ISAAC ROSENBERG

[April-May 1915]   87 Dempsey St
                                                             Stepney E

MY DEAR MARSH

Forgive my weak and selfish letter. I should not have disturbed you at all but one gets so bewildered in this terrible struggle. Thank you for showing my things to Abercrombie and thinking of that now. He has not written yet. I can come if you like Tuesday or any day. I will come Tue if you do not write.

Yours sincerely

ISAAC ROSENBERG

[June 4th, 1915]   87 Dempsey Street
                                                             Stepney E

DEAR MR SCHIFF

Here are some poems I've had printed.[2] I am selling them at half [a] crown a book. I am also enclosing a sketch for a play,[3] which may interest you; but I want this back as I have no spare copies.

Hope you enjoyed your holiday. We just missed being blown to pieces by a bomb the other night, a factory near by was burnt to pieces and some people killed.

Yours sincerely

ISAAC ROSENBERG

You will notice I've torn out a page in the book. The poems were very trivial and I've improved the book by taking them out.

---

[1] The death of Rupert Brooke
[2] *Youth*   [3] *Moses*

87 Dempsey Street
Stepney E
DEAR MR SCHIFF
Thank you for your P.O. I am sending you another copy and one to
Mr Clutton Brock[1] as you asked me. I am very glad you have taken the
trouble to read my things and have found something you like in them—
most people find them difficult and wont be bothered to read into them.
What people call technique is a very real thing, it corresponds to con-
struction and command of form in painting. Rossetti was a supreme
master of it in poetry and had no command of form whatever in painting.
My technique in poetry is very clumsy I know.

I wonder whether Mr Clutton Brock could get me some Art writing
to do for any journals he is connected with. I shall mention it in writing
to him.

I am thinking of enlisting if they will have me, though it is against all
my principles of justice—though I would be doing the most criminal thing
a man can do—I am so sure my mother would not stand the shock that I
don't know what to do.

Yours sincerely
ISAAC ROSENBERG

[*July 1915*] 87 Dempsey Street
Stepney E

DEAR MR SCHIFF
I heard from Mr Clutton Brock and he says he likes my things. If I
have the letter I will send it to you. He writes he is overworked but was
kind enough to go through them (I should think with care) and mentions
those he likes most. I do not know whether you are still away, but when
you are in town and you care to see my pictures you can let me know.

Gertler has a remarkable painting at N.E.[2] which puts him easily next
to John amongst our painters. John has a very fine head of B. Shaw,
vivid and alive and serious. Gertler's appears clever beside the high
seriousness of his.

Yours sincerely
ISAAC ROSENBERG

[*July 1915*] 87 Dempsey Street
Stepney E

DEAR MR SCHIFF
Do you mind sending the enclosed to Mr Clutton Brock. I did not
answer his letter as I mislaid it and your card has made me think of it. I

---

[1] Arthur Clutton-Brock (1868-1924) essayist, art critic and journalist, was
Literary Editor of *The Speaker* 1904-06, and for many years a regular contributor
to *The Times Literary Supplement*. In 1908 he joined *The Times* as art critic, and
continued to write for it on a variety of subjects for the rest of his life.

[2] The New English Art Club Exhibition

believe they are getting up a show of Gaudier's[1] work—at least they are talking of it but nothing is settled as far as I know. I do not know his work but I met him once. He gave one a good impression. It is awful bad luck.

Yours sincerely
ISAAC ROSENBERG

[*September 1915*]   87 Dempsey Street
Stepney E

DEAR MR SCHIFF
    I sent you two drawings I hope you will like, though I had meant to do a composition but have not been able to in my present state of mind. I have decided not to think of painting—at least until I have achieved some kind of (no matter how small) independence, by doing what is called an honest trade—I am going to learn something and in a few months I may start earning a little. Painting was once an honest trade, now the painter is either a gentleman, or must subsist on patronage —anyway I won't let painting interfere with my peace of mind[.] If later on I haven't forgotten it I may yet do something. Forgive this private cry but even the enormity of what is going on all through Europe always seems less to an individual than his own struggle.

Yours sincerely
ISAAC ROSENBERG

The drawings will follow

[*October 1915*]   87 Dempsey Street
Stepney E

DEAR MR SCHIFF
    In my last letter I wrote you I was learning 'an honest trade'. I don't know whether I told you what it was but what I meant was that I was learning to do work that I would not be put to all sorts of shifts and diplomatics to dispose of. It is very mechanical work though my skill in drawing is of great use in it. It is process work—preparing blocks for the press—but it is very unhealthy having to be bending over strong acids all day—and though my chest is weak I shall have to forget all that. But I

---

[1] Henri Gaudier (1891-1915) was a gifted sculptor and draughtsman, born in France, who came to London in 1911 with Sophie Brzeska, and began using their joint name. He was a Founder Member of the London Group, and exhibited in numerous exhibitions at that time, including the Allied Artists' Association 1913, Roger Fry's *Grafton Group* exhibition of 1914, and (posthumously) the *Vorticist Exhibition* 1915. He had by then enlisted in the French army and been killed on June 5th of that year.

have yet to learn it and when I have learnt it it may take some time before I find work. I am attending an evening school where this work is taught and it may take some months to learn as the hours at the school are so few. I also have to pay this evening school, it is not very much but it is more than I can afford. You have shown that you are interested in me so I thought you would not mind lending me the 10 shillings to pay as it is so very little and I could so easily return it as soon as I get work. I hope you will not think this impudence, but all my friends seem to have disappeared. I hope very soon and by this means that I shall need none.

I am sending some small poems I have managed to write in my awful state of mind, or rather as a relief from it.

Yours sincerely
ISAAC ROSENBERG

[*October 1915*]   87 Dempsey St
                                                           Stepney E

DEAR MR SCHIFF

Thank you for the cheque which is as much to me now as all the money in America would be to the Allies. When I am settled I hope you will allow me to return it either in drawings or money. I expect to know enough for my purpose in 2 months, and I will let you know how I get on. As to what you say about my being luckier than other victims I can only say that one's individual situation is more real and important to oneself than the devastation of fates[1] and empires especially when they do not vitally affect oneself. I can only give my personal and if you like selfish point of view that I[,] feeling myself in the prime and vigour of my powers (whatever they may be) have no more free will than a tree; seeing with helpless clear eyes the utter destruction of the railways and avenues of approaches to outer communication cut off. Being by the nature of my upbringing, all my energies having been directed to one channel of activity, crippled from other activities and made helpless even to live. It is true I have not been killed or crippled, been a loser in the stocks, or had to forswear my fatherland, but I have not quite gone free and have a right to say something.

Forgive all this bluster but—salts for constipation—moral of course.

Yours sincerely
ISAAC ROSENBERG

I have not seen or heard of Bomberg for ages but he was pretty bad 5 months ago.

---

[1] R clearly wrote 'fates' but this was presumably a slip of the pen for 'states'.

[*1915 ?October*]   87 Dempsey Street
                                                     Stepney E

DEAR MR SCHIFF

    I shall send you a drawing either this week or next for your cheque, which I hope you will like—I should like to write much more but I don't feel I can now. I will try and write a letter when I send the drawing.

    I have changed my mind again about joining the army. I feel about it that more men means more war,—besides the immorality of joining with no patriotic convictions.

    Thank you very much for your cheque.

Yours sincerely
ISAAC ROSENBERG

On Y.M.C.A. notepaper, headed 'H.M. Forces on Active Service'

[*October 1915*]   Priv. I. Rosenberg
                                                     Bat. Bantam, Regt. 12th Suffolk,
                                                     New Depot, Bury St. Edmunds

DEAR MR SCHIFF,

    I could not get the work I thought I might so I have joined this Bantam Battalion (as I was too short for any other) which seems to be the most rascally affair in the world. I have to eat out of a basin together with some horribly smelling scavenger who spits and sneezes into it etc. It is most revolting, at least up to now—I don't mind the hard sleeping the stiff marches etc but this is unbearable. Besides my being a Jew makes it bad amongst these wretches. I am looking forward to having a bad time altogether. I am sending some old things to the New English and if they get in you may see them there. I may be stationed here some time or be drafted off somewhere else; if you write I will be glad to hear[.]

Yours sincerely
I. ROSENBERG

[*October 1915*]   12th Suffolks
                                                     Bantam Bat.
                                                     New Offices Recruiting Depot
                                                     Bury St Edmunds

DEAR MARSH

    I have just joined the Bantams[1] and am down here amongst a horrible rabble—Falstaff's scarecrows were nothing to these. Three out of every 4 have been scavengers[,] the fourth is a ticket of leave. But that is

---

[1] In this letter R misspelt 'Bantam' as 'Bantaam', but since he quickly learnt the correct form, as subsequent letters show, it seemed pointless to perpetuate the error here.

nothing—though while I'm waiting for my kit I'm roughing it a bit having come down without even a towel. I dry my self with my pocket handkerchief. I don't know whether I will be shifted as soon as I get my rigout—I thought you might like to hear this. I meant to send you some poems I wrote which are better than my usual things but I have left them at home where I am rather afraid to go for a while—I left without saying anything. Abercrombie did not write to me, I hope it is not because he disliked my things. If that is not the reason I should like to send him my new things. Can you tell me anything of Gertler.[1]

Yours sincerely
ISAAC ROSENBERG

[*October 1915*]   22648
                          C Company, 12th Suffolk Bantams
                          Bury St Edmunds

DEAR MR SCHIFF

You are very good to send me that note. Money is very handy and we get too little of it here. Half of what I get goes to my mother. When I spoke to you of leave I don't think I mentioned that I did not tell my mother I had joined and disappeared without saying anything. It nearly killed my mother I heard[,] and ever since she has been very anxious to see me. I send you here a photo which I think is pretty alive.

What you say about your nephews I dare say is just, but I have been used to this sort of thing and know the kind of people I am with well. I should have been told to soften my boots and I would not have had this damned bother. I now find everybody softens their boots first and anybody would be crippled by wearing them as I have done. I shall let you know when I am in London.

Yours sincerely
ISAAC ROSENBERG

[*Early November 1915*]   Military Hospital
                                Depot, 12th Suffolk Bantams
                                Bury St Edmunds

DEAR MR SCHIFF

Don't be frightened at the heading. In running before the colonel I slipped on some mud and gravel and cut my both hands rather badly. But I shall be right enough in a few days. I shall find out the name of

[1] See footnote[4] to p. 204

the Colonel before I send this letter. Of course if some kind of sense of difference could be established between myself and the others, not that my sensitiveness should not be played upon but only that unnecessary trouble shouldn't be started. I don't object to severe duties or menial and filthy work as it hardens one. As I won't get paid till I am in kharki[1] which business takes some time it seems (I've been here over a week and have had to do all the duties of new recruits in my civies and have come quite unprepared expecting to get them the day I joined) naturally your present is very handy. It will do for some shaves and suppers etc. I hope to be well and get the kharki in a few days. I don't know yet whether I am staying here or will be sent down to Aldershot. I will write more when I know. I wanted to join the RAMC[2] as the idea of killing upsets me a bit, but I was too small. The only regiment my build allowed was the Bantams.

Yours sincerely
I Rosenberg

Priv. I. Rosenberg

[*November 1915*]   12th Suffolk Bantams
Military Hospital, Depot, Bury St Edmunds

Tuesday night

Dear Mr Schiff

I am still in the hospital and expect to be for at least two days more, so though I have your present for which many thanks, I am unable to make any use of it, but it won't be long before I will be unable to make any more use of it, as it will be used. Just now I don't quite know where I can keep books. I have with me Donne's poems and Brown's 'Religion De Medici' and must carry both in my pocket. I have drawn some of the chaps in the hospital and I can see heaps of subject matter all over. If you could send any small books or news that might interest me I think I could find a place for them. A small box of watercolours would be handy. I cannot get one in this town. I can only get Sundays off so have no chance of finding out as the evenings are pitch black and no shops are visible. Cigarettes or any small eatable luxuries also help to make things pleasanter. Any sketches I may do I will send though I don't think I'll be in the frame of mind for doing decent work for some time. The only thing (and it is very serious to me) that troubles me is my mother is so upset about me. It was this thought that stopped me from joining long ago.

I hope you are happy with your work. Any kind of work if one [can] only be doing something is what one wants now. I feel very grateful at your appreciation of my position, it keeps the clockwork going. To me this is not a result but one motion of the intricate series of activities that all combine to make a result. One might succumb[,] be destroyed—but one might also (and the chances are even greater for it) be renewed,

---

[1] R's phonetic spelling, which he later amended.
[2] Royal Army Medical Corps.

made larger, healthier. It is not very easy for me to write here as you can imagine and you must not expect any proper continuity or even coherence. But I thought you might like to hear how I am placed exactly and write as I can. If I could get a very small watercolour box with a decent sketch block, pencil, paper about 12 × 10, I might do something Sundays. The landscape is quite good. Hospital incidents are good but I may not be here more than two days. If you could send anything at once I'd get it here. They'd give it me if I had left. With cigarettes I could make myself more liked, and eatables I'd like myself. Cakes chocolates etc. I hope you don't mind this but though they would do this for me at home I don't like my mother to feel I haven't everything I want.

Yours sincerely
I ROSENBERG

[*November 1915*] 12th Suffolk Bantams
 Military Hospital
 Depot, Bury St Edmunds

DEAR MR SCHIFF

Many thanks for the paints and sketch book which I received yesterday and are just the things I wanted. I sketched an invalid in the blue uniform but I must give it to him—I got a deal of pleasure in painting after so long a rest. I expect I'll be out of the hospital Tuesday[,] my hands seem to be so slow to heal. We are pretty near starved in this damned hospital and there is no one to complain to. There are no books to read and one must not stir from the room. I'm impatient to get out. This militarism is terrorism to be sure. Again many thanks for the paints.

Yours sincerely
I ROSENBERG

[*Postmarked December 1, 1915*] 12th Suffolk Bantams
 Military Hospital
 Depot
 Bury St Edmunds

Sat night

MY DEAR MARSH

I have only just got your letter. They kept it back or it got mislaid—anyway it only reached me today. First not to alarm you by this heading I must tell you that while running before the colonel I started rather excitedly and tripped myself coming down pretty heavily in the wet grit and am in the hospital with both my hands cut. I've been here since last Sat and expect to be out by about the beginning of the week. It is a nondescript kind of life in the hospital and I'm very anxious to get out and be doing some rough kind of work. Mr. Schiff, sent me some watercolours and I amuse myself with drawing the other invalids. Of course I

222

must give them what I do but I can see heaps of material for pictures here. The landscape too seems decent though I haven't seen anything but the Barracks as this accident happened pretty near at the start.

I hope you were not annoyed at that fib of mine but I never dreamt they would trouble to find out at home. I have managed to persuade my mother that I am for home service only, though of course I have signed on for general service. I left without saying anything because I was afraid it would kill my mother or I would be too weak and not go. She seems to have got over it though and as soon as I can get leave I'll see her and I hope it will be well. It is very hard to write here so you must not expect interesting letters [though] there is always behind or through my object some pressing sense of foreign matter, immediate and not personal which hinders and disjoints what would otherwise have coherence and perhaps weight. I have left all my poems including a short drama with a friend and I will write to him for them when I shall send them either direct to Abercrombie or to you first. I believe in myself more as a poet than a painter. I think I get more depth into my writing. I have only taken Donne with me and don't feel for poetry much in this wretched place. There is not a book or paper here, we are not allowed to stir from the gate, have little to eat, and are not allowed to buy any if we have money— and are utterly wretched (I mean the hospital). If you could send me some novel or chocolates, you would make me very happy. I think I will be here (in the hospital) till Tuesday night as it is Sunday tomorrow, and if the doctor says Monday I can leave the hospital, it means Tuesday night. You will get this Mon and I will have a whole day left me to eat a box of choloates in; it is only a short winters day.

Yours sincerely
ISAAC ROSENBERG

[October-November 1915]

22648
C Company Bantam Bat.
12th Suffolk
Bury St. Edmund[s]

MY DEAR MARSH

I suppose my troubles are really laughable, but they do irritate at the moment. Doing coal fatigues and cookhouse work with a torn hand and marching ten miles with a clean hole about an inch round in your heel and bullies swearing at you is not very natural. I think when my hands and feet get better I'll enjoy it. Nobody thinks of helping you—I mean those who could. Not till I have been made a thorough cripple[.] An officer said it was absurd to think of wearing those boots and told me to soak it thoroughly in oil to soften it. Thank you for your note, we get little enough you know, and I allow half of that to my mother (I rather fancy she is going to be swindled in this [?] rat trap affair) so it will do to get to London with. You must now be the busiest man in England and I am sure would hardly have time to read my things, besides you won't

like the formlessness of the play.[1] If you like you can send them to Abercrombie and read them when you have more time. I don't think I told
you what he said, 'A good many of your poems strike me as experimental and not quite certain of themselves. But on the other hand I
always find a vivid and original impulse; and what I like most in your
songs is your ability to make the concealed poetic power in words come
flashing out. Some of your phrases are remarkable; no one who tries to
write poetry would help envying some of them.' I have asked him to
sit for me—a poet to paint a poet. All this must seem to you like a blur
on the window, or hearing sounds without listening while you are thinking. One blur more and I'll leave you a clean window—I think we're
shifting to Shoreham in a week.

Yours sincerely,
Isaac Rosenberg

22648

[*Early December 1915*]   Company C, Bat. Bantam,
                                     Regt. 12th Suffolks, Bury St Edmunds

Dear Mr Schiff

I have a spare moment and am using it to write to you. I feel very
bucked this week and as you are interested in my poems I think it will
please you too. A letter reached me from Lascelles Abercrombie who I
think is our best living poet—this is what he says. 'A good many of
your poems strike me as experimental and not quite certain of themselves. But on the other hand I always find a vivid and original impulse;
and what I like most in your songs is your ability to make the concealed
poetic power in words come flashing out. Some of your phrases are remarkable; no one who writes poetry would help envying some of them.'
You must excuse these blots[—]I'm writing from pandemonium and with
a rotten pen. I felt A. would sympathise with my work. I haven't been able
to draw—we get no private time. The money you sent me I was forced
to buy boots with as the military boots rubbed all the skin off my feet and
I've been marching in terrible agony. The kind of life does not bother
me much. I sleep soundly on boards in the cold; the drills I find fairly
interesting, but up till now these accidents have bothered me and I am
still suffering with them. My hands are not better and my feet are hell.
We have pups for officers—at least one—who seems to dislike me—and
you know his position gives him power to make me feel it without me
being able to resist. When my feet and hands are better I will slip into
the work but as I am it is awkward. The doctor here too, Major Devoral,
is a ridiculous bullying brute and I have marked him for special treatment when I come to write about the army. The commanding officer is
Major Ogilvie and his adjutant Captain Thornhill. If you happen to
know them, all I would want is leave for a weekend to see my mother. I

---

[1] Presumably one of the early drafts of *Moses*

have asked and was told if I got it now I should have none Xmas so I have put it off. I think we go to Shoreham next week.

Yours sincerely
ISAAC ROSENBERG

I believe I have some pictures in the N.E. but I fancy they are catalogued as Bomberg's but I'm not sure.

[*October-November 1915*]

22648
C Company Bantam Bat.
12th Suffolk
Bury St. Edmund[s]

MY DEAR MARSH

I received a letter today (sent over a week ago) from Abercrombie and I feel very flushed about it. He says no one who tries to write poetry would help envying some of my writing. Since I wrote you I have had more mishaps. My feet now are the trouble. Do you know what private's military boots are? You are given a whole armourys shop to wear—but by God—in a few hours my heels were all blistered and I've been marching and drilling in most horrible pain. I drew three weeks pay and had some money sent me from home and bought a pair of boots 3 or four sizes too large for me my feet had swelled so. Besides this trouble I have a little impudent schoolboy pup for an officer and he has me marked—he has taken a dislike to me I dont know why. I sent pictures to the New English but I think they have got me mixed up somehow with Bomberg as they wrote me my things were accepted addressing me Isaac Bomberg.

Could you send me a pound to buy boots with and to get to London with [by] Xmas if my devil of an officer will give me leave as I must get another pair when my feet are better. You can have the pick of any drawing I do after this if I get clear, for it. Has Winston Churchill's change made any change to you? I suppose you find a lot to do in these times.

Yours sincerely
ISAAC ROSENBERG

[*December 1915*]

Pte I Rosenberg
No 22648
Platoon No 3
12th Suffolks. Hut No 2
Depot. Bury St Edmunuds

MY DEAR MARSH

I have devoured your chocolates with the help of some comrades and am now out of the hospital. I have been kept very busy and I find that the actual duties though they are difficult at first and require all

R 225

one's sticking power are not in themselves unpleasant, it is the brutal militaristic bullying meanness of the way they're served out to us. You're always being threatened with 'clink'. I am sending you my little play and some poems. The play I mean to work at when I get a chance. I also enclose a photograph of one of my S African drawings. When you have read the poems will you send them to Abercrombie[,] that is if you think he won't be annoyed.

Yours sincerely

I ROSENBERG

Who is the author of Erebus.[1] I have a marvellous poem by him.

To Miss Seaton [from Bury St. Edmunds, December 1915]

Thanks for your letter and your books which they sent me from home. It is impossible to read as we are, and I don't expect to get proper leisure for reading till this rotten affair is over. My feet are pretty nigh better, and my hands, and I am put down for a Lance-Corporal. The advantage is, though you have a more responsible position, you are less likely to be interfered with by the men, and you become an authority. I expect to be home for four days shortly. I don't know whether I told you Lascelles Abercrombie sent me a fine letter about my work, which made me very bucked. There is nobody living whose praise could have pleased me so much. I have some pictures at the N.E.A.C., one of which is likely to be sold.

[*Late December 1915*]	22648 C Company 12th Suffolk Bantams Bury St Edmunds

MY DEAR MARSH

I am going home on leave Friday and shall have four days in town. I don't know whether you have had time to send my things to L.A.[2] but if not, could you send them to me at 87 Dempsey St so that I might correct them and send them on myself. I am getting on so well that I have been offered a stripe, but I declined. What is Gertler doing? I feel a bit tired to write, and I expect you are too [to] read a long letter. We are being drilled pretty stiffly.

Yours sincerely

ISAAC ROSENBERG

87 Dempsey St
Stepney E

[1] I have not been able to discover the author of this book or poem.
[2] Lascelles Abercrombie.

[*Late December 1915*]   87 Dempsey St
                                          Stepney London E   *Thurs.*
DEAR MR SCHIFF
    I shall be home for 4 days from tomorrow, Fri, as you asked me to
let you know. I must be looking smart, for I was offered a stripe which I
declined. I have some more pictures at home if you care to see, though I,
since I have joined[,] have hardly given poetry or painting a thought. I
feel as if I were casting my coat, I mean, like a snake or butterfly. Here's
another one of myself, not much like a poet—I'm afraid.

                         Yours sincerely
                              ISAAC ROSENBERG

                                          22648
[*Late December 1915*]   C Company
                                          12th Suffolk Bantams
                                          Bury St Edmunds
MY DEAR MARSH
    I have sent on the poems to L.A. I sent this one as well which I
like.[1] But it is something else I want to write about. I never joined the
army from patriotic reasons. Nothing can justify war. I suppose we must
all fight to get the trouble over. Anyhow before the war I helped at
home when I could and I did other things which helped to keep things
going. I thought if I'd join there would be the separation allowance for
my mother. At Whitehall it was fixed up that 16/6 would be given including the 3/6 a week deducted from my 7/-. Its now between 2 and 3
months since I joined; my 3/6 is deducted right enough, but my mother
hasn't received a farthing. The paymaster at barracks of course is no use
in this matter. I wonder if you know how these things are managed and
what I might do.
                         Yours sincerely
                              ISAAC ROSENBERG

[*Late December 1915*]   22648
                                          C Company, 12th Suffolk Bantams
                                          Bury St Edmunds
DEAR MR SCHIFF
    Thanks for your letter. I will try and write to Bomberg. If you wish
to buy my thing you can have it for 5 guineas. I am anxious to sell as my
mother has received no separation allowance yet and half of my money
is deducted which should go to her and it is most difficult to get satis-
factory reasons. I have written to Marsh to see whether he would know
what to do in the matter.
                         Yours sincerely
                              ISAAC ROSENBERG

---

[1] 'Marching—as seen from the left file' (see p. 95).

[*Late December 1915*]

22648
C Company
12th Suffolk Bantams
Bury St Edmunds

My Dear Marsh

I think this is a decent photo of me and if anything were to happen[,] that would be as far as I got.[1] They talk of sending us out in Spring.

Yours sincerely
Isaac Rosenberg

[*Postmarked January 5, 1916*]

22648
12th South Lancashires
A Coy. Alma Barracks
Blackdown Camp
Farnborough

My Dear Marsh

I have been transferred to this reg and am here near Aldershot. Thanks for writing to W.O. I believe my people are getting my 6d a day deducted from my 1s, but not the allowance. We get very little food you know and sometimes none, so if one has only 6d (and often for unaccountable reasons it is not even that) you can imagine what it is like. If I had got into a decent reg that might not have mattered, but amongst the most

[1] Possibly the photograph reproduced above, a print of which was found among Annie Wynick's papers.

unspeakably filthy wretches, it is pretty suicidal. I am afraid, though, I'm not in a very happy mood—I have a bad cold through sleeping on a damp floor and have been coal fatigueing all day (a most inhuman job). You must be very busy.—It is a great pity this conscription business, besides the hope it will give to the enemy to have brought England to that step.

I am sorry you didn't like that poem; I thought I had hit on something there.

Yours sincerely
ISAAC ROSENBERG

I have heard it is not difficult to get a commission. Do you know anything about it?

24520
A Coy, 12th South Lancs
Alma Bks, Blackdown Camp
Farnborough, Hants.

[*Postmarked January 29, 1916*]

MY DEAR MARSH

I don't remember whether I told you I'd got transferred to this lot and am now near Aldershot. We are having pretty rigourous training down here and the talk is we are going out the middle of next month. Except for the starvation rations and headachy moments I get its not so bad down here. I have just been inoculated and asked for 48 hours leave (we get 48 hrs excused duties) and could not get it. I was told it was a privilege one could insist on, but of course I could not go home without a pass. I sent my poems to Abercrombie about a month ago and have not heard. I hope they won't get lost as I have no copies and I think they're the best things I've done. I added some lines to the Marching poem which you will think vague but I like them.

Yours sincerely
ISAAC ROSENBERG

24520
A Coy, 12th South Lancs
Alma Bks, Blackdown Camp
Farnborough, Hants

[*Early 1916*]

DEAR MR SCHIFF

Thank you for your letter and present, (particularly as I've been unlucky this week and lost 5/- through the post). The latter will be turned into food, which means fitness, and that means proper work. My troubles at the beginning were mostly caused by unsufficient food; one felt inert, and unable to do the difficult work wanted; until I got my people to send food from home. The authorities are quite aware of the state of things, but as the authorities have not got to eat of our food, their energy in the matter is not too obvious. I am known as a poet and artist, as our second in command is a Jewish officer who knows of me from his people. I have other copies of those poems I sent you so you needn't return them.

Mr Clutton Brock's address I've lost, though of course, I would be very glad of his interest. I will keep you informed of my whereabouts should we shift, and send you anything I think worth reading, though we get really no time to write or think[.]

Yours sincerely

ISAAC ROSENBERG

To Lascelles Abercrombie

March 11, 1916

24520
A Coy, 12th South Lancs
Alma Bks, Blackdown Camp
Farnborough

DEAR SIR

Your letter was sent to me from home and it gave me a lot of pleasure. I really wonder whether my things are worth the trouble you have taken in analysing them, but if you think they are, and from your letter, you do, of course I should feel encouraged. I send you here my two latest poems, which I have managed to write, though in the utmost distress of mind, or perhaps because of it. Believe me the army is the most detestable invention on this earth and nobody but a private in the army knows what it is to be a slave.

I wonder whether your muse has been sniffing gunpowder.

Thank you for your good wishes.

Yours sincerely

ISAAC ROSENBERG

[1916, ?March]

24520
A Coy, 12th South Lancs
Alma Bks, Blackdown Camp
Farnborough, Hants

DEAR MR SCHIFF

I have been in this reg about 2 months now and have been kept going all the time. Except that the food is unspeakable, and perhaps luckily, scanty, the rest is pretty tolerable. I have food sent up from home and that keeps me alive, but as for the others, there is talk of mutiny every day. One reg close by did break out and some men got bayoneted. I don't know when we are going out but the talk is very shortly. I have written two small poems[1] since I joined and I think they are my strongest work. I sent them to one or two papers as they are war poems and topical

---

[1] 'Spring 1916' and 'Marching—as seen from the left file' (see pp. 102 and 95).

but as I expected, they were sent back. I am afraid my public is still in the womb. Naturally this only has the effect of making me very conceited and to think these poems better than anybody else's. Let me know what you think of them as I have no one to show them to here.

Yours sincerely
ISAAC ROSENBERG

To Miss Seaton [from Blackdown Camp, Farnborough, Spring 1916]

Thanks very much for the bread and biscuits, which I enjoyed very much. I am in another regiment now, as the old one was smashed up on account of most of the men being unfit. We that were left have been transferred here. The food is much better, but conditions are most unsettling. Every other person is a thief, and in the end you become one yourself, when you see all your most essential belongings go, which you must replace somehow. I also got into trouble here the first day. It's not worth while detailing what happened and exposing how ridiculous, idiotic, and meaningless the Army is, and its dreadful bullyisms, and what puny minds control it. I am trying to get our Passover off, which falls Easter. If I do I'll let you know. The bother is that we will be on our ball-firing then, and also this before-mentioned affair may mess it up. This ball-firing implies we will be ready for the front. I have been working on 'Moses'—in my mind, I mean—and it was through my absent-mindedness while full of that that I forgot certain orders, and am now undergoing a rotten and unjust punishment. I'm working a curious plot into it, and of course, as I can't work here, I jot little scraps down and will piece it together the first chance I get.

[Mid-May 1916]

22311
A Coy, 11th(S) Batt K.O.R.L.
Alma Bks, Blackdown Camp
Farnborough

DEAR MARSH

I have not heard from you and did not expect to, as you must be full up with work. I've also had very little inclination to write to anybody though I've been very eager to hear from all. We are pretty certain to be off the beginning of June and are having our last leave this week. I've got quite used to the thing by now though naturally I hate the restraints. The food in this Reg is much better than the other. I am having a small pamphlet printed of a play[1] and some small poems, all written

[1] *Moses.* The title page reads *Printed by The Paragon Printing Works, 8 Ocean Street, Stepney Green, E.* This is thought to have been an imprint established by Reuben Cohen, a friend of R's, who had the use of Narodiczky's printing machines, and who most likely set the type of *Night and Day* and *Youth*.

since I joined; and I want you to make allowance for the play as I had to write it in a very scrappy manner and even got into trouble through it. It made me a bit absent minded and you know what that means in the army. I expect it will be ready in 2 weeks.

If you are answering this immediately write to

87 Dempsey St
Stepney E

as I think I'm having my 6 days furlough from Friday.

[No signature]

[*Postcard postmarked May 19 1916*]

I will be at Raymond B[1] Mon morning. Have got six days. I'll bring some proofs of my play[2] which will amuse you. The printer is superb. He's made quite an original thing of it, and given me a million hints for new things. The plot is droll. There is a famine in Egypt caused by the superabundance of slaves who eat up all the food meant for the masters. To prevent this, all the back molars of the slaves are drawn, so they eat less. The plot works round this.

I. ROSENBERG

Berg Collection

[*Last week of May 1916*]

22311
A Coy, 11th Batt., K.O.R.L. Regt.
Blackdown Camp

DEAR MR SCHIFF

I have not written to you for some time because there was nothing much new to write about. We are going overseas at last, some day this week—I fancy Thursday, but whether its France or the Coloured Countries I couldn't say. I will write to you from wherever I am. I have had another pamphlet printed of poems as I felt that would be the safest way of keeping my best work if anything should happen. I have not seen the book myself but I believe it is finished by now and I will ask my people to send on a copy to you. When you have seen that, if you would like a bound copy or some for friends, I am selling some to make up the cost of printing—which is not yet paid for. You could write to Miss A. Rosenberg, 87 Dempsey St. Stepney E. but say nothing of my being away as it would pain my mother. A friend sent me a nice letter from Trevelyan the poet[3] (brother of the socialist M.P.) in which he mentions me and

---

[1] Raymond Buildings, Grays Inn, London, where Marsh lived.   [2] *Moses.*

[3] R. C. ('Bob') Trevelyan (1872-1951). Poet and translator. Published numerous volumes of verse between 1898 and 1947, as well as translations of many Greek and Latin poets and dramatists. R spelt his name the way it is pronounced, Trevellyan, in some subsequent letters, but since he spelt it correctly here I have silently corrected it elsewhere. It says much for Trevelyan's catholic taste and generous nature that he responded so warmly to R's very different kind of poetry.

my poems as being 'startlingly fine'. He has not seen my new things yet. For the rest I am in splendid condition and feel ready for the rotten job I'm about.

Yours sincerely

ISAAC ROSENBERG

To Israel Zangwill

[*Late May, 1916*]

22311

A. Coy, 11th (S) Batt., K.O.R.L.

Alma Bks.

Blackdown Camp.

DEAR SIR,

I hope you will excuse this liberty I take in sending my poems to you. I believe you will be interested in 'Moses.' I have not worked him out as a character quite in the way I wished, because I had to hurry to get it finished before I went out. I was not able to correct proofs either. We are going overseas this week. If you are pleased with my book and think friends will like it they are for sale at 1s. each or in cloth, 4/6d. This is only to pay the printer. I thought it necessary to get them printed to prevent them getting lost.

Yours sincerely,

ISAAC ROSENBERG

If books wanted send here for them:
Miss A. Rosenberg,
87 Dempsey Street,
Stepney,
London E.

To R. C. Trevelyan

[*Last week of May, 1916*]

22311

A Coy

11th (S) Batt. K.O.R.L. Regt.

Blackdown Camp

DEAR SIR

My friend Rodker[1] told me you liked my poems and wanted a copy. I am enclosing one for you and one for Mr Bottomley (who is the most

---

[1] John Rodker (1894-1955) author, translator, poet and publisher, was the son of an East End Jewish corset-maker, and slightly better off than the other two members of the original group of Whitechapel friends that R joined—Joseph Leftwich and Samuel Winsten. It was they who, in Leftwich's words, 'used to walk up and down the Mile End Road and the Whitechapel Road . . . with our noses stuck in books and our heads in the clouds'. Gifted and highly intelligent, though ordinary in looks, Rodker was nevertheless very successful with women and married three or four times. R's splendid portrait of Rodker's wife Sonia is reproduced as Colour Plate XV. Towards the end of his life Rodker ran a successful small publishing business, the Imago Press, concentrating on works of psycho-analysis and related subjects.

233

real poet living in England). They will also send you from home copies (one for Bottomley) of some new poems which I've written since I joined. You will excuse the printers errors as I was not able to correct them. We are leaving for overseas this week (Thursday) but if you write soon I expect I'll get the letter; or write to my people for me Miss A. Rosenberg. 87 Dempsey St. Stepney. London. E. but don't say anything of my being away as my people are Tolstoylians and object to my being in khaki. My reason for 'castrating' my book before I sent it was simply that the poems were commonplace and you would not have said: 'You do it like a navvy' but, 'You do it like a bank clerk.' You have made me very pleased by liking my work and telling me B liked them.

If my people send you a copy bound in cloth you won't mind paying for it, I'm sure[,] as I have not paid the printer yet. 3/6 will do.

Yours sincerely
ISAAC ROSENBERG

[*Probably May 27, 1916*]   [*No address*]

DEAR MARSH
It was a pity I came late that morning but it could not be helped and I was so anxious to rush my printer through with my poems before I left England. Anyway we're off at last, either tomorrow or Mon. (its Sat now and we've handed in all our surplus kit and are quite ready). I'll write them at home to send you a copy of my poems, one called 'Spring 1916'[1] I particularly like, and I think you will. But some poems will be in cloth and I am charging for those to make up the cost of printing. If you want any will you write me when I let you know where I am. They are 4/6 each. The king inspected us Thursday. I believe its the first Bantam Brigade been inspected. He must have waited for us to stand up a good while. At a distance we look like soldiers sitting down, you know, legs so short.

Yours sincerely
ISAAC ROSENBERG

[*Early June, 1916*]   [*No address*]

DEAR MR ABERCROMBIE
I am sending you copy of new poems. I hope you'll like them. We're off tonight overseas. As soon as we land anywhere I'll let you know as I'd like very much to hear they pleased you.

Yours sincerely
ISAAC ROSENBERG

[1] See p. 102.

Some of these books are for sale to make up cost of printing if friends of yours should want any. Send Miss A. Rosenberg, 87 Dempsey St, Stepney E. Don't mention my being abroad.

[*Postmarked June 15, 1916*]   22311 Pte I Rosenberg
                                                  A. Coy 11th(S) Batt. K.O.R.L
                                                  British Expeditionary Force

DEAR MR TREVELYAN

My sister sent me on your letter, which has made me feel very conceited and elated. It is strange why people should be so timid and afraid to praise on their own, and yet so bold to criticise. I know my faults are legion; a good many must be put down to the rotten conditions I wrote it in—the whole thing was written in barracks, and I suppose you know what an ordinary soldier's life is like. Moses symbolises the fierce desire for virility, and original action in contrast to slavery of the most abject kind. I was very sorry to hear about Bottomley being bad. I hope by the time this reaches you that will be a thing to joke about. If I get through this affair without any broken bones etc, I have a lot to say and one or two shilling shockers, that'll make some people jump. Here's a sketch of our passage over.[1] If you see Mrs Rodker please ask her to write to me about R. as I believe R is in prison.

The above address will or should find me.

> Yours sincerely
> ISAAC ROSENBERG

We are in the trenches now and its raining horribly.

To Miss Seaton [*from France, June 1916*]

We made straight for the trenches, but we've had vile weather, and I've been wet through for four days and nights. I lost all my socks and things before I left England, and hadn't the chance to make it up again, so I've been in trouble, particularly with bad heels; you can't have the slightest conception of what such an apparently trivial thing means. We've had shells bursting two yards off, bullets whizzing all over the show, but all you are aware of is the agony of your heels ... I had a letter from R. C. Trevelyan, the poet ... He writes: 'It is a long time since I have read anything that has impressed me so much as your "Moses" and some of your short poems ...' He confesses parts are difficult, and he is not sure whether it's my fault or his.

---

[1] 'The Troop Ship', see p. 100.

[*June 1916*]   22311
                                            11th (S) Batt. 40th division
                                            K.O.R.L. Regt.
                                            B.E.F. France

My Dear Marsh

You know we mustn't say very much now we're over the water but as soon as I get a chance I'll try and give you some idea of what's happening to me. Up to now nothing very important has happened, nothing more terrible than uncomfortable regrets at not having learned this infernal lingo when I had the chance. I had a letter from a friend who knows Trevelyan. This letter was from Trevelyan to my friend about my poems—not my recent things. G. Bottomley happened to be staying with him at the time and they both thought some of my things 'startlingly fine'. My new things are miles ahead of those. Write me if you can and if anything occurs to you useful in the trenches that I'm not likely to get here could you send me.

                                     Yours sincerely
                                            Isaac Rosenberg

Here's sketch of passage over.

                        ['The Troop Ship']

I came across your second Georgian book lately.[1] Why didn't you say anything to me about it. I'm mad to read a play by Bottomley. Is Binyon in London or France?

To Gordon Bottomley [postmarked June 12, 1916]

If you really mean what you say in your letter, there is no need to tell you how proud I am. I had to read your letter many times before I could convince myself you were not 'pulling my leg'. People are always telling me my work is promising—incomprehensible, but promising, and all that sort of thing, and my meekness subsides before the patronizing knowingness. The first thing I saw of yours was last year in the Georgian Book, 'The End of the World'. I must have worried all London about it —certainly everybody I know. I had never seen anything like it. After that I got hold of 'Chambers of Imagery'. Mr Marsh told me of your plays, but I joined the Army and have never been able to get at them. It is a great thing to me to be able to tell you now in this way what marvellous pleasure your work has given me, and what pride that my work pleases you. I had ideas for a play called 'Adam and Lilith' before I came to France, but I must wait now.

---

[1] *Georgian Poetry 1913-15*, in which the first item was Bottomley's play 'King Lear's Wife'.

22311 A Coy
11th Batt. K.O.R.L.
3 Platoon.
B.E.F.

MY DEAR MARSH

I sent you a letter and a copy of my book when I reached here, but am doubtful whether you got it, as several letters I sent off at the time, I know got mislaid. I am aware how fearfully busy you must be, but if poetry at this time is no use it certainly won't be at any other. Miss Asquith seems to think this too, and I half believe it is at your suggestion. R. C. Trevelyan is a friend of yours I believe. He wrote me a most flattering letter about my 'Moses'. He said no new thing has impressed him so much for a long time. Bottomley admires my work too, and that has pleased me more than if I were known all over the world. We made straight for the trenches and have spent a wet time and dry one there. I'll write you out a dramatic thing of the trenches some time and shan't say anything here. I sketched myself in a dug out but lost it. Here's it rough. If you have anything to say about my poem do write me as soon as you get time. I am busy too but I write. Of course the work I'm busy at doesn't matter as much as yours—I mean its not so responsible but do write.

Here's a sketch very slight I've done here.

Yours sincerely
ISAAC ROSENBERG

[*No date*]

22311 A Coy 3 platoon
11th K.O.R.L. B.E.F.

DEAR MRS COHEN

We are on a long march and I'm writing this on the chance of getting it off; so you should know I received your papers and also your letter. The notice in the Times of your book is true—especially about your handling of metre. It is an interesting number. The Poetry Review you sent is good—the articles are too breathless, and want more packing, I think. The poems by the soldier are vigorous but, I feel a bit common-place. I did not like Rupert Brooke's begloried sonnets for the same reason. What I mean is second hand phrases 'lambent fires' etc takes from its reality and strength. It should be approached in a colder way, more abstract, with less of the million feelings everybody feels; or all these should be concentrated in one distinguished emotion. Walt Whitman in 'Beat, drums, beat', has said the noblest thing on war.

I am glad Yeats liked your play: His criticism is an honour. He is the established great man and it is a high thing to receive praise from him. Don't talk of Noyes[1]—he only cloys. I always think of some twopenny bazaar when I read him.

---

[1] Alfred Noyes (1880-1958) poet and novelist. His early, patriotic verse, with its easy sentiment and barrel-organ rhythms, not surprisingly sickened R.

I am thinking of a Jewish play with Judas Macabeas for hero. I can put a lot in I've learnt out here. I hope I get the chance to go on with it. I've freshly written this thing—red from the anvil.[1] I have a good one in the anvil now but it wants knocking into shape. Thanks very much for the papers[.]

Yours sincerely
ISAAC ROSENBERG

To Gordon Bottomley [postmarked July 23, 1916]

Your letter came to-day with Mr. Trevelyan's, like two friends to take me for a picnic. Or rather like friends come to release the convict from his chains with his innocence in their hands, as one sees in the twopenny picture palace. You might say, friends come to take you to church, or the priest to the prisoner. Simple *poetry*—that is where an interesting complexity of thought is kept in tone and right value to the dominating idea so that it is understandable and still ungraspable. I know it is beyond my reach just now, except, perhaps, in bits. I am always afraid of being empty. When I get more leisure in more settled times I will work on a larger scale and give myself room; then I may be less frustrated in my efforts to be clear, and satisfy myself too. I think what you say about getting beauty by phrasing of passages rather than the placing of individual words very fine and very true.

[Late July 1916] Pte I Rosenberg 22311
c/o 40th Divisional Coy Salvage Officer
B.E.F. France

DEAR MR SCHIFF

I was most glad to get your card today together with the papers. It is a hard job to get any decent literature out here and it has never occurred to any of my friends to send any to me; (though they have sent me things more urgent and necessary, such as chocolates etc) Still, up to now I have had no leisure at all, not a moment for books, but by some curious way, some queer change in my military programme has taken place, and now I do get time to read—but there is nothing to read. I am sending you this portrait of the militant poet a bit changed ay! Also my sister will send you a trench poem of mine. I think I'll also enclose copy of G. Bottomley's letter to me. I wonder whether you have any of his plays to send me. He was my great god of poetry the moment I read 'The End of the World' in 'Georgian book', and I immediately bought a small book of his and that was the only book I had with me since I joined till I came to France where I lost it somehow. I am distressed about your state of mind, but refrain from philosophizing. I know Cornwall but not Devonshire. I've found Cornwall in Spring gorgeous and I've done a

---

[1] 'August 1914'

good deal of sketching there. I do not know Trevor Blakemore's[1] work though I know his name and his opinion of my work would interest me greatly. It is fine of you to show my work about so, as it may do me a deal of good after the war if I get established some way. My plan is to teach drawing at a school a few days in the week, which leaves plenty of leisure to write, as I am convinced I am more deep and true as a poet than painter. I am glad Bomberg has done something definite at last, I do hope nothing will happen to him out here, more than ever. Who has he married? What division is he in? I might run across him.

The above address is fairly permanent as far as I know. If you write I am pretty sure to get it, and I am bucked up when I hear from friends.

Yours sincerely
ISAAC ROSENBERG

Aug 4th, [1916]   [*Address in final paragraph*]

MY DEAR MARSH

I have only just received your letter, which has been lying about for the last week before it was given to me. By now, you must have read a letter I wrote on behalf of a friend, and sent to Whitehall to reach you during the day, as it was so pressing. I trust you have been able to do something; as it is rough luck on the poor fellow. I was most glad to get your letter and criticism. You know the conditions I have always worked under, and particularly with this last lot of poems. You know how earnestly one must wait on ideas, (you cannot coax real ones to you) and let as it were, a skin grow naturally round and through them.[2] If you are not free, you can only, when the ideas come hot, seize them with the skin in tatters raw, crude, in some parts beautiful in others monstrous. Why print it then? Because those rare[3] parts must not be lost. I work more and more as I write into more depth and lucidity, I am sure. I have a fine idea for a most gorgeous play, Adam and Lilith. If I could get a few months after the war to work and absorb myself completely into the thing, I'd write a great thing.

I am enclosing a poem[4] I wrote in the trenches, which is surely as simple as ordinary talk. You might object to the second line as vague, but that was the best way I could express the sense of dawn.

[1] Trevor Ramsey Villiers Blakemore (*c.*1880-1953). A noted Edwardian wit and *bon viveur*, and an accomplished poetaster with a gift for intricate versification. It is difficult to imagine that R's poetry would have meant much to him.

[2] Altered by R from '(you cannot coax them to you) and let as it were, a skin grow round them'.

[3] R substituted 'rare' for 'beautiful' in the original.

[4] 'Break of Day in the Trenches'; although 'A Worm fed on the heart of Corinth' appears to have been enclosed in the same letter.

Since I wrote last I have been given a job behind the lines and very rarely go into the trenches. My address is c/o 40th Divisional Coy Officer. B.E.F. Pte I Rosenberg 22311. It is more healthy but not absolutely safe from shells as we get those noisy visitors a good many times a day even here.

Yours sincerely
ISAAC ROSENBERG

[*August 1916*]   [*No address*]

DEAR MR SCHIFF

Thank you for your letter which gave me great pleasure. With your letter was a post card sent a week or so before the letter but which only reached me now. Trevor Blakemore's letter was a good one and I enjoyed the manner of it. What he says is good, also[,] but though I agree with most part of it about over involved simplification etc. I think we would be at loggerheads in our ideas of technique. I mean to make my next play a model of lucidity. I have never read 'King Lear's Wife'.[1] (Is that the book you're sending me, because Marsh, who brought the book out, gave me the first Georgian B; however, either would delight me.) 'The End of the World'[2] in the first Georgian Book stands by itself in the language. I do not think there is any modern poet with the subtlety and energy of mind and art that Bottomley has. John Drinkwater, I could never read, he seems so dull to me and Rupert Brooke has written one fine poem with depth, 'Town and country'.[3] I don't like his other work much, they remind me too much of flag days. I am so glad you are in a happy place and the weather is all you wish it to be. Gertler once told me you had written a novel and I look forward to seeing it when I get back, and the new one. Prose is so diffuse and has not the advantages of poetry. The novels I like best are those terrific conceptions of Balzac, and one I read of Stendhal's. Hardy I think is a better poet than novelist. There is so much unessential writing one puts in a novel and yet which must be there, at the same time, that makes me regard novel writing as a mistaken art.

I will write the moment I receive the book. Did I acknowledge your papers?

Yours sincerely
I ROSENBERG

---

[1] By Gordon Bottomley. R was shortly to read it with enthusiasm in the 2nd volume of *Georgian Poetry*.

[2] See footnote 4 to letter to Marsh on p. 199.

[3] See Rupert Brooke's *Poems* 1911, p. 37. 'Town and Country' is a rhetorical, rather obscure, pseudo-metaphysical poem, now deservedly forgotten. But it is not difficult to see why its far-fetched imagery appealed to R.

MY DEAR MARSH

You didn't get my letter because it was never sent; however time has put it all to rights again and there's no need to bother you about it. Thank you for showing my thing to Rothenstein.[1] I value his praise very much.

G. Bottomley sent me 'King Lear's Wife'. I do think it magnificent as a play and some stunning poetry in it too. There are few men living who could whack that as a play.

We are kept pretty busy now, and the climate here is really unhealthy; the doctors themselves can't stand it. We had an exciting time today, and though this is behind the firing line and right out of the trenches there were quite a good many sent to heaven and the hospital. I carried one myself in a handcart to the hospital, (which often is the antichamber to heaven.)

Binyon wrote me a letter about *Moses* with the paternal rod half raised in one hand[2] and some sweets and chocolates in the other. But it was a letter I feel grateful for and very good criticism. He says my poetry comes out in clotted gushes and spasms. He has been to France and is back in England now.

Write me if you get time as you know a letter (especially Strakers Stationery) is a bit—a very tiny bit like London.

I ROSENBERG

DEAR MR SCHIFF

Your Georgian B. has arrived at last; many many thanks. I pounced on King Lear's Wife, and though it was not more than I expected, it was not less. The only fault I can find is in the diction. It has the aspect of talking to children, in some places.

Goneril is marvellously drawn. Lear is a bit shadowy perhaps, but altogether as a poetic drama, it is of the very highest kind. The conception of Lear making love to the servant beside the bedside of his dying wife is unsurpassable.

In one way I do not think the play equal to some things in 'Chambers of Imagery'; at least I never got that startling pleasure from the play as I did from those. Rupert Brooke's poem on Clouds is marvellous; his style offends me; it is gaudy and remini[s]cent. The second half of the

---

[1] Sir William Rothenstein (1872-1945), painter and draughtsman. Studied at the Slade and later in Paris. Was an official War Artist in France 1917-18, and later Principal of the Royal College of Art.

[2] R originally wrote 'for my hindquarters' but struck it out.

second line, and the whole of the 4th line are so uninteresting. Fogetting these it is a really wonderful thing. I also received your packet of papers which I've had no time yet to look into. I trust you've heard well of your nephews. I wonder how Bomberg behaves. I *must* write to him.

Is the novel growing? I am a bad midwife to ideas just lately and only bring out abhortions.

Yours sincerely
I Rosenberg

[*August 1916*]

[*No address*]

Dear Mr Schiff

Many thanks for your letter and the papers. I'll wait till I get back to England to learn French as I can't concentrate on it here. The French poets I think have given a nasty turn to English thought. It is all Café Royal poetry now. The Germans are far finer though they are fine through Baudelaire. Heine, our own Heine, we must say nothing of. I admire him more for always being a Jew at heart than anything else. Personally I am very fond of our Celtic Rabelais. Of Butler I know very little, but Shaw in spite of his topsy turvy manner seems to me to be very necessary. Anyhow his plays are the only plays I can stand at the theatre. I mean of course of the plays that are played on the stage. He has no subtlety, no delicate irony, none of the rarer qualities. But his broad satire is good.

Yours sincerely,
I. Rosenberg

[*August 1916*]

22311
A Coy 3 Platoon
11th K.O.R.L. B.E.F.

My Dear Marsh

I know the terrible length of my new address will make an excellent excuse for not replying; I hope however, it will not frighten you. I am back again in the trenches. I have a notion the Artist rifles have been somewhere about because I fancy I recognized a Fitzroy Street flea, but I couldn't swear to it. I have been forbidden to send poems home, as the censor won't be bothered with going through such rubbish, or I would have sent you one I wrote about our armies, which I am rather bucked about. I have asked the 'Nation' to print it, if they do, you will see it there. The 'Georgian book' was sent out to me here. Brooke's poem on 'Clouds' is magnificent.[1] Gordon Bottomley has been writing me warm letters. He is a great man and I feel most pained about his condition. Do you know anything about artists out here to disguise things, landscape

---

[1] The reference is to the sonnet of that name included on p. 59 of *Georgian Poetry 1913-15*, and previously published in *1914 and Other Poems*, p. 37, where it is subscribed 'The Pacific, October 1913'.

sheds etc. Col S J Solomon[1] is their Chief I believe and I know him a bit. I wonder if I'd be any good at it. Who would I have to approach about it. Do write.

Yours sincerely

ISAAC ROSENBERG

[*Late August 1916*]   [*No address*]

DEAR MR SCHIFF

As soon as I had sent my letter off to you I wrote this little thing. I believe Mr Massingham[2] will like it better than the other you showed him, though I of course prefer the other. I am not sending it to any other paper.

How is the novel progressing.

Yours sincerely

ISAAC ROSENBERG

[*Late August 1916*]   22311
                                                A Coy, 3 Platoon, 11th K.O.R.L.
                                                B.E.F.

DEAR MR SCHIFF

I sent the poem to Mr Massingham. Nation. It makes things so complicated when there is no reply, as one can't show it elsewhere. I am back in the Trenches now and my address is altered as you notice. Thank you for Lawrence offer but cloth books are so bulky and impossible out here. I have sent home the Georgian book. I know his poems a little and admire his power, but not his outlook. I suppose he is the necessary spokesman for people that way inclined. It is a pity you are chucking your novel, but of course, you would know best. I read an excellent poem in the Westminster Gazette,[3] it got the prize there; it begins

'Me and Bill and Ginger'

do you know who wrote[4] it? Its by someone at the front.

---

[1] Solomon J. Solomon, R.A. (1860-1927), served with the Royal Engineers as head of Camouflage 1916-18. He was the brother of Mrs Delissa Joseph, who helped send R to the Slade, and uncle of Ruth Löwy whom R drew in 1912 (see Monochrome Plate 6(b)).

[2] H. W. Massingham (1860-1924), journalist and political commentator, was editor of the *Nation* 1907-23.

[3] *The Saturday Westminster Gazette* was originally a penny Liberal evening paper, started in 1893 in competition with the old *Pall Mall Gazette*. Under the editorship of J. A. Spender from 1896-1922 it was renowned for the high standard of its political and literary criticism.

[4] The Prize was offered 'for a song for a Camp Concert'. In the event, it was divided between the poem R liked, signed 'Etien', and another. The identity of the former was not revealed, but in his Report on the competition the Editor said his 'song came in an envelope passed by the censor and stamped by the B.E.F. Field Post Office'. For the full text of 'Me and Bill and Ginger' see *The Saturday Westminster Gazette* for August 5th, 1916.

I am sorry I can't date my letters as you ask but I never know the date and one can't choose your own time as to sending letters. I generally write when I see the postman coming to collect, if I get the chance.

Yours sincerely
ISAAC ROSENBERG

[1916 ?August]

22311
A Coy 3 platoon 11th K.O.R.L.
B.E.F.

DEAR MR SCHIFF

Thanks very much for papers. I liked the article on the Somme Cinemas; Of course Chesterton[1] on Zangwill[2] was nearer home; but C seems sly and certainly anti Jewish. We are having rotten wet weather in the trenches, mucky and souzing and cold. I don't think I've been dry yet, these last 3 days. Bottomley is a permanent invalid and lives quietly in the North of England. I don't think he's ever troubled much about his work though they have made more headway in Yankeeland than here. I think him in many ways our best poet. He has an extraordinary dramatic power and quite new. There is a lovely delicacy about his work as if shaken about strength, as powerful as any of those sledge hammer bawlers which many people will accept alone for strength. His enfeebled condition is a great loss to literature as it lessens his output.

Yours sincerely,
ISAAC ROSENBERG

I forgot to mention the rejected masterpiece. Its adventures must have been various and many, to judge by the interminable length of time it took to reach me again; it must have been handled by angels too, for the printless pressure of their fingers on the paper could be felt but not seen. Gordon Bottomley thought the lines from 2 to 5 first rate poetry, but thought the whole thing seemed like a long interjection. Well, I had meant to go on with it.

[1] Gilbert Keith Chesterton (1874-1936) poet, prose writer and journalist, was a prolific author of books on a variety of subjects, from philosophy and sociology to detective fiction. In 1922 he became a Catholic convert, which may explain the anti-Jewish bias which R detected.

[2] Israel Zangwill (1864-1926) Jewish novelist, playwright and journalist. Very early in R's career Zangwill was shown some of R's poems but apparently made no response. This was very unlike him, for he was well known for his active encouragement of young Jewish writers and artists, and there are grounds for believing that at one point he intervened on R's behalf with Carl Hentschel, the process-engraver for whom R worked after leaving school. Zangwill, who numbered Thomas Hardy, Bernard Shaw and S. L. Bensusan among his friends, has been called 'the first and still the greatest story writer on Jewish themes in this century' for his *Children of the Ghetto* and similar books in which he vividly evoked the East End of those days. See Joseph Leftwich's biography of Zangwill, and his 1976 Tower Hamlets Lecture: *Israel Zangwill—Isaac Rosenberg.*

22311. A Coy. 11th Batt. K.O.R.L. rgt
3 Platoon
British Expeditionary Force
France

DEAR MR TREVELYAN

My sister sent me your letter on, which I answered; but as certain other letters I sent off at the same time went astray I surmise that one was lost as well, so I am writing again. The other side of this sheet is a very crude sketch of how I look here in this dugout.[1] I'll write out at the end of this letter a little poem[2] of the troop ship where I try to describe in words the contortions we get into to try and wriggle ourselves into a little sleep. Of course if you're lucky and get a decent dugout you sleep quite easily—when you get the chance, otherwise you must sleep standing up, or sitting down, which latter is my case now. I must say that it has made me very happy to know you like my work so much; very few people do, or, at least, say so; and I believe I am a poet.

Here in the trenches where we are playing this extraordinary gamble, your letter made me feel refreshed and fine. I hope Bottomley is quite better by now—he is a man whose work (I have only read 'Chambers of Imagery') has made me feel more rare and delicately excited feelings, than any poetry I have ever read. The little poem 'Nimrod' the image in the first stanza to me is one of the most astonishing in all literature. Another thing that seems to me too astounding for comment, is Abercrombie's Hymn to Love.

I hope we may some day be able to talk these things over.

Yours sincerely
ISAAC ROSENBERG

[No date]
22311 A Coy. 3. Platoon
11th. Batt. K.O.R.L.
B.E.F.

DEAR SONIA

I have been anxious to hear from you about Rodker. I wrote to Trevelyan (he thinks me a big knut at poetry) and asked him for news but I fancy my letter got lost. Write me any news—anything. I seem to have been in France, ages. I wish Rodker were with me, the infernal lingo is a tragedy with me and he'd help me out. If I was taciturn in England I am 10 times so here; our struggle to express ourselves is a fearful joke. However our wants are simple, our cash is scarce, and our time is precious, so French would perhaps be superfluous. I'd hardly believe French manners are so different to ours, but I leave all this for conversation. Here's a little poem a bit commonplace I'm afraid.[3]

Yours sincerely
ISAAC ROSENBERG

[1] See overleaf.   [2] See 'The Troop Ship', p. 100.
[3] 'In the Trenches' (see p. 102).

[*1916 ?October*]

22311 A Coy 3 Platoon
11th K.O.R.L. B.E.F.

Dear Miss Lowy,

I did not send K.L.W. as I hadn't the chance and am most glad
you had already read and liked it. We have been on the march almost all

246

the time since I last wrote to you and it has been impossible to do anything one wanted to do. King Lear's Wife is remarkable. The conception of the king's love making at the bedside of his dying wife is marvellous. I chiefly admire the simple beauty of the writing and the characterization of Goneril—hard and beautiful. If you can, do get his 'Chambers of Imagery'. I like some things there perhaps better than the play. He wrote me when he read my 'Moses' that the 'Ah Kolue' speech, and two or three other speeches was the 'very top of poetry'.

He is a permanent invalid and it gives him hell to write much. He has written me most warm letters out here and I feel really happy when I hear his work is enjoyed.

I spent my wild little pick-a-back days in Bristol; was born there, too. I have some vague far away memories of the name of Polack in connection I fancy with Hebrew classes and prizegiving. It pleases me much that my poems are liked in my natal place—a fate so opposite to the usual—but probably that is because they are unaware of it being my natal place.

G.B. has urged me to write Jewish Plays. I am quite sure if I do I will be boycotted and excommunicated, that is, assuming my work is understood. My 'Moses' is a hard pill to swallow and should I get the chance of working on it and amplifying it as I wish—it will be harder still. Mrs. Cohen sent me her book. It is interesting but my idea of poetry is something deeper than that. She sent me papers too and I notice there Gilbert Cannan[1] has written a novel called 'Mendel'. I fancy as far as I can make out, Gertler is the hero. Gertler is or was on very friendly terms with Cannan, and lived with him a long time. Cannan is very clever and is ranked very high as a satirical novelist, a kind of Piccadilly Voltaire. I must stop now as we have no more lights.

Yours sincerely
ISAAC ROSENBERG

To Harriet Monroe [*1916 ?October*]

Could you let me know whether a poem of mine 'Marching' has been printed by you, as I understood from J. Rodker, it was accepted. I have no means of knowing, or seeing your magazine out here, I have lost touch with Rodker . . . I am enclosing a poem or two written in trenches[2] . . .

---

[1] Gilbert Cannan (1884-1955) was a prolific writer of plays, short stories, poems and novels, no less than 28 of which appeared between 1909 and 1924. He was also a gifted translator. The novel to which R refers above, *Mendel* (1916), was indeed a portrait of the young Gertler and his affair with Dora Carrington. It caused considerable resentment among them, and other friends of Cannan's portrayed in the book. In 1924 he became mentally deranged and spent the last 30 years of his life in institutions. He has been called a tragic example of 'a genius that never developed'.

[2] They were 'Break of Day in the Trenches' and 'The Troop Ship'.

MY DEAR MARSH

You complain in your letter that there is little to write about; my complaint is rather the other way, I have too much to write about, but for obvious reasons my much must be reduced to less than your little. My exaggerated way of feeling things when I begin to write about them might not have quite healthy consequences.

I was most glad to hear about Bottomley. He has been writing me warm letters and I was greatly pained to find so fine a nature possessing so frail a hold on health and I am always most anxious about him and to hear anything of him.

My Lilith has eloped with that devil proc[r]astination, or rather, labours of a most colos[s]al and uncongenial shape have usurped her place and driven her blonde and growing beauty away. I have written something that still wants knocking into shape. I feel too tired to copy it out, but later on I will, if you care to see it. I came across that poem on clouds by poor Rupert Brooke. It is magnificent indeed, and as near to sublimity as any modern poem.

The poem I like best of modern times is Abercrombie's Hymn to Love. It is more weighty in thought, alive in passion and of a more intense imagination than any I know. I was amused to hear of your gardening experiment. I suppose one must get interested in things different to our usual interests and get our thoughts shaken up a bit nowadays or it would be Hell going on. Do write when you can.

> Yours sincerely
> ISAAC ROSENBERG

To Laurence Binyon, [*Autumn 1916*]

It is far, very far, to the British Museum from here (situated as I am, Siberia is no further and certainly no colder), but not too far for that tiny mite of myself, my letter, to reach there. Winter has found its way into the trenches at last, but I will assure you, and leave to your imagination, the transport of delight with which we welcomed its coming. Winter is not the least of the horrors of war. I am determined that this war, with all its powers for devastation, shall not master my poeting; that is, if I am lucky enough to come through all right. I will not leave a corner of my consciousness covered up, but saturate myself with the strange and extraordinary new conditions of this life, and it will all refine itself into poetry later on. I have thoughts of a play round our Jewish hero, Judas Maccabeus. I have much real material here, and also there is some parallel in the savagery of the invaders then to this war. I am not decided whether truth of period is a good quality or a negative one. Flaubert's 'Salambo' proves, perhaps, that it is good. It decides the tone of the work, though it makes it hard to give the human side and make it more living. However, it is impossible now to work and difficult even to think of poetry, one is so cramped intellectually.

[*No date*]   Pte I Rosenberg
                                                        [Address deleted
                                                         by the censor.]
DEAR MR TREVELYAN
     Your letter came with a second one of Bottomley's. His first was all praise and his second all criticism; but his criticism was higher praise than any praise I had been given before. His letter was full of fine writing and useful tips and I feel very grateful for it, and to you for first showing my things to him. I had been meaning to write to him for some time, in fact, when I first read him, but I always thought to myself,—wait till you have something worthy to show him! It was only coming out to France and the risk of being knocked over made me print the poems hurriedly.
     I have never read B's plays though Mr Marsh told me of them, but the war interfered and I have read no literature for the last year, till I got yours and B's letters. I have asked my sister to send you a poem Bottomley liked—'Break of day in the trenches'[.] Perhaps the end is not quite clear and wants working on. I have an idea for a book of war poems. I have already written a few small things but have plans for a few longish dramatic poems. Abercrombie's 'Hymn to Love' is I think, the great thing of modern times, and far above anything else of his I know. Bottomley is more profound and a purer artist—but the Hymn to Love wants some licking. Thank you for showing my work about, I am naturally anxious for discerning people to read my things.

                                         Yours sincerely
                                               ISAAC ROSENBERG
I have not heard from J.R.[1] and am glad he is not in trouble.

[*Postmarked November 20, 1916*]   22311 A Coy 3 Platoon
                                            11th K.O.R.L. B.E.F.
DEAR MR TREVELYAN
     I had just written to Mr Bottomley when your letter reached me last week. Perhaps you were still with him when my letter arrived (if it did arrive) and read the little poem I sent. Just as a reminder that poetry is still alive in my brain. We are pretty busy and writing letters is most awkward, but after some rough days in the trenches, here before the comfortable glare of the camp fire I cannot help using these few odd minutes to answer your letter. It was a treat to get something about something from home. I cannot now enter into your arguments though that kind of fighting is more in my line than trench fighting—

[1] John Rodker

249

I am writing this chiefly to let you know I am still safe, and to thank you for your letter. I am most eager to see Bottomley's new work and the rest in your annual. I read Moore's Sicilian Idyll in the first Georgian book and it is great.[1] That is all I know of Moore. Judith and the Hymn to Love made me think Abercrombie the first poet in the world. If there is any chance of getting home I'll certainly let you know—though things are so vague and in the air we never know whats going to happen for two minutes together.

Yours sincerely
ISAAC ROSENBERG

[*Probably December 1916*]   [*No address*]

MY DEAR MARSH

If I get two letters from one friend I get none from another. Well— I have not been out here six months for nothing—I have learnt to be a Stoic and say nothing. We hear very little of what's going on in England, but I did get a rumour of great changes in the government which may affect you. I wish I were in England just for a while, particularly now that I feel run down and weakened. I am also wishful to meet Gordon Bottomley some day. I hear Abercrombie is over-working himself and doing himself no good; a condition of being I can claim to rival him in. Gibson's 'Battle' was sent to me and delighted me.[2] It is as good as Degas. In a way it seems a contradiction that a thinker should take a low plane as he does there[,] instead of the more complex and sensitive personality of a poet in such a situation. Most who have written as poets have been very unreal and it is for this reason, their naturalness, I think Gibson's so fine. The Homer for this war has yet to be found— Whitman got very near the mark 50 years ago with 'Drum Taps'. I don't know what these Government changes will mean to you but do write if you can and let me know.

Yours sincerely
ISAAC ROSENBERG

Berg Collection

[*No date*]   [*No address*]

DEAR RODKER,

What on earth is happening to you and why are you so secret about things. Your letter made me quite wild to know what was up. However perhaps you've got to be quiet. I've had some lovely letters from G

---

[1] See T. Sturge Moore, *Georgian Poetry 1911-12*, p. 137.

[2] Wilfred Wilson Gibson, a minor Georgian poet whose work appeared in all 5 volumes of Marsh's *Georgian Poetry*.

Bottomley. It is rough luck on him that he's so poor in health. That must be the reason he doesn't produce very much. I had a box of Turkish from Miss Pulley and if you see her you can tell her that the war has been worth while since its been the cause of this enormous pleasure to me—Of course a poet must put it on a bit thick. Turn over for a patriotic gush[,] a jingo spasm

POZIÈRES

Glory! glory! glory!
British women, in your wombs you plotted
This monstrous girth of glory, this marvellous glory.
Not for mere love delights Time meant the profound hour
When an Englishman was planned.
Time shouted it to his extremest outpost.
The illuminated call through the voided years
Was heard, is heard at last,
And will be heard at the last
Reverberated through the Eternities,
Earth's immortality and Heavens.

I am sending this to Sonia as you gave no address.

ROSENBERG

[*Postmarked January 18, 1917*]   [*Address given below*]

MY DEAR MARSH

My sister wrote me she would be writing to you. She'd got the idea of my being in vile health from your letter addressed to Dempsey St, and naturally they at home exaggerated things in their minds. Perhaps though it is not so exaggerated. That my health is undermined I feel sure of; but I have only lately been medically examined, and absolute fitness was the verdict. My being transfer[r]ed may be the consequence of my reporting sick, or not; I don't know for certain. But though this work does not entail half the hardships of the trenches, the winter and the conditions naturally tells on me, having once suffered from weak lungs, as you know. I have been in the trenches most of the 8 months I've been here, and the continual damp and exposure is whispering to my old friend consumption, and he may hear the words they say in time. I have nothing outwardly to show yet, but I feel it inwardly. I don't know what you could do in a case like this; perhaps I could be made use of as a draughtsman at home; or something else in my own line, or perhaps on munitions. My new address is

Pte I R 22311
7 Platoon F. Coy
40th Division
Works Battalion
B.E.F.

251

I wrote a poem some while ago which Bottomley liked so, and I want you to see it, but I'm writing in most awkward conditions and can't copy it now. 'Poetry' of Chicago printed a couple of my things[1] and are paying me. I should think you find the Colonial Office interesting particularly after the war.

I hope however it leaves you leisure for literature; for me its the great thing.

Yours sincerely
ISAAC ROSENBERG

[*Postmarked February 8, 1917*]　　　　　　　　　　　[*Address given below*]

MY DEAR MARSH

I was told the other day by the Captain that he had heard from you about me. He had me examined, but it appears I'm quite fit. What I feel like just now—I wish I were Tristram Shandy for a few minutes so as to describe this 'cadaverous bale of goods consigned to Pluto'. This winter is a teaser for me; and being so long without a proper rest I feel as if I need one to recuperate and be put to rights again. However I suppose we'll stick it, if we don't there are still some good poets left who might write me a decent epitaph.

I've sketched an amusing little thing called 'the louse hunt', and am trying to write one as well.[2] I get very little chance to do anything of this sort but what I have done I'll try and send you. Daumier or Goya are far in perspective.

How do [you] find the Colonial Office after the Treasury?

Yours sincerely
ISAAC ROSENBERG

Pte I. R. 22311
7 Platoon F. Coy 40th Division
Works Batt. B.E.F.

I'll send on the poem G.B. liked so much, next time I write.

To Gordon Bottomley [*February 1917*]

Your letters always give me a strange and large pleasure; and I shall never think I have written poetry in vain, since it has brought your friendliness in my way. Now, feeling as I am, cast away and used up, you don't know what a letter like yours is to me. Ever since November,

---

[1] 'Marching' and 'Break of Day in the Trenches' both appeared in the December 1916 issue of *Poetry: A Magazine of Verse* (Chicago) edited by Harriet Monroe, to whom Ezra Pound and later John Rodker had recommended R's work.

[2] See the poem 'Louse Hunting' on p. 108.

when we first started on our long marches, I have felt weak; but it seems to be some inscrutable mysterious quality of weakness that defies all doctors. I have been examined most thoroughly several times by our doctor, and there seems to be nothing at all wrong with my lungs. I believe I have strained my abdomen in some way, and I shall know of it later on. We have had desperate weather, but the poor fellows in the trenches where there are no dugouts are the chaps to pity. I am sending a very slight sketch of a louse-hunt. It may be a bit vague, as I could not work it out here, but if you can keep it till I get back I can work on it then. I do believe I could make a fine thing of Judas. Judas as a character is more magnanimous than Moses, and I believe I could make it very intense and write a lot from material out here. Thanks very much for your joining in with me to rout the pest out, but I have tried all kinds of stuff; if you can think of any preparation you believe effective I'd be most grateful for it.

To Gordon Bottomley [*postmarked April 8, 1917*]

All through this winter I have felt most crotchety, all kinds of small things interfering with my fitness. My hands would get chilblains or bad boots would make my feet sore; and this aggravating a general run-down-ness, I have not felt too happy. I have gone less warmly clad during the winter than through the summer, because of the increased liveliness on my clothes. I've been stung to what we call 'dumping' a great part of my clothing, as I thought it wisest to go cold than lousy. It may have been this that caused all the crotchetiness. However, we've been in no danger—that is, from shell-fire—for a good long while, though so very close to most terrible fighting. But as far as houses or sign of ordinary human living is concerned, we might as well be in the Sahara Desert. I think I could give some blood-curdling touches if I wished to tell all I see, of dead buried men blown out of their graves, and more, but I will spare you all this.

[*Postmarked April 25, 1917*]   [*Address given below*]

MY DEAR MARSH

My sister wrote me you have been getting more of my 'Moses'. It is hardy of you, indeed, to spread it about; and I certainly[1] would be distressed if I were the cause of a war in England; seeing what warfare means here. But it greatly pleases me, none the less, that this child of my brain should be seen and perhaps his beauties be discovered. His creator is in sadder plight; the harsh and unlovely times have made his mistress, the flighty Muse, abscond and elope with luckier rivals, but surely I shall

---

[1] R originally wrote 'assuredly' but substituted the less grandiose adverb.

hunt her and chase her somewhere into the summer and sweeter times. Anyway this is a strong hope; Lately I have not been very happy, being in torture with my feet again. The coldness of the weather and the weight of my boots have put my feet in a rotten state. My address is different now

Pte IR 22311
7 Platoon
120th Brigade Works Coy
B.E.F.

There is more excitement now, but though I enjoy this, my feet cause me great suffering and my strength is hardly equal to what is required.

I hear pretty often from G. Bottomley and his letters are like a handshake: and passages are splendid pieces of writing. Have you seen Trevelyan's 'Annual' which G.B. writes me of?

Do write me when you can.

Yours sincerely
ISAAC ROSENBERG

[Postmarked May 8, 1917]   [No address]

MY DEAR MARSH

We are camping in the woods now and are living great. My feet are almost healed now and my list of complaints has dwindled down to almost invisibility. I've written some lines suggested by going out wiring, or rather carrying wire up the line on limbers and running over dead bodies lying about.[1] I don't think what I've written is very good but I think the substance is, and when I work on it I'll make it fine. Bottomley told me he had some very old poems in The Annual but of course its too bulky to send out here. Your extract from his 'Atlantis' is real Bottomleyian. The young Oxford poets you showed my things to I've never come across yet, and I'll soon begin to think myself a poet if my things get admired so.

I'm writing to my sister to send you the lines as she will type several copies.

Yours sincerely
I R

I trust the colonial office agrees with you

[Postmarked May 27, 1917]   [No address]

MY DEAR MARSH

I liked your criticism of 'Dead mans dump'. Mr Binyon[2] has often sermonised lengthily over my working on two different principles in the

[1] A clear reference to the inception of R's greatest poem 'Dead Man's Dump'
[2] Laurence Binyon, see footnote on p. 192.

same thing and I know how it spoils the unity of a poem. But if I couldn't before, I can now, I am sure, plead the absolute necessity of fixing an idea before it is lost, because of the situation its conceived in. Regular rhythms I do not like much, but of course it depends on where the stress and accent are laid. I think there is nothing finer than the vigorous opening of Lycidas for music; yet it is regular. Now I think if Andrew Marvell had broken up his rhythms more he would have been considered a terrific poet. As it is I like his poem urging his mistress to love because they have not a thousand years to love on and he can't afford to wait. (I forget the name of the poem)[1] well I like it more than Lycidas.

I have written a much finer poem which I've asked my sister to send you.[2] Don't think from this I've time to write. This last poem is only about 70 lines and I started it about October. It is only when we get a bit of rest and the others might be gambling or squabbling I add a line or two, and continue this way. The weather is gorgeous now and we are bivouacked in the fields. The other night I awoke to find myself floating about with the water half over me. I took my shirt off and curled myself up on a little mound that the water hadn't touched and slept stark naked that night. But that was not all of the fun. The chap next to me was suddenly taken with Diarrhoea and kept on lifting the sheet of the Bivouac, and as I lay at the end the rain came beating on my nakedness all night. Next morning, I noticed the poor chap's discoloured pants hanging on a bough near by, and I thought after all I had the best of it.

I fancy you will like my last poem, I am sure it is at least as good as my Kolue speech,[3] and there is more of it.

Yours sincerely
Isaac Rosenberg

[Postmarked May 29, 1917]   [No address]

My Dear Marsh

I hope you have not yet got my poem 'The Amulet' [which] I've asked my sister to send you. If you get it please don't read it because its the merest sketch and the best is yet to come. If I am able to carry on with it I'll send you it in a more presentable fashion. I believe I have a good idea at bottom. Its a kind of 'Rape of the Sabine Women', idea.

---

[1] 'To His Coy Mistress'.

[2] Almost certainly 'Daughters of War', see p. 112.

[3] See *Moses*, the last 23 lines of Scene I beginning 'Ah! Koelue!' Marsh considered this Rosenberg's best work to date, and included it in *Georgian Poetry 1916-1917*. Strangely, there is no reference on the Contents page, as there is in the case of the other contributors, to the source from which the lines were taken. Marsh, for all his genuine endeavours to help R, evidently thought *Moses* too insignificant a publication to be worth a mention, in this or subsequent editions of G.P. 1916-17 as late as 1922.

Some strange race of wanderers have settled in some wild place and are perishing out for lack of women. The prince of these explores some country near where the women are most fair. But the natives will not hear of foreign marriages and he plots another rape of the Sabines, but he is trapped in the act. Finis. But I fancy poetry is not much bothering you or anybody just now. I've heard of the air raids and I always feel most anxious about my people. Yet out here, though often a troublesome consolation, poetry is a great one to me. G. Bottomley sent me some knock-outs. 'Atlantis' is one of the grand poems in our language;[1] and came to me as the news of a great victory might come. I am still with the R.E.s and go up the line every night, unloading barbed wire etc. In the afternoon we load the stuff. So I have the morning to sleep in, unless I happen to be doing some punishment for my forgetfulness; and then I must do that in the morning. Though furloughs are going about in our Div, it may be a good while before my turn comes.

Yours sincerely
ISAAC ROSENBERG

7th June [1917]   [Address as below]

DEAR MOTHER
    I have not had a letter since well over a week and hope things are all right at home. My new address is Pte I Rosenberg

22311
11th K.O.R.L.
c/o 229 Field Coy.
Royal Engineers,
B.E.F.

I will send a poem if I can't manage it in this letter, in the next, I want typed and sent back to me[,] not to be shown to anyone, as I want to work on it before it is seen. The weather is still marvellous though last night it lightninged a good deal, it was good to see.
    Send me a pencil or chalk pencil. What is Dave doing and Elkon[?][2] I hope Peretz's[3] boys are good and no trouble. If they are good[,] things should be lively[.]

Love to all
ISAAC

---

[1] Bottomley's poem first appeared in his *An Annual of New Poetry, 1917*, from which Marsh reprinted it in *Georgian Poetry 1916-17*, p. 165.

[2] R's brothers, both of whom were in the army and in France.

[3] Rabbi Peretz was a relative of R's on his father's side. See his portrait by R, at Monochrome Plate 1 (a).

13. Portrait of Marda Vanne. Pencil. Drawn in S. Africa. 1914   12″ × 11″

14. (a) Head of a Woman, full-face.
Chalk. c. 1914   12″ × 9½″

14. (b) The Artist's Father. Pencil.
1915   9″ × 6″

To Edward Marsh [*June 1917*]

I am now fearfully rushed, but find energy enough to scribble this in the minute I plunder from my work. I believe I can see the obscurities in the 'Daughters',[1] but hardly hope to clear them up in France. The first part, the picture of the Daughters dancing and calling to the spirits of the slain before their last cries have ceased among the boughs of the tree of life, I must still work on. In that part obscure the description of the voice of the Daughter I have not made clear, I see; I have tried to suggest the wonderful sound of her voice, spiritual and voluptuous at the same time. The end is an attempt to imagine the severance of all human relationship and the fading away of human love. Later on I will try and work on it, because I think it a pity if the ideas are to be lost for want of work. My 'Unicorn' play is stopped because of my increased toil, and I forget how much or little I told you of it. I want to do it in one Act, although I think I have a subject here that could make a gigantic play. I have not the time to write out the sketch of it as far as it's gone, though I'd like to know your criticism of it very much. The most difficult part I shrink from; I think even Shakespeare might:—the first time Tel, the chief of the decaying race, sees a woman (who is Lilith, Saul's wife), and he is called upon to talk. Saul and Lilith are ordinary folk into whose ordinary lives the Unicorn bursts. It is to be a play of terror—terror of hidden things and the fear of the supernatural. But I see no hope of doing the play while out here. I have a way, when I write, to try and put myself in the situation, and I make gestures and grimaces.

To Gordon Bottomley [*postmarked July 20, 1917*]

My sister wrote me of your note, and it made me very glad to feel you thought in that way about my poem, because I liked it myself above anything I have yet done. I know my letters are not what they should be; but I must take any chance I get of writing for fear another chance does not come, so I write hastily and leave out most I should write about. I wished to say last time a lot about your poem, but I could think of nothing that would properly express my great pleasure in it; and I can think of nothing now. If anything, I think it is too brief—although it is so rare and compressed and full of hinted matter. I wish I could get back and read your plays; and if my luck still continues, I shall. Leaves have commenced with us, but it may be a good while before I get mine. We are more busy now than when I last wrote, but I generally manage to knock something up if my brain means to, and I am sketching out a little play.[2] My great fear is that I may lose what I've written, which can happen here so easily. I send home any bit I write, for safety, but that can easily get lost in transmission. However, I live in an immense trust that things will turn out well.

[1] The poem entitled 'Daughters of War' (see p. 112)
[2] 'The Unicorn'

The other poems I have not yet read, but I will follow on with letters and shall send the bits of—or rather the bit of—a play I've written. Just now it is interfered with by a punishment I am undergoing for the offence of being endowed with a poor memory, which continually causes me trouble and often punishment. I forgot to wear my gas-helmet one day; in fact, I've often forgotten it, but I was noticed one day, and seven days' pack drill is the consequence, which I do between the hours of going up the line and sleep. My memory, always weak, has become worse since I've been out here.

[*1917, ?July*]

22311 Pte I Rosenberg
11th K.O.R.L. Regt.
Attached 229 Field Coy, R.Es.
B.E.F. France

Dear Mr Schiff

I was most glad to hear from you. I have just received your letter and its useful enclosure for which many thanks. I say I was most glad— but that is not quite true—your letter is too bitter. I did not get your letters in France and I often wondered about you, but things are so tumultuous and disturbing that unless one has everything handy, like an addressed envelope a pencil and a moment to spare one cannot write letters. One's envelopes get stuck and useless with the damp and you cannot replace them. I managed to jot down some ideas for poems now and then but I wont send them to you because they are actual transcripts of the battlefield and you wont like that, anyway just now. I do hope you have exaggerated your feelings and are not so low in spirits as your letter makes out. We manage to keep cheerful out here in the face of most horrible things but then, we are kept busy, and have no time to brood. I hope your wife is well. My sister and my mother wish you well.

Yours sincerely
Isaac Rosenberg

I am sending you a good photo of myself in a day or two.[1]

[*Postmarked July 30, 1917*]   [*Address given below*]

My Dear Marsh

I'm glad you've got your old job again and are Winston Churchill's private sec. once more, though it will be a pity if it will interfere with your literary projects. I thought that would happen when I heard he'd become Minister of Munitions. I can imagine how busy you will be kept and if

[1] Possibly the photograph reproduced facing p. 128 of *Isaac Rosenberg: The Half-used Life* by Jean Liddiard (Gollancz: 1975).

J. R. July
France 1917

you still mean to go on with your memoir and G.P.[1]; you perhaps can imagine me, though of course my work pretty much leaves my brain alone especially as I have a decent job now and am not as rushed and worked as I was in the trenches. I will be glad to be included in the Georgian Book, and hope your other work won't interfere with it. I've asked my sister (she recognises your helplessness about me, but I hope you were not too annoyed at her persistence; although I was; when I heard of it) not to send the Amulet because I've changed the idea completely and I think if I can work it out on the new lines it will be most clear and most extraordinary. Its called 'The Unicorn' now. I am stuck in the most difficult part; I have to feel a set of unusual emotions which I simply can't feel yet. However if I keep on thinking about it it may come. We may not begin a letter with our address but work it in the text; I generally forget about it as I go on writing.

Pte I.R. 22311
11th K.O.R.L.
Attached 229 Field Coy R.E.s.
B.E.F.

I think with you that poetry should be definite thought and clear expression, however subtle; I don't think there should be any vagueness at all; but a sense of something hidden and felt to be there; Now when my things fail to be clear I am sure it is because of the luckless choice of a word or the failure to introduce a word that would flash my idea plain, as it is to my own mind. I believe my Amazon poem[2] to be my best poem. If there is any difficulty it must be in words here and there[,] the changing or elimination of which may make the poem clear. It has taken me about a year to write; for I have changed and rechanged it and thought hard over that poem and striven to get that sense of inexorableness the human (or inhuman) side of this war has. It even penetrates behind human life for the 'Amazon' who speaks in the second part of the poem is imagined to be without her lover yet, while all her sisters have theirs, the released spirits of the slain earth men; her lover yet remains to be released. I hope however to be home on leave, and talk it over, some time this side of the year. In my next letter I will try and send an idea of 'The Unicorn'.

If you are too busy don't bother about answering;

Yours sincerely
Isaac Rosenberg

To Gordon Bottomley [postmarked August 3, 1917]

I don't think I'll get my play complete for it in time, though it will hardly take much space, it's so slight. If I could get home on leave I'd

[1] Georgian Poetry.
[2] 'Daughters of War', see p. 112.

work at it and get it done, no doubt, but leaves are so chancy. It's called 'The Unicorn'. Now, it's about a decaying race who have never seen a woman; animals take the place of women, but they yearn for continuity. The chief's Unicorn breaks away and he goes in chase. The Unicorn is found by boys outside a city and brought in, and breaks away again. Saul, who has seen the Unicorn on his way to the city for the week's victuals, gives chase in his cart. A storm comes on, the mules break down, and by the lightning he sees the Unicorn race by; a naked black like an apparition rises up and easily lifts the wheels from the rut, and together they ride to Saul's hut. There Lilith is in great consternation, having seen the Unicorn and knowing the legend of this race of men. The emotions of the black (the Chief) are the really difficult part of my story. Afterwards a host of blacks on horses, like centaurs and buffaloes, come rushing up, the Unicorn in front. On every horse is clasped a woman. Lilith faints, Saul stabs himself, the Chief places Lilith on the Unicorn, and they all race away.

[*Received August 11, 1917*]   [*No address*]

DEAR FATHER

Ray[1] wrote me card of the air raid, also your letter. Your miracle amused me very much and the story of the honey delighted me. I hope to be home before the new year but leaves are going very slowly in our division. So its no use building on it. Mrs. Herbert Cohen sent me a little book compiled by the Chief Rabbi of Jewish interest. There are good bits from the Talmud and from some old writers. A very little bit by Heine, nothing by Disraeli and a lot by Mr. Hertz and a few more rash people; I admire their daring, if not their judgement. Mrs. Cohen has paid all the expenses and a fuller anthology is coming out shortly; I hope some restraint and caution will be used this time. I think you will find Heine's poems among my books, there is a beautiful poem called 'Princess Sabbath' among them, where the Jew who is a dog all the week, Sabbath night when the candles are lit, is transformed into a gorgeous prince to meet his bride the Sabbath.

I mention this because there is a feeble imitation of this in the anthology. If I am lucky and get home this side of the year you might keep Dave's breeches for me.

Love to all
ISAAC

[*1917. ?August*]   [*Address given below*]

MY DEAR MARSH

Is the poem clearer now? I felt the opening was the weak part and have struggled hard with it.

[1] Rosenberg's youngest sister, Rachel (1894-1976), the fourth of his parents' six children, who later became Mrs Lyons.

261

I am sure once you get hold of it you will find it my best poem and most complete, most epic. I haven't had the chance to work on 'The Unicorn' but will send you the central idea soon.

G. Bottomley wrote me Mr Abercrombie is a shell inspector now at Liverpool, but is living in Arabia between whiles, but says nothing of Parnas[s]us. I shall have to find another daughter of war who elopes with his soul and the background will be a munition factory. Doubtless my usual obscurity will be serviceable this time, and save me from the wrath of a jealous wife.

Pte I R, 22311. 11th K.O.R.L.
attached 229 Field Coy. R.Es. B.E.F.

I hope your job keeps you fit.

Yours sincerely
ISAAC ROSENBERG

[*Between 16 and 26 September 1917*]   87 Dempsey St
                                                        Stepney E
DEAR MR SCHIFF

I am home on leave for 10 days. I called at your place but as you are away, I write this. I trust you're fit and having a good time also Mrs Schiff. I'll write a longer letter shortly.

Yours sincerely
ISAAC ROSENBERG

To Gordon Bottomley, [on leave, September 21, 1917]

The greatest thing of my leave after seeing my mother was your letter which has just arrived . . . I wish I could have seen you, but now I must go on and hope that things will turn out well, and some happy day will give me the chance of meeting you . . . I am afraid I can do no writing or reading; I feel so restless here and un-anchored. We have lived in such an elemental way so long, things here don't look quite right to me somehow; or it may be the consciousness of my so limited time here for freedom—so little time to do so many things bewilders me. 'The Unicorn', as will be obvious, is just a basis; its final form will be very different, I hope.

[*September 26, 1917*]   [*No address*]

DEAR MR TREVELYAN

I rec your play and Annual. Thank you very much. The play is gorgeous, one of the chiefest pleasures of my leave days; and for this I thank you indeed. The ideas are exactly what we all think out there—

and the court martial of the Kaiser and kings etc might have been copied from one of ours. The fun and the seriousness is splendidly managed together and I only wish the thing had the power of its purpose—I suppose it will be in the end through such literature that we will get satisfaction in the end—just as the French Revolution was the culmination of Revolutionary literature. I have not had the chance of looking at the Annual yet but will do so before I go back.

Yours sincerely
ISAAC ROSENBERG

[*1917, ?October*] 22311
A Coy 3 Platoon 11th K.O.R.L.
B.E.F.

DEAR FATHER

I am glad you are satisfied with my Yomtov[2] energy. I had a letter from Minnie[3] which I've answered. I suppose you will be home for the winter now. I am short of stationery so can't write much, but everything is contained in 'I'm fit'. Will write home as soon as I get stationery.

ISAAC

18th Oct. [*1917*] 22311 Pte I Rosenberg
11th K.O.R.L. Att 229 Field Coy R.E.
Lines B.6. 51 General Hospital
B.E.F. France

DEAR MR TREVELYAN

My sister sent your letter on to me here. I liked your letter and very much your little boy's verses. 'And the wind blows so violent' takes me most; I hope he will always go direct to nature like that and not get too mixed up with artifice when he has more to say about nature. I brought your play back with me but I'm afraid its lost now. I lent it to a friend in the Batt but that day I fell sick and was sent down here to hospital[.] My sister is sending on Lucretius and I have time now to read so I will write you how it strikes me. Your play was all I read at home—I read it in bed—the rest of my time I spent very restlessly—going from one place to another and seeing and talking to as many people as I could. G. Bottomley sent me nearly all the poems in the annual before so I knew

---

[1] *Yomtov*, yiddish for 'holiday'
[2] R's eldest sister, Minnie Horvitch

them. 'Atlantis' is an immense poem—and as good as anything else he has done. I saw friends of J.R. while on leave, and I don't know whether he's having a worse time than us; I hardly think so—Anyway, we're all waiting[.]

Yours sincerely
ISAAC ROSENBERG

[*1917, ?November*] [*Address as given below*]

DEAR MOTHER

Rec Parcel—everything in it champion—but really there is no need to send butter, eggs or Borsht, just now, at any rate. I suppose we get our food much easier than you—and in this village we get any amount of extra. I have not heard from Samuels so don't know whether he is Colonel of the Batt. I applied for a transfer about a month ago but I fancy it fell through. I shall apply again. Neither Mrs. Cohen or Löwy have written to me though I have written. You can let them have my new address if you care to. Did you come across any notices of my thing in the Georgian Book? I don't know who the Sergeant was Annie saw— several are on leave now—they mostly live in the North of England though. I hope our Russian cousins are happy now. Trotsky, I imagine will look after the interests of his co religionists—Russia is like an amputated limb to our cause and America is the cork substitute: I doubt whether she is more. 8 Platoon B Coy 1st Batt. K.O.R.L. B.E.F.[.] I hope you manage to get things all right and comfortably. We hear such rotten tales about home. Love to all

ISAAC

To Miss Seaton [*written in Hospital, Autumn 1917*]

I was very glad to have your letter and know there is no longer a mix-up about letters and suchlike. Always the best thing to do is to answer at once, that is the likeliest way of catching one, for we shift about so quickly; how long I will stay here I cannot say: it may be a while or just a bit. I have some Shakespeare: the Comedies and also 'Macbeth'. Now I see your argument and cannot deny my treatment of your criticisms, but have you ever asked yourself why I always am rude to your criticisms? Now, I intended to show you ———'s letters[1] and why I value his criticisms. I think anybody can pick holes and find unsound parts in any work of art; anyone can say Christ's creed is a slave's creed, the Mosaic is a vindictive, savage creed, and so on. It is the unique and superior, the illuminating qualities one wants to find—

---

[1] Probably Gordon Bottomley's, but possibly R. C. Trevelyan's.

discover the direction of the impulse. Whatever anybody thinks of a poet he will always know himself: he knows that the most marvellously expressed idea is still nothing; and it is stupid to think that praise can do him harm. I know sometimes one cannot exactly define one's feelings nor explain reasons for liking and disliking; but there is then the right of a suspicion that the thing has not been properly understood or one is prejudiced. It is much my fault if I am not understood, I know; but I also feel a kind of injustice if my idea is not grasped and is ignored, and only petty cavilling at form, which I had known all along was so, is continually knocked into me. I feel quite sure that form is only a question of time. I am afraid I am more rude than ever, but I have exaggerated here the difference between your criticisms and ———'s. Ideas of poetry can be very different too. Tennyson thought Burns' love-songs important, but the 'Cottar's S.N.' poor. Wordsworth thought the opposite.

[*Late 1917*]   22311 Pte I Rosenberg 11th K.O.R.L. Att 229 Field Coy R E Lines B.6. 51 General Hospital B.E.F. France

DEAR MR TREVELYAN

Your Lucretius arrived in all its beauty of type and cover. It is a noble poem and I wish it were printed in a more compressed form so that one could have it in the pocket and read it more. It does not sound like a translation the words seem so natural to the thought. Hamlet's enquiring nature so mixed with theology, superstition, penetration, may be more human and general—But Lucretius as a mood, definite, is fine, proud philosophy. I can say no more than I got deep pleasure from it and thank you very much. I'm reading some Shakespeare—Sturge Moore, G. Bottomley[,] H. G. Wells—Sturge Moore delights me[1]—they are only small things I mean as number of words go,—but he is after my own heart. You know what I think of G.B. And that old hawker of immortality how glad one feels, he is not a witness of these terrible times—he would only have been flung into this terrible distruction, like the rest of us. Anyway we all hope it'll all end well.

Yours sincerely
ISAAC ROSENBERG

To Miss Seaton [written in Hospital, November 15, 1917]

London may not be the place for poetry to keep healthy in, but Shakespeare did most of his work there, and Donne, Keats, Milton, Blake—I think nearly all our big poets. But, after all, that is a matter of personal likings or otherwise. Most of the French country I have seen has

---

[1] T. Sturge Moore (1870-1944) poet and wood-engraver. His classically orientated verses appeared in numerous anthologies of the twenties and thirties.

been devastated by war, torn up—even the woods look ghastly with their shell-shattered trees; our only recollections of warm and comfortable feelings are the rare times amongst human villages, which happened about twice in a year; but who can tell what one will like or do after the war? If the twentieth century is so awful, tell me what period you believe most enviable. Even Pater points out the Renaissance was not an outburst—it was no simultaneous marked impulse of minds living in a certain period of time—but scattered and isolated.

[*To the same, November-December 1917*]

Many thanks for book and chocolate. Both are being devoured with equal pleasure. I can't get quite the delight in Whitman as from one poem of his I know—'Captain, my Captain'. I admire the vigour and independence of his mind, but his diction is so diffused. Emerson and not Whitman is America's poet. You will persist in refusing to see my side of our little debate on criticism. Everybody has agreed with you about the faults, and the reason is obvious; the faults are so glaring that nobody can fail to see them. But how many have seen the beauties? And it is here more than the other that the true critic shows himself. And I absolutely disagree that it is blindness or carelessness; it is the brain succumbing to the herculean attempt to enrich the world of ideas.

[*8th Dec. 1917*]

22311 Pte. I. Rosenberg
11th. K.O.R.L.
LINES B.6.
51, General Hospital
B.E.F. France.

DEAR LEFTWICH,[1]
I am in hosp and have been here for about 2 months—lucky for me— I fancy—as I got out of this late stunt by being here. My brother Dave in the Tanks got a bullet in his leg and is also in hosp—also my wilder brother in the S.A.H.A.[2] is in hosp. And now your letter has been buffeted into hosp, and that it has reached me must be looked upon as one of the miracles of this war. I know Isaacs,[3] who I like—but his poetry

[1] Joseph Leftwich, poet, biographer, translator and gifted writer in many other fields both English and Yiddish, was born in 1892 of Polish Jewish parents. He was thus 2 years younger than R, whom he met in Whitechapel in 1911. Subsequently, with Rodker and Winsten, he invited R to join their 'group'. Like the others, Leftwich quickly appreciated R's unusual gifts, and over a long life has consistently sought to advance appreciation of R's work. (See also under *Acknowledgments* and *Introduction*.)

[2] Elkon Rosenberg, R's youngest brother, who had enlisted in the South African Horse Artillery.

[3] Jacob ('Jack') Isaacs (1896-1973), scholar and critic, met R at the Café Royal when the latter was on leave in September 1917. He was to become Professor of English Language and Literature at Queen Mary College, University of London, 1952-64. He gave the opening address when the 1959 Rosenberg Exhibition at Leeds University was transferred to the Slade School, London.

didn't appear to me much good—but then, when he showed it to me I was on leave and poetry was quite out of my line then and possibly the poetry in them may have been too delicate and subtle for me to discover at the time. We never spoke about Whitman—'Drum Taps' stands unique as War Poetry in my mind.

I have written a few war poems but when I think of 'Drum Taps' mine are absurd. However I would get a pamphlet printed if I were sure of selling about 60 at 1s each—as I think mine may give some new aspects to people at home—and then one never knows whether you'll get a tap on the head or not: and if that happens—all you have written is lost, unless you have secured them by printing. Do you know when the Georgian B. will be out? I am only having about half a page in it—and its only an extract from a poem—I don't think anybody will be much the wiser. Whats the idea of my joining your J affair,[1] its no use to me out here, is it? Besides after the war, if things go well—I doubt whether I'd live in London. But you can put me down if you like.

I. ROSENBERG

[*Postmarked January 26, 1918*]   *My address is on the other side*

MY DEAR MARSH

I have been in topsy turveydom since I last saw you and have not been able to write. Even now it is in the extremest difficulties that I'm writing this. I wanted to talk about the Georgian Book[2] which I had sent over to me but have not had time to more than glance through. I liked J. C. Squire's poem about the 'House' enormously and all his other poems. Turner's[3] are very beautiful and Sassoon has power. Masefield seemed rather commonplace, but please don't take my jud[ge]ment at anything because I have hardly looked at them. I am back in the trenches which are terrible now. We spend most of our time pulling each other out of the mud. I am not fit at all now and am more in the way than any use. You see I appear in excellent health and a doctor will make no distinction between health and strength. I am not strong. What has happened to your Life of Rupert Brooke. Is it out yet. I suppose you are kept very busy.

Yours sincerely

I ROSENBERG

Address Pte I Rosenberg 22311
    4 Platoon A Coy
    11th K.O.R.L.
    B.E.F.

[1] This was the Jewish Association of Arts and Sciences, which Leftwich had invited R to join.

[2] *Georgian Poetry 1916-17*. Three poems by J. C. Squire were included in the third G.P., all taken from *The Lily of Malud*.

[3] W. J. Turner (1889-1945), poet, playwright and music critic.

To Miss Seaton [dated February 14, 1918]

We had a rough time in the trenches with the mud, but now we're out for a bit of a rest, and I will try and write longer letters. You must know by now what a rest behind the line means. I can call the evenings—that is, from tea to lights out—my own; but there is no chance whatever for seclusion or any hope of writing poetry now. Sometimes I give way and am appalled at the devastation this life seems to have made in my nature. It seems to have blunted me. I seem to be powerless to compel my will to any direction, and all I do is without energy and interest.

[? *February 23, 1918*]   22311 Pte I R
8 Platoon, B Coy. 1st K.O.R.L.
B.E.F.

Dear Rodker

I did not know you were a fixture or I'd have written direct to the Settlement. I don't see the papers so your news is *news*. However we're expecting to go up the line soon, after some weeks rest. I'd like to read Elliott's[1] work but I hardly get a chance to read letters sent to me. If we get any time there is no seclusion and always interruptions. I am very glad you can read and if you write to my sister for Hueffer's book I daresay she'll find it for you. I'll mention it in my next letter also. Address Miss A. Rosenberg 87 Dempsey St Stepney. E.
Mine is 22311 Pte I R 8 Platoon, B Coy. 1st K.O.R.L. B.E.F.

I suppose I could write a bit if I tried to work at a letter as an idea—but sitting down to it here after a day's dull stupefying labour —I feel stupefied. When will we go on with the things that endure?

Yours sincerely
Isaac Rosenberg

To Gordon Bottomley [postmarked February 26, 1918]

I wanted to send some bits I wrote for the 'Unicorn' while I was in hospital, and if I find them I'll enclose them. I tried to work on your suggestion and divided it into four acts, but since I left the hospital all the poetry has gone quite out of me. I seem even to forget words, and I believe if I met anybody with ideas I'd be dumb. No drug could be more stupefying than our work (to me anyway), and this goes on like that old torture of water trickling, drop by drop unendingly, on one's helplessness.

[1] The reference is presumably to T. S. Eliot, whom Rodker would have been very likely to recommend to R. *Prufrock*, Eliot's first volume, was published in 1917.

DEAR RODKER

I could not answer your last letter as immediately as I wished because of a lot of unexpected things. Things happen so suddenly here that really nothing is unexpected—but what I mean is quite a lot of changes came on top of each other and interfered with my good epistolary intentions. I hope you still keep the same good spirits of your last letter and that the work is not beyond your strength. My work is but somehow we blunder through. From hospital I went back to the line and we had a rough time with the mud. Balzac could give you the huge and terrible sensations of sinking in the mud. I was in the trenches a month when our Batt broke up and I am now in another Batt of our regiment. When you write again write to

> Pte I Rosenberg 22311
> 8 Platoon. B. Coy
> 1st Batt K.O.R.L.
> B.E.F.

Just now we're out for a rest and I hope the warmer weather sets in when we go up the line again. It is quite impossible to write or think of writing stuff now, so I can only hope for hospital or the end of the war if I want to write. In hospital I saw the Georgian Book. Turner is pretty good—but somehow I seem to have lost all sense of discrimination and everything seems good. My own is so fragmentary that I think it were better left out. I hear it is selling well. You have got an article on Trevelyan, I hear. He sent me his Comedy which I liked very much. I know little of his other work.

Yours sincerely
ISAAC ROSENBERG

To Gordon Bottomley [*dated March 7, 1918*]

I believe our interlude is nearly over, and we may go up the line any moment now, so I answer your letter straightaway. If only this war were over our eyes would not be on death so much: it seems to underlie even our underthoughts. Yet when I have been so near to it as anybody could be, the idea has never crossed my mind, certainly not so much as when some lying doctor told me I had consumption. I like to think of myself as a poet; so what you say, though I know it to be extravagant, gives me immense pleasure.

To Miss Seaton [*March 8, 1918*]

I do not feel that I have much to say, but I do know that unless I write now it will be a long time before you hear from me again, without something exceptional happens. It is not very cold now, but I dread the wet weather, which is keeping off while we are out, and, I fear, saving itself up for us. We will become like mummies—look warm and lifelike, but a touch and we crumble to pieces. Did I send you a little poem, 'The Burning of the Temple'? I thought it was poor, or rather, difficult in expression, but G. Bottomley thinks it fine. Was it clear to you? If I am lucky, and come off undamaged, I mean to put all my innermost experiences into the 'Unicorn'. I want it to symbolize the war and all the devastating forces let loose by an ambitious and unscrupulous will. Last summer I wrote pieces for it and had the whole of it planned out, but since then I've had no chance of working on it and it may have gone quite out of my mind.

[*March 1918*]   [*Address given below*]

DEAR DAVE

We've been very busy lately and I've not been able to answer your letters. I'm now back in reserves and know that even this poor scrawl will be better than nothing and you will understand it as but the vanguard of a host. I wanted to write a battle song for the Judaens but so far I can think of nothing noble and weighty enough. I wrote a slight poem which I will send in next letter.

My address now is[1]

> Pte I R 22311
> 6 Platoon B Coy
> 1st K.O.R.L. B.E.F.

I do hope you get your leave for Pasach[2] and the Stepney business will be over by then.

[1] The letter clearly says 6 Platoon, as does the final letter to Marsh (p. 272), but this was almost certainly a misunderstanding on R's part (see the next letter and his previous letters to Rodker.)

[2] The Passover festival.

Best love
ISAAC

[*March 1918*]   [*Address given below*]

DEAR DAVE

I had a letter from you yesterday but lost it before I could properly read it. So can't reply to the actual wording. Have you my new address

> Pte I R 22311
> 8 Platoon B. Coy. 1st K.O.R.L. B.E.F.

I had the Georgian Book sent out to me but was obliged to return it when I went up the line—it was so bulky. I could have sent it on to you but I never thought of it. Perhaps you may find one of your lot has it.

There is some good stuff in it but very little. Gordon Bottomley stands head and shoulders above the rest.

I'm not saying this because he wrote me there were few pages in the book as beautiful as mine. His 'Atlantis' in this Georgian Book is one of the most beautiful of modern poems. There is a rotten poem by Herbert Asquith[1] and some paltry stuff by very good poets. Masefield is far from his best. 18 writers are included altogether. J.A. is having a lark I see.

Best love
ISAAC

[Postmarked March 7, 1918]   *[Address given below]*

MY DEAR MARSH

I see my sister has been on the warpath again, and after your scalp in her sisterly regard for me. They know my lackadaisical ways at home and have their own methods of forcing me to act. I have now put in for a transfer to the Jewish Batt—which I think is in Mesopotamia now. I think I should be climatized to the heat after my S. African experience. I'll let you know if I get it. I am now in

8 Platoon, B Coy
1st. K.O.R.L. B.E.F.

as our old Batt broke up.

I saw the G.B.[2] It does not match the first G.B. nor indeed any of the others in my mind. But I put that down to the War of course. Turner is very poetic. Masefield sentimentalizes in too Elizabethan a fashion. There is a vivid poem about Christ in the Tower I remember I liked very much.[3] And of course G.B.'s 'Atlantis' stands out. I saw the book about 3 months ago and not for long. I was going into the trenches then. What have you done with your 'Life of R.B.'[4] is it complete yet[?]

I'm sending this letter to Ministry of Mun. because I sent a letter a month or so ago to Raymond Buildings and got no answer. If you are very busy do try and drop just a line so that I know you've rec my letter.

Yours sincerely
I ROSENBERG

[1] *The Volunteer.* Very far from being a 'rotten' poem, but one can understand R's dislike of what he mistakenly took to be Asquith's 'class' approach to war.

[2] The third volume of *Georgian Poetry*.

[3] 'The Tower' by Robert Nichols. See *Georgian Poetry 1916-17*, p. 71.

[4] Marsh's projected life of Rupert Brooke.

My Dear Marsh

I think I wrote you I was about to go up the line again after our little rest. We are now in the trenches again and though I feel very sleepy, I just have a chance to answer your letter so I will while I may. Its really my being lucky enough to bag an inch of candle that incites me to this pitch of punctual epistolary. I must measure my letter by the light. First, this is my address

> 22311 Pte I R.
> 6 Platoon B Coy 1st K.O.R.L.
> B.E.F.

We are very busy just now and poetry is right out of our scheme. I wrote one or two things in hospital about Xmas time but I don't remember whether I sent them to you or not. I'll send one, anyhow.

During our little interlude of rest from the line I managed to do a bit of sketching—somebody had colours—and they weren't so bad, I don't think I have forgotten my art after all. I've heard nothing further about the J.B.[1] and of course feel annoyed—more because no reasons have been given me—but when we leave the trenches, I'll enquire further. I don't remember reading Freeman.[2] I wanted to write a battle song for the Judaens but can think of nothing strong and wonderful enough yet. Here's just a slight thing.[3]

I've seen no poetry for ages now so you mustn't be too critical—My vocabulary small enough before is impoverished and bare.

> Yours sincerely
> I Rosenberg

[1] The Jewish Battalion.

[2] John Freeman, a minor Georgian poet whose work featured prominently in Marsh's anthologies from the 3rd volume on.

[3] ' Through these Pale Cold Days', the last poem Rosenberg wrote. He was killed in action the day before this letter got posted.

In 1967 Professor Robert H. Ross of Washington State University put forward in *The Georgian Revolt*, p. 173, the theory that the poem which R enclosed in the above letter was 'Returning, We Hear the Larks'. This he stated was "according to the evidence" of an undated letter to Marsh that Ross saw in the Berg Collection in 1955, which was not included in CW. From the quotations he gave from it, the letter is the one printed on p. 250, which indeed was not included in CW. But since the letter was certainly written in 1916 ("I have not been out here six months for nothing") it is hard to see what relevance it can have to a poem that R sent Marsh on 28 March 1918. Moreover, there is clear proof that 'Returning, We Hear the Larks' was written long before that, for R sent a TS copy of it to John Rodker in summer 1917.

15. (a) The First Meeting of Adam and Eve. Chalk. 1915 $9\frac{3}{4}''\times10\frac{7}{8}''$

15. (b) Head of a Woman.
Black Chalk. c. 1912 $8\frac{1}{8}''\times7\frac{7}{8}''$

16. Self-Portrait in a Steel Helmet. Black Chalk and gouache on brown wrapping paper. Probably 1916 $9\frac{1}{2}'' \times 7\frac{3}{4}''$

PROSE
AND FRAGMENTS OF PROSE

ON A DOOR KNOCKER[1]

[February 1911]

This is essentially an age of romance. We no longer dream but we live the dream. Romance is no more a dim world outside the ordinary world, whose inhabitants are only poets and lovers, but wide, tangible and universal. Poets no longer hold exclusive monopoly of the clouds, but whosoever pleases (except the poet generally) can soar aloft on the wings of an aeroplane beyond the reach and ken of man. No longer is it the poet who brags of the rushing chariot of the whirlwind, for he alone is unable to afford a motor. In fact, the positions are reversed. The philistine has become the romanticist, and the poet the philistine; and he actually presumes to deny the purity of their romanticism on the grounds that achieving the ideal destroys the ideal, and the charm of existence is the illusion of it. Wherever we turn we see the unmistakable atmosphere of romance and strangeness, of a delightful incongruity, that might be a Japanese fantasy. The ragged newsboy bartering news and information to the gentleman in the high hat. The gentleman in the high hat benevolently making a picture of himself for us to enjoy the spectacle; and see, this charming young lady decked out as a draper's front window, as if this were some merry carnival. In this age of romance we are bent so profoundly on romancing ourselves that we have little time to notice the romances of others. We read novels, true; but they are Hardy, Zola, Turgenev; dreadfully realistic, so as to get more zest from the romance of life, by contrast with this ugly realism. Few ever dream of considering— say—the romance of a door knocker. Its romantic pre-existence—its long subterraneous sojourn in purgatorial mines; its awakening to light, and the kingdom of man; the gradual stages of its development, make of it an object supremely romantic. We will take the knocker as it is, and study it in its aspect and relation to modern conditions; it must be worth while, having had such romantic development. We will see how the manners and customs, the tendencies of the age are reflected in the knocker.

A door knocker is the symbol of an unfinished civilization and an aloof and unassertive aristocracy. Its imperiousness is unquestioning, its meek acquiescence to convention a record of the sham of custom. It is the signpost of politeness and the negative to precipitate familiarity. It is a proof of the decay of religion, for it shows our want of faith in man, and consequently of the God in man. What forces are set in motion by it? In our family alone (there are no servants) its summons is generally the signal whereby the entire faculties of the junior members are exerted in

---

[1] There are two typescripts of this piece. T1, which CW followed, has only a few minor typographical corrections by R. T2, on the other hand, has a number of emendations to the concluding sentences, some of which are not wholly clear, and about which R wrote in pencil at the foot of the page: 'Please forgive my treatment of last paragraph. It wants retyping to make quite clear.' I hope that the three words which I have inserted (in square brackets) make R's revised intentions plain.

tremendous efforts to ignore and despise its imperiousness. Ah! what a type then of power desolate! of man beating at the doors of knowledge and clamouring vainly at the gates of the unseen. And in repose, what a sense of infinite patience and a world of energy lying dormant—useless, like genius when the circumstances to bring it into light are wanting. It is kissed by the sun and rain, by day and by night, and endures the frost and thunder with supreme immovable dignity.

The comparative insignificance of the knocker lies in the fact of its functions being so startlingly obtrusive that the cause itself is obscured; an important contrast to the chimney pot in this. The chimney pot glares at you—fixes you. It is the last stage, the final result of a series of causes that only minister to its service; whereas the knocker is the beginning—the cause of a certain result. It is the touchstone of character. How timidly the timid use it? How impetuously the impetuous? How gently the gentle-hearted? Before the knocker all self-consciousness is abandoned and the natural and spontaneous is brought into play. It is a type of prostitution, for it is sold to all men; of helplessness, for it lies where all can wreak their will on it; of power, for it sets great forces in motion; of aristocracy, for it is lordly and imperious; of democracy, for it makes no distinction between low and high; of wealth, for like gold, it is the means of opening doors at its magic touch. It is the link of fraternity whereby so many of divergent aims and minds touch hands. Sometimes knockers are peculiarly identified with the families of the houses to which they are attached, and the fate and fortune of the knocker is the fate and fortune of the family. In one family I know, whose reverses and ill fortune were something miraculous, the knocker invariably found its way behind the door, and the only disposition it ever showed to knock when it was in its place was to fall and knock the head off of a millionaire relation, who had just discovered them, and they were obliged to pay for his funeral. In another, the knocker was the cause of suicide. A friend of mine of aesthetic tastes, visiting his affianced, took prejudice to the knocker, because of its exceedingly ugly shape, and so fastidious was he that he would not knock; but finding the door open, and being of that passionate precipitate nature that despises convention, rushed in, and conceive his horror when he beheld his beloved in the embrace of a man (it happened to be her long lost brother just returned), and, infuriated, he dashed out and went straight to the river (not even stopping to pick up his hat), and there ended his sorrows . . .

A knocker is so enchantingly romantic and real; so human in its pathetic helplessness; so divine in its terrible significance of power, that we might sum up in it the epitome of humanity. Man, with his vast power over destiny, yet controlled by destiny. Man, with death in his hands yet in the hands of death. Power that is powerless. Sleeping mechanism that is ready to leap and crash at a touch.

Thus far we have seen the knocker as a symbol of general tendencies and vitalities of the present, and an important factor in the lives and destinies of individuals. Let us see in it a prophetic far-reaching symbol of the religion of the future. The only serious drawback is its variety of type; but this of course, would depend on the aesthetic leanings and fashions of the future generation. When we consider that the symbol of the Christian religion was erstwhile a sign of degradation, a gallows; how idealism has converted this type of human degradation into a symbol of divine beatific sanctity, does it need a great wrench of credulity to believe that a door knocker, which has so tremendous a significance, and is so much more infinitely romantic in form, might take its place and stand for the new religion. When culture has completed its emancipation from barbarism, [and] Christianity with its limitations, its self-sacrifice, its strange mendicant idealisation of poverty, its crown and banner of austere primitive barbarism the cross [has become] a thing that has been; and a religion, generous, large in its conception of humanity, refined yet homely, usurp the vacated throne; the door knocker its sceptre.

RUDOLPH

[April 1911]

Poor Rudolph! He was an artist and a dreamer—that is, one whose delight in the beauty of life was an effective obstacle to the achievement of the joy of living; whose desire to refine and elevate mankind seemed to breed in mankind a reciprocal desire to elevate him to a higher and still higher—garret. Though a nearer view of heaven and though a poet, he would have preferred a less lofty dwelling place to preserve, what he facetiously termed his ancestor's remains, from the chill November weather—but so it was. In this garret, in the dim waning light God could see day by day the titanic wrestlings of genius against the exigencies of circumstances, the throbbings of a sensitive organism, touched to emotion at the subtlest changes on the face of nature; the keen delight simply in endeavour, the worship and awe of genius before the altar of genius. But day after day of unrequited endeavour, of struggle and privation, brought depression, and in the heaviness of his spirit the futility of existence was made manifest to him. Often inspiration was dead within, and all his aspirations and ideals seemed to mock at his hollow yearning. In his social and spiritual isolation, in his utter desolation he felt as if he was God's castaway, out of harmony with the universe, a blot upon the scheme of humanity. Life appeared so chaotic, so haphazard, so apathetic—O! it was miserable. He—a spark struck from God's anvil, he—who could clasp the Heavens with his spirit—to whom Beauty had revealed herself in all her radiance—and to what end? What purpose was there in such wasted striving—and supposing success did come would it be sufficient recompense for the wasted life and youth, the starved years—the hopelessness of the barren Now?

In one of these moods he strayed to the National Gallery. It was Students' Day, and he wandered round without being able to concentrate himself on his old loves and longings, till at length he sat down on a seat brooding and revolving 'the fragments of the broken years .... He was awakened from his reverie by hearing a feminine voice saying 'O! please don't rise, oblige me.' He looked up and saw a lady at an easel gazing intently at him and painting.

'I am painting the interior and you just happen to fit in well, I won't be many minutes,' she called out to him.

'O! certainly,' murmured Rudolph, 'as long as you like.' She was a pleasant faced lady of about thirty five, rosy and buoyant, and he wondered what her work would be like. He thought what a strange thing Art was, life was. Around were the masters, to whom Art was life, and life meant Art. Here were the dilettanti to whom Art was a necessity as an alternative to the boredom of doing nothing; an important item in the ingredients that go to make up culture.

She was soon finished and asked Rudolph to see it, which he accordingly did, and was and expressed himself greatly struck by the result.

'Dutch in idea and influence and yet exceedingly modern' he told her.

She assented, and then in a tone of defiant confession 'Do you know I thank Van Eyck the greatest artist that ever lived. I adore him because he makes the commonplace so delightfully precious.'

'I think a picture should be something more' protested Rudolph. 'Van Eyck is interesting to me just as a pool reflecting the clouds is interesting, or a landscape seen through a mirror. But it is only a faithful transcript of what we see. My ideal of a picture is to paint what we cannot see. To create, to imagine. To make tangible and real a figment of the brain. To transport the spectator into other worlds where beauty is the only reality. Rossetti is my ideal.'

She smiled, amused at his enthusiasm.

'But why go out of the world for beauty when we can find beauty in it?'

'I admit an artist with imagination might make a most exquisite picture out of what may seem most uncompromising in nature. But it is his imagination, his refinement of sentiment, that only uses the object itself as a basis to give expression to his vision. Why then were we given the creative faculty? What, if not this, is the meaning of God?'

The lady laughed. 'I have a nephew who used to think like you, until he saw Degas, and now he raves over the beauty of ugliness. He said to me, "We are all idealists when we are young. We begin in the clouds and as we are slipping away from existence we come nearer to existence in thought and feeling. We are born with wings but we find our feet are safest." Perhaps you have heard of him, Leonard Harris, the poet.'

'Leonard Harris! he could never have said that,' incredulously exclaimed Rudolph, and added: 'Though the expression sounds his. Surely Heaven hasn't got too bright for him.'

'Anyway that's how he talks now. Do you know him?' she asked.

'No, but I should very much like to,' he replied eagerly.

'Well, I shall talk to him about you. Are you an artist?' she questioned. 'You certainly have the artistic spirit.'

'I am unfortunately.'

'Why unfortunately? It is a golden gift.'

277

'A golden gift; but I could not exchange it for a pair of shoe laces if I wanted to. Unless one has the golden means the gift is only one of misery.'

'You are young to be a pessimist.'

'I am not old enough to be an optimist. When I will have experienced occasion for optimism I will be one.'

She looked concerned. 'Dear dear, you are young to talk like that. I think that if one has the golden means, and everything made smooth for him, one does not try so much; that is why the geniuses are always those who have had great difficulties to contend against.'

He smiled bitterly. 'When one has to think of responsibilities, when one has to think strenuously how to manage to subsist, so much thought, so much energy is necessarily taken from creative work. It might widen experience and develop a precocious mental maturity, of thought and worldliness, it might even make one's work more poignant and intense, but I am sure the final result is loss, technical incompleteness, morbidness and the evidence of tumult and conflict.'

'Well, it may be so,' she admitted half doubtingly. 'But you must see my nephew on those matters. I will talk to him and leave you his address in case you'd care to write to him.'

'I'd write this moment. I too am a poet.'

'Yes! How nice. Well, send your poems. I myself am not very poetical in my tastes. In any case you'll hear from me, as I cannot let a sinner so young go on sinning,' she said smilingly as she bade him goodbye.

'Then I shall owe my good fortune to my wickedness. The way of the world, Madam.'

Some time after this Rudolph received a letter from Leonard Harris, to whom he had sent his poems, inviting him to dine with him the following evening. Rudolph immediately wrote back accepting the invitation, and in the elation caused by the turn fortune seemed to be taking with him, rushed off to communicate the wonderful intelligence to a friend.

'And you've accepted the invitation?' his friend asked sceptically.

Rudolph looked at him. 'Why—I never waited to finish reading the letter before I answered.'

His friend shook his head pityingly. 'You simple Simon. Do you know what a wealthy supper is? Evening dresses, immaculate shirt fronts, diamond pins, and sparkling patent boots. If you don't look as if you'd just stepped out of a fashion plate you're a pariah, you'll be trampled on, pulverised. And probably the whole family will be there. You haven't even got an ordinary dress. Why, I'd sooner think of dropping through a chimney pot than going.'

Rudolph rubbed his cheek, perplexed; this view of the case had never presented itself to him.

'Then what shall I do?' he questioned disconsolately. 'Can't you suggest something in my dire extremity? Go I must; even if it's in this,' pointing to his transparent alpaca, which had the appearance of a Turkish carpet, for he had used it as a palette once or twice by mistake.

'Good God! If you can pretend that you mistook the invitation for one to a fancy-dress ball it might work. But I'll tell you what. My landlady, who as you know is very sweet on me, possesses a husband, who possesses an evening dress, which God knows what he uses for, unless it's to hide a hole in the wall which they want no one to see; for I've lived there two years and that suit has never shifted. It's in a state of remarkable preservation except for some green paint spots on the shoulder little Madge dropped on [it] when the house was being repaired; but that wouldn't notice in the evening. She'll lend it me if I say it's for myself.'

'Dave, you've saved me. Thou art indeed a friend in need. But you must have a swell landlord.'

'He seems to have some mysterious connections with 'igh society, from what I can make out from his missis. I rarely see him.'

Next day Dave brought the prize round. He had succeeded in borrowing it without much difficulty, but with a caution from the landlady to be careful, as it was a particular favourite of her ole man's, being the one in which he had captivated and conquered his Mary Ann, it being so precious that he would not wear it but look at it only to remind him of their honey days.

The suit was laid out, and Rudolph proceeded to make his entrance into the uniform of a gentleman, into which he completely disappeared. When gradually his limbs one by one emerged from its recesses, and he had managed to extricate his head from the vacuity, he desired to know Dave's unbiased impression as to its decorative qualities. After careful examination from all points of view, Dave delivered judgment to the effect that he thought its decorative qualities immense, but that one was inclined to lose sight of the object it was intended to decorate.

'Do you really think it is slightly too big?' queried Rudolph anxiously; 'I feel somehow I am lost in it. But don't you think it will make me look bigger?'

'It might, if one could see you, but I think we can do it with pins. I expect it'll look a little creasy but it won't notice at night.'

'And these green spots, are they noticeable?'

'O! they won't notice at night.'

'And now, the shirt front. Didn't she have one?'

'Well, he couldn't keep the shirt front for two years. Possibly he might if he had foreseen this emergency. I don't know what to suggest unless we buy one. We may get one at the pawnbroker's shop. You might even exchange your alpaca for one, these stains won't notice in this light.'

Thus arrayed in swallow-tail and shirt front, enveloped by his friend's overcoat, with his portfolio under his arm, and the inevitable sombrero on his head, the transformed Rudolph set out on his way to Harris. This was just the opportunity he desired; now he would assert himself. For one night the evening dress was his, for one night would he revel in the privileges it meant. He felt transformed, transfigured; and in his sense of power he mentally pictured society as a beautiful lady, deferential and smiling, showering flowers and delights. . . . These thoughts were counteracted by a sudden inrush of natural shyness; of embarrassment; and he suddenly felt bewildered and mute in the presence of this beautiful creature. While he listened to her mellifluous voice, masculine voices seemed to respond in rich tones, and elegant forms of perfect ease made him appear to shrink—shrink but unable to escape. 'St John's Wood', he heard the conductor call, and he rushed out just in time. He soon found the house and rang. The servant after inquiring his name asked him to follow and announced him. A young man came out, shook hands and pulled him in. After the preliminaries of introduction and the inevitable weather discussion, Rudolph undid his portfolio and arranged his drawings round the room, then stood by to explain and elucidate where elucidation was necessary, which was not seldom; for he painted on the principle that the art of painting was the art of leaving out, and the pleasure in beholding a picture was the pleasure of finding out. Where he had not left out the whole picture, sometimes it was successful. After he had inculcated Harris with a sense of the sacred supremacy of his principles and proved his principles without justifying his pictures, and bewildered and mystified him into acceptance of his creed with a suspicion of its results, Harris found breath to ejaculate, 'I should say you take more trouble in defending your pictures than in painting them.' 'Yes!' flashed Rudolph. 'A religion may be the conception of a moment but it takes ages to spread. Propaganda is a necessary evil.'

At supper, Mrs Harris asked Rudolph whether his father had literary or artistic propensities. Rudolph smiled, 'The only deviation into artistic endeavour I have ever seen my father make was when he, in a frenzy of inspiration, turned and decorated my left eye most beautifully in blue and black (which decorative effect, unfortunately, I was not in a condition to appreciate, not being able to see it), and he accompanied that extraordinary feat with a fervour of exuberant flowery language. The most complete combination of poetry and painting I have ever experienced. But otherwise our genealogical tree has not many blossoms of genius. I am the first to scandalise the family with a difference. They consider it perfectly immoral to talk and think unlike them—and—well what can I do—they show their sense of superiority by being ashamed of me!'

'Perfectly atrocious,' broke in young Harris. 'But as I am rather interested in heredity I am curious to know whether you acquired your taste for art and literature after or before your father's (private or public) exhibition of his skill.'

'Oh! domestic exhibition. I had always practised it to some extent. I wanted to do a sketch of Romeo and Juliet. I got my father to pose for Romeo, and the servant girl for Juliet. When it was finished my mother came across it and of course thought I had sketched my father kissing the servant girl as I had seen it. Well, I have told you the consequences. It was a practical demonstration of his abhorrence for realism—and preference for decoration. I have altered my style since.'

'A sure proof,' gravely asserted Harris, smothering laughter, 'that the genius of the child is sprung from seed in the parent.'

Rudolph assented. 'But my father also had mature qualifications which have descended to me. I have inherited from him a remarkable genius for taciturnity and an amazing facility for forgetting things. Just now I am exercising the latter to exorcise the former.'

The plates clattered with the laughter: under its cover Miss Lily said sweetly to Rudolph 'Len says you also write.'

'I am afraid I must plead guilty.'

He almost flushed, while young Harris said 'You should see his verses, mother, he writes beautifully.'

'Which do you prefer, writing or drawing?' inquired Mrs. Harris.

'Drawing when I must write, writing when I must draw,' replied Rudolph becoming flippant.

'Then you never enjoy either, as you must do what you don't want to do: I condole with you!' sympathised Harris with mock pathos on his face.

'No need!' retorted Rudolph. 'I enjoy my disappointment and laugh at myself.'

From this glimpse of Rudolph we might surmise he was one of those superficial wits who are like bottles of soda-water just being opened, and never open their mouths but to fizzle like a chinese cracker. This apparent superficiality was the natural consequence of a super-selfconsciousness, a desire not to frustrate expectation, and a lack of sustaining inspiration to keep up with desire. Constructively and inherently he was serious, because he was an enthusiast—and because he was an enthusiast the comic in his nature would run riot once begun. Wit is the flash of the knit brows of a refined intellect, capped by the smile of achievement. Superficiality is the easy snatch at wit when the knit brows refuse to work, and in him the comic always strove to snatch: sometimes happy, sometimes not.

Brought up as he had been: socially isolated, but living in spiritual communion with the great minds of all the ages, he had developed a morbid introspection in all that related to himself, and a persistent frivolousness in relations with others; a dark book for his bedside and a gaudy one for the street. The development of temperament had bred a disassociation from the general run of the people he came in contact with, that almost rendered him inarticulate when circumstances placed him amongst those of more affinity to himself, from disuse of the ordinary faculties and facilities of conversation. Naturally these circumstances would be such where his vanity suggested he had a reputation to sustain, and he would be perpetually on the strain to say something clever. He was totally lacking in the logic of what might be called common sense, but had a whimsical sort of logic of his own which was amusing till it became too clever, and then—patience was a crime.

Now although Rudolph was in the conversational mood, and felt that in the small talk of the table he was acquitting himself well, he was not wholly at his ease. Some of the pins of his evening dress had come out and he had a feeling of general discomfort, and that they were all looking at him and eyeing his suit particularly. He was beginning to curse inwardly the artificialities of convention, the forms that bound each man to be a mechanical demonstration of its monotony, extremely aggravated at not having made more sure of the arrangement of his temporary disguise. When they adjourned for coffee he was afraid to rise lest he would disappear and only an evening dress be seen walking about. He held his chair in front of him as he manoeuvred gingerly along.

'And how do you find people take your poetry?' Harris was saying to him. Rudolph sat down. 'My poetry? well I find that the poet is to the mass so respected that they consider his creations too sacred even to look at. It would be profanation to open a book of poems. The beggar who carries a menagerie in his rags and the poet are the most respected characters we have. Veneration is carried so far that contact with them is unthought of.'

'I have not been so fortunate as you in that respect,' replied Harris. 'Since I published my poems I have been practically suffocated by the pressure of contact. I am in the throes of a—'

He was interrupted by a crash behind. He turned; the butler had dropped the tray with the coffee and was glaring at Rudolph, and his mouth was open in astonishment.

'What is it?' exclaimed Rudolph amazed. 'Surely there is no need to be terrified at so trivial an accident.'

'There is,' broke in Harris. 'It would be an accident if he did not drop it. You are always dropping things, Henry, and—'

'Er—er—I beg pardon, sir,' stammered Henry 'and turning to Rudolph, 'I . . . I . . . I . . . you . . . I don't know how to explain myself—' and he pointed to the suit, 'you are wearing my clothes,' he gasped out.

'Wha . . . what do you mean?' almost whispered Rudolph, oppressed by vague misgivings.

They all stood by, dumbfounded at the strange scene.

The butler pointed to the spots.

'You see these spots, five of 'em, heart shaped. Those very spots were done by my little niece Madge two years ago. That was the very suit I wore when

[A passage is missing here]

the crestfallen Rudolph as by degrees he made himself visible. My extraordinary choice . . . my situation rendered . . . my point of observation was somewhat confusing. I did not notice the ladies.' They were all laughing uproariously while Rudolph, having recovered his self-possession, explained the situation.

'You see, Henry', put in Harris, 'Mr. Rudolph was under the impression that he was going to a fancy-dress ball; and he borrowed the suit on account of the spots from your lodger.'

Rudolph interposed. 'I'm sorry, Henry, that your wife has suffered on my account, and I hope you feel more comfortable in your property than I do. And I can't help thinking that if you had paid more attention to your property, and not allowed those spots to find their way on, there would have been no necessity for this disturbance. Besides, your latest additions in coffee stains, although they may be very creditable to your decorative capabilities, do not show a just sense of the relative values of time and place. It positively destroys the harmony. However, Henry, I forgive you.'

It was two hours past midnight when he got out into the street and he experienced a wonderful feeling of rejuvenation. The air was tingling and pure, and he walked under the limpid heaven as under a vague, vast tree. The golden lamplights hung in narrowing perspective and shimmered and scintillated on the iridescent bluish pavement. He walked along, the shadowy trees of the park appearing to creep beside him. Some outcasts of the night slept on benches, some looked wistfully: the miserable blasted fruit of this tree of heaven. Praises rang in his ear, fragments of wit, flashes of lyric, and night played vibrations on the chord of emotion. His mind was in a whirl. His past—what a horrible waste of God's faculties—unused. If he had only been taken up and moulded; but life had been cruel to him. Now she showed signs of remorse and atonement. He was young, upon the threshold of life. Life would hold the doors for the golden stairs. Chamber after chamber of the house of delight would be thrown open to him and he would wander in the gardens of pleasure holding the hand of love. The fountains of song would make perpetual music and they would glide down the rivers of twilight in an ecstasy of repose. Glimpses of undulating robes, shimmer of pearl, gleam of dresses, creamy arms and gleaming shoulders—ah! life! was it not time?

And now the dawn broke quietly and rich upon his dream. The vast blue flower of heaven over the dark rim of quaint angular buildings changed dreamily into broken gold and green and rose. The pearly waves of shimmering twilight seemed rising like a tide to meet the dawn, into the light which stole inch by inch the kingdom that was night's.

THE PRE-RAPHAELITE EXHIBITION

[Notes for an article, Winter 1911-12]

Whether it is intentional on the Director's part or unconscious, the present exhibition of the Pre-Raphaelite Brotherhood running side by side with Alfred Stevens is a perfect antithesis and brings into projectivity the significance of the Pre-Raphaelite Brotherhood. Here we have two great activities—both reactions against a school of sickly . . . that was existent, both [of them] an indignant protest against the art around, and both a revival, a return to the principle of a form of art apparently forgotten and obsolete, and yet both utterly different. The Pre-Raphaelite Brotherhood, temperamentally disgusted with the affectations, the low sentiment, the want of spiritual fervour and sincerity which was guiding Art, saw all this in the early Italians, and taking nature as material and guide, formed themselves on the principles of . . . They were fascinated by the almost childishness, the naiveness, the genius of their outlook on nature, and the esoteric feeling, the purity and earnestness, and strove to see these qualities in nature, and interpret nature on these principles.

Alfred Stevens, also disgusted . . . not from the Pre-Raphaelite point of view, took another standpoint. He felt the lack of largeness, dignity and style in art, and he turned to the greatest stylist of all, Michael Angelo, not as a guide and index whereby to see the dignity of nature but . . .

His ideal was the simplicity of a giant, the large languor of grandly-moulded limbs, and titanic sweep of contour in design. Purity of design to him meant harmonious and sinuous arrangement, to compel nature into a preconception of balance. Thus the soul's hunger for perfection sought and found in two temperaments a realisation. The Pre-Raphaelites had the acquiescence of a body perhaps because the path was more natural; Alfred Stevens with his sense of monumental, academic design was alone.

What strong and sympathetic lovers of nature these were. How nature is enhanced and how lovingly and earnestly each exquisite blade of grass, each petal assumes a beauty, a fragrance, an importance, and is yet subsidiary to the entire effect. Often the sentiment is trivial and mean, as in many of Millais' and Hughes', but enough is compensated by the treatment, the evident delight in earnest endeavour.

In looking at Simeon Solomon's[1] work we are brought face to face with a psychological contradiction that is not uncommon in the history of art; the antagonism of the relation of art to conduct. In natures like Simeon Solomon's, who know life only through their art, beyond their art their faculties for the controlling and management of their life are undeveloped; they have poured their souls out with creation and possess none for actuality.

In 1850 three young Academy students[2] were furiously discussing art round the tea-table at the house of the youngest. One, who was evidently the dominating[3] spirit, and to whom the others were somewhat deferential considering the tense state they were in, spoke in a rich loud voice of Keats and the glowing colour of Botticelli and the passion of soul in art, of the correct soullessness of Raphael—'O, if he hadn't lived';[4] then art had continued uninterrupted—of the crying need of a return to the men before Raphael.

Before they parted for the night they had planned to work a subject

[1] Simeon Solomon (1841-1905) pre-Raphaelite painter and disciple of Rossetti, was the son of the first Jew to become a Freeman of the City of London. He acquired some notoriety through his association with Swinburne, and enjoyed some success through the latter's friends in the literary and artistic circles of London and Oxford. He died of alcoholism in St. Giles's workhouse.

[2] They were Holman Hunt, J. E. Millais and D. G. Rossetti.

[3] R actually wrote 'domineering 'but presumably meant 'dominating', as in CW.

[4] R originally wrote, in lieu of 'the correct soullessness of Raphael', 'the detestable, deplorable, excruciating impositions of Mulready, Etty'; but evidently thought better of it.

on the principles of earnestness and fundamental literalness and exactness to subject and nature. The subject chosen was from Keats, Lorenzo and Isabel.[1] Millais' drawing is here. It is incredible for his age, and disregarding age it is amazing. For psychological accuracy, consistency and continuity of thought, for variety of minute accessories and yet subordinated to the main interest, and for charm of executive quality, it is remarkable.

The cream of the collection is Rossetti's pen-and-ink drawings for Tennyson, etc. The wealth of design, the poetic exuberance of the idea, and the extraordinary dramatic and fervid execution of them, make them unique in art.

The most astonishing for technical achievement is Millais' 'Mariana at the Moated Grange'. It is Dutch in idea, in minuteness of detail and exquisiteness of finish, but it possesses a richness, a daringness, an arrangement of colour that Dutch art never attained to.

Ingenuity of imagination is the prime requisite in their design. They recognised the limitation of the grand style of design and widened the possibilities of natural design. They imagined nature, they designed nature. They were so accurate in design that the design is not felt; and yet though it defies criticism from the naturalistic side we are projected into an absolutely new atmosphere that is real in its unreality.

When I say the naturalistic I mean it in its absolute sense, in the sense that Velasquez painted and Rembrandt, in the sense [that] the post-impressionists paint. Each of these saw nature in their own way and interpreted it so. All are as truthful to nature and all as unlike each other, in so much as the artist was bent more or less on a particular effect in nature which appealed more to his temperament. Velasquez aimed for realising light as affected by atmosphere.[2] Rembrandt saw nature as one effective chiaroscuro which brought into relief the character and psychology. The post-impressionists paint nature according to the sensation a perception produced upon them, and the Pre-Raphaelites combine all these qualities.

UNCLE'S IMPRESSIONS IN THE WOODS AT NIGHT[3]

[1911-12]

The moon shed its clear effulgent beam upon a scene of sylvan beauty wrapped in its garments of night.

I smiled with glee as a gentle breeze came softly whirring round me, fanning me with its light and delicate touch, and dispelling the heat of a summer's night. The trees, my companions for years, invested with new

---

[1] See R's painting of Lorenzo's murder at Colour Plate IX.

[2] R originally wrote 'Velasquez emphasised the atmosphere, the envelope'.

[3] Not in CW. Text from R's original typescript in BL, presented by Lady Gollancz (née Ruth Löwy).

life this beautiful still night, intermingled a soothing, incessant rustling of their leaves with the slight noises which arose now and then from an awakened insect.

The trees around me stood in ghostly array, huge blotches of shadow in the night shades, but here and there inexpressibly lovely and fairylike, when a beam outlined and touched with a silvery light, a leaf, a twig, or a notch of the gnarled bark.

No daylight could make these trees look lovelier, thought I.

The golden light of the sun with its bold, artistic touch, transforming dull greens into golden magnificence, flooding with its arrogant beneficence a peaceful vale, could not compete, thought I, with the gentler splendour of his sister Moon.

The Lady of the Moon showed me a study of silver and black. Thus the night as the daytime has a peculiar atmosphere of its own. Here, everything was still: a prolonged silence, an unearthly stillness, stole over the woods. The silence was broken by an impudent insect, the watchman of the night, who curious to know why all was so still called to its sleeping companions. A little babel arose, yet sweet and appropriate to the woods. It pleased me to think that I was not alone in noting the wonders of Nature by night. Again silence fell, to be interrupted as before by the insect life which dwelt at my feet. They were innumerable, but having respect for my age, they did not often drop in upon my meditation. I like the little things though, and when they ask me to tell them events I have seen in bygone ages, they listen entranced till I cease.

Thus my thoughts ran on in the same groove as they had run on years before, and still, I looked at the Lady touching up a little pool with her wand. The inky blackness of the pool would have disguised its presence but those light touches accentuated the undulations of each ripple, revealing its presence as She revealed each tree. Thus my friends were not merged into the shadows, but with becoming dignity stood out individually and displayed their noble proportions. I ceased thinking and with the rest of the world around me slept.

ROMANCE AT THE BAILLIE GALLERIES[1]

The Works of J. H. Amschewitz[2] and the late H. Ospovat[3]

[Summer 1912]

If one were to walk into the Baillie Galleries, Bruton Street, without knowing the names of the artists, the children of whose brain we are

---

[1] The above review was published in *The Jewish Chronicle* of May 24, 1912, retitled 'At the Baillie Gallery' and with minor modifications.

[2] See footnote on p. 43.

[3] Henry Ospovat (1877-1909), illustrator and draughtsman, came of Russian Jewish parents who settled in Manchester. A student at the Royal College of Art, where he was much influenced by the Pre-Raphaelites, he went on to illustrate the works of Matthew Arnold, Browning and Shakespeare. His *Shakespeare's Sonnets* and *Shakespeare's Songs* were published by John Lane in 1899 and 1901.

dealing with here, one would not suspect for a moment the Jewish parentage of this remarkable progeny.

Whether this is something to be deplored or not is beside the question here, as it is the inevitable result of ages of assimilation and its blame (if a defect) is to be placed on the causes that made us a race, and unmade us as a nation. Yet though these causes have deprived us of any exclusive atmosphere such as our literature possesses, they have given that which nothing else could have given. The travail and sorrow of centuries have given life a more poignant and intense interpretation, while the strength of the desire of ages has fashioned an ideal which colours all our expression of existence. We find this exemplified in the work before us. Where nature has inspired, the hold on life is strong, but there is an added vitality, the life of ideas, and, as all great and sincerely imaginative work must be, the result is more real. Life that is felt and expressed from the immediate fires of conception must naturally be more convincing than what is merely observed and described from without. First is the portrait of a young poet, gazing as if out of 'dream dimmed' eyes, holding the pen in his hand, apparently waiting for an inspiration.[1] This he doubtless does as a protest against the legendary unpractical habits of poets. With such prudence and foresight, so long-headed a precaution as the pen implies, no poet surely could incur the stigma of impracticability.[2] It is well studied, except for the mannered and unpleasant way the forms of the shadows repeat themselves, which makes it appear as though style were aimed at rather than exact interpretation. The portrait of Michael Sherbrooke is a most vivid and vivacious rendering of this frank good-humoured modern Roscius. Those who know the original know what a living likeness it is of a mood of a man whose moods are so many. The ease and fluency of the handling, so consistent with the buoyancy of the expression, is characteristic of the spontaneous unlaboured technique, which Mr. Amschewitz knows as well how not to abuse. Then there is the portrait of the painter's mother, a sympathetic and most gracious piece of painting. The scheme is one of gold and black, rich, yet reserved, beautiful in delicate treatment of the lace diapery, besides being a most human piece of subtle portraiture. The series of illustrations to 'Everyman' show, perhaps more than any isolated treasure, the remarkable fertility of Mr. Amschewitz's versatile and extraordinary powers. Here he combines a vehement yet orderly dramatic intuition with (to the artist) the larger issues of decorative fitness and harmony. One perhaps might have preferred the text to be illustrated in a purer and more fervid religious spirit. The passion of sense is here more than the passion of soul. But that is merely personal preference. The wealth and opulent colour of some, the restrained delicacy of others, notably No. 10 for this, the breadth, spaciousness, and dignity in the conception of one or two, No. 13

---

[1] Clearly a reference to the Amschewitz portrait of R, reproduced on the back flap of this book's dust wrapper.

[2] CW substituted 'unpracticality' for the word R used, although the latter has more dictionary authority than the former. So I have restored it.

particularly, make the series an extraordinary achievement. Then we come to the landscapes. Some, unaffected fantasies, where nature is used simply as a basis for creation, others, faithful transcripts of recognisable localities, but seen through a richly glowing temperament. They all have the authority and air of experience, autobiographical records of moods, lovely and glad, tinged with the merest grace of melancholy—moods sunny and joyous, brooding and pensive, retiring and shy, or sombre with presentiment of storm and tragedy. There is no space except just to mention as another phase of this artist's talent the powerful black and white study 'The hungry' for its intensity, the yearning tragedy that is its motive.

The works of H. Ospovat shown here are entirely comprised of pen-and-ink illustrations to Matthew Arnold, Browning, and some Shakespeare sonnets. They are very forcible and beautiful interpretations, and show a keenness of insight, and sympathetic appreciation of the poets, wonderful in their way. His influences are apparent, and it seems to me that though he possessed in a great measure the poetic feeling and refinement of the Pre-Raphaelite school of illustrators, he lacked the tenderness and charm of their execution, their patient and honest endeavour for exactness. Sometimes his work recalls Fred Walker, sometimes Rossetti, but neither at their best. When he is personal, as in the 'Last ride together', 'The wandering Jew', he shows a strength sweetened by refinement that is very rare.

EMERSON

[Fragment, ?1913]

The great poets of the earth have been mainly intellects with a kind of coarseness engrained. At the most delicate and rare there is a sense of solidity and bulk, close knit, that is like some unthinkably powerful chemical contained in some dewlike drop. We question a poet like Shelley because we feel this lack of robustness where we do not question Keats or Donne or Blake. We ask in a poet a vigorous intellect, a searching varied power that is itself, and an independent nature.

We know our poem by its being the only poem. The world is too full of echoes and we seize on the real voice. Does it happen that the real voice is sometimes not heard or is mistaken for an echo? It not infrequently happens that the real voice, sickened by echoes and shy of its own sound, withdraws and only calls to ears it is its delight to call to. The Masters must needs have the whole earth for their bough to sing on or they burst their throats, but there are voices humbler in their demands, but nowise less imperious in their result. That ebullition of the heart that seeks in novel but exact metaphor to express itself, the strong but delicate apocalyptical imagination that startles and suggests, the inward sanity that controls and directs—the mainspring of true poetry—is Emerson's. Does he possess in any eminent degree, does he possess at all, that manly intellect, that solidity and bulk, which is the certificate of legitimacy for a great poet?

We have here no tradition—no tricks of the trade. Spontaneity, inspiration, abysmal in its light, is the outer look these poems have to the eye. The words ebulliate and sparkle as fresh as a fountain. But we are always near a brink of some impalpable idea, some indefinable rumour of endlessness, some faint savour of primordial being that creeps[1] through occult crevices and is caught back again. We know nothing better than Shakespeare's lyrics that have this suggestiveness in perfection:

> Full fathom five thy father lies;
> Of his bones are coral made:
> Those are pearls that were his eyes:
> Nothing of him that doth fade,
> But doth suffer a sea-change
> Into something rich and strange.
> Sea-nymphs hourly ring his knell . . .

Or from the sonnets:

> Not mine own fears, nor the prophetic soul
> Of the wide world dreaming on things to come . . .

*　　　*　　　*

This man paved the way for Whitman. His freedom, his daring, his inspiration, in Whitman's hands became a roadway right through humanity.

ART[2]

[Summer 1914]

PART I

We all, more or less, feel a work of art, and I should like in this paper to find a sort of philosophic connection between one's thoughts and work created by mind.

---

[1] R originally wrote 'some indefinable savour of endlessness, some faint rumour that creeps . . .' but improved the passage by introducing the words 'of primordial being' and the interchange of 'savour' and 'rumour' which this entailed.

[2] There are several versions of this Lecture, including an almost complete ink holograph which the 1937 editors followed virtually verbatim. But the printed text which appeared in *South African Women in Council*, in the issues of December 1914 and January 1915, differs from the holograph in several ways, not all merely punctuational. As R not only had plenty of time in which to tidy the Lecture up for press (he first wrote to Marsh about it in July or August 1914), and since there are one or two further corrections to the printed version in his own hand, I have assumed that the latter, rather than the holograph, should be regarded as the authentic text. *South African Women in Council* was a monthly journal 'for the Cultured Woman', owned and edited by Mrs Agnes Cook.

I also want to say a word on modern aims; and no doubt all here have heard of the fermented state of culture now in Europe. The multiplexity, and elaborately interwoven texture of modern life; the whole monstrous fabric of modernity is rapidly increasing in complexity, and art, which is a sort of summing up, and intensification of the spirit of the age, increases its aims accordingly. A great genius is, at once, the product and the creator of his age. It is in him that a marked stage of evolution is fulfilled. His ideas are absorbed and permeate, even when the natures who feel them are not large enough to contain them. These ideas weaken as they become absorbed into the indrawing and everwidening complexities of life, and no longer have their original force, and a new stimulus is necessary. So we have these new movements and their energetic repudiation of preceding movements. To make my point clear I shall be obliged to run roughly through the evolution of art, before I can speak of its present state.

We all have impressions from nature. Our consciousness of these impressions is life. To express and give shape to such impressions on our consciousness, by artificial means, is art. Man's natural necessities, his instinct to communicate his desires, and feelings, found shape in corresponding signs and sounds; symbols which, at first crude, gradually developed and refined. Special emotions found expression in the nearest and most sufficient ways. Singing and dancing for joy—for awe and worship, the reverential mien and solemn incantation. Victories, festivities, marriage, love, all these were occasions for art. Shouting became singing; more and more rhythmical and orderly. From the expression of private joy and sorrow, it told tales of others' joys and woes. It became art. Hunters whose eyes were keen and hands were skilful, gloating over the image of the power they chased, strove to record it, cutting sharply with their rude hunting knives on the stone of their rough cave dwelling. Architecture developed, then sculpture as a natural result. We begin with high culture at the Egyptians. A land of high profound, austere philosophy—their art expressed their priestly natures. Art went hand in hand with their religion, grave and austere. With a profound knowledge of form and perfect craftsmanship, all their energies were directed to express deity, an abstraction of simple, solemn profundity, the omnipresent spirit. Their art was angular and severe.

The Greeks followed, more idealistic they cultivated a more effeminate conception of beauty, an idea of grace, of rounded forms, suavity. Body's strength and body's beauty, was the ideal of this lovely land, and this pagan philosophy has produced art, beautiful indeed, but of no intensity, no real hold on man's spirit.

We are moved by a work of art. Is an artistic emotion similar to an ordinary emotion got from actual life? Is fear, horror, pride, called into play? Yet we are moved, aesthetically. What moves us? Just as figures stand for quantities, so we have subtle but intelligible symbols to correspond to the most delicate and imperceptible shade of emotion; and it is by bringing these varied symbols into a coherent unity that a work of art is constructed. To detach a part from nature, and give it the completeness of the whole, by applying to that part the principle of rhythmic law that is instinctive in our consciousness, and harmonises us to the exterior nature. A law of repetition and contrast, continuity in variety. It is this principle that our consciousness responds to. Art becomes by this, a living thing, another nature, a communicable creation. To convey to all, in living language, some floating instant in time, that mixing with the artist's thought and being, has become a durable essence, a separate entity, a portion of eternity. Art widens the scope of living by increasing the bounds of thought. New moods and hitherto unfelt particles of feeling are perpetually created by these new revelations, this interfusion of man's spirit, eager to beget, and crowd existence with every finer possibility. Thus art is an intensification and simplification of life, which is fragmentary, and has no order and no coherent relationship to us, until it has passed through the crucible of Art. Science explains nature physically by atoms; philosophy explains life morally, but art interprets and intensifies life, representing a portion through the laws of unity that govern the whole.

How do we know a vital composition? We know it by its newness and by its rightness. Do you know Blake's drawing of 'The Song of the Morning Star'? Do you know why it was not conceived before Blake? Yet it is as natural and magnificent a conception as the Sun, as familiar and holy when we are with it as the name of God in our hearts, and as mysterious and holy, and as new.

Perhaps it is irreverent to analyse, but as we are endeavouring to discover a principle in art, we must see how the most inspired art (and no art is perfect without appearing inspired) conforms to this principle.

It is a vital composition because its content is an infinite idea expressed coherently in a definite texture. The spaces harmonise in unexpected ways, the forms are expressive and consistent, the gestures are rhythmical, but surprise us, as though one's own private thought, too secret even to reveal to ourselves, were suddenly shown to us from outside. It is a limitless idea, responsive to the emotion but ungraspable by the intellect. A poem contains in itself all it would convey, which is infinity. This is brought about through movement, the rapid succession of images and thoughts, as in nature itself. Painting is stationary, it only begins a process of thought, it suggests. But you think outside the painting, not in it. Now this brings us to a point I wish to insist on. In appreciating a picture, it is the general tendency to confuse literary ideas with painting ideas. An idea in painting is only one because it cannot be put into words, just as an idea in music can only receive form through the medium of sound. Each art has its own special ideas and special qualities to express them, though they all have a common basis, the expression of emotional truth.

Incident, in a picture, can give some sort of human interest, it might even be that which has inspired the artist to his rhythmical arrangement, but the emotional truth underlying is brought about by insistence on the plastic unity, the beauty and harmony purely of shapes and forms.

If one takes nature as a standpoint, to a cold judgment, how whimsical and odd it is to see limbs suspended in motion, expressions wrought to the utmost limits of intensity, and remaining so. But pictures depend on gestures and expressions. True, but the gesture must be part of some unfathomable, preponderating idea, hovering on the borderland of revelation. We are struck by no particular gesture, but some rhythmical and unexpected quality that helps in some tentative way our approach to this idea. Art has never received purer or higher utterance than the Italian primitives gave it. No formal, cold, lifeless arrangement, but some elaborately organised pattern, instinct with some vital conception, rich with variety of texture; simple in result. Every space brimful of meaning; touched with adumbrations of some subtly felt idea. Clear and definite in form, their whole outlook was expressiveness. Nature had no other significance to them save as a means to symbolise some more intimate nature. Sometimes their passion for something deeper and occult, something never seen by eye or thought of man, led them a little out of the way, to bring back fantastic blossoms and things strange and curious, but which men might like or be angered by as with a child's or a woman's whim. But always their vision of beauty was pure and entire, and their failures rose from their eagerness to obtain a more intimate and profounder sense of her. It was this wishfulness to know, this passionate hunger to reach into the inmost heart of things, by men of such depth, and profundity; this deep imaginative understanding of natural things that drove them burningly to give the clearest utterance to their conclusions of destiny. Art gradually took on different aims. The School founded by Giotto, which might be called the naturalistic school, nature being their immediate inspiration, gave place to a more scholarly group of painters, whose idea of life was largely woven up with Greek culture and learning, Botticelli and Mantegna being the chief.

We come now to Leonardo Da Vinci, a mind of unhuman vastness, of the deepest poetry, and extraordinary logic and invention. Too fertile in his ideas to ever go through with one completely, he has yet left us some single achievements which stand supreme in Art. He might be said to have invented Chiaroscuro, for he was enamoured of the mystery of shadow. He was enamoured of all mysteries, and strove to fathom most, and in art made many revelations of form. His drawings, particularly of women's heads, for perfect loveliness and pure realisation of form have never been surpassed—few indeed have ever come near them. In the Primitives the paintings are in a light bright key, the shadows are light and pearl, and the lights delicate rose. Their patterns of colour are definite, and subordinated to the linear effect. But Leonardo, eager to express mystery, the elusiveness of natural aspects, particularly the smiling of women, sought in shadow a symbol of this. You might call his pictures colour monochromes.

PART II

Then we have Michael Angelo whose solitary spirit sought in huge titanic limbs and volcanic energy of motion, to express the grandeur of his conceptions of nature. Sculpturesque, architectural, within these arbitrary bonds he unloosed his vast writhing universe, and poured his lonely cries into the void. With the Primitives, true decoration passed. Art became more and more concerned with the aspect of things. Plastic unity was achieved, not as in the Primitives, by linear design, by expressive spaces and clearly defined planes, but by tonal relationship of shapes of dark and light. Sloven in their form, the work of the Venetians is soft and inexpressive. Their colour is artificial, and has neither the refinement, truth, nor variety of the Primitives. Their designs are almost always commonplace, picturesque, and grandiose; always sensuous, clever and pleasant, seldom noble and profound—never intense.

With Velasquez we reach the beginning in painting of a new epoch, the objective attitude. Truth to him was not a reaction of the concrete on his sensitiveness in such a way as to become new and unlike—and yet the same. His truth was more the practical truth of the mirror; and yet so clear was his understanding that, even as the sun is drawn into the dark roots of the earth, so his soul too was drawn beneath the surface and gave birth to new combinations. I will say nothing of Rembrandt, who of all artists came nearest to realising the highest of all, the union of the abstract and concrete, the purest interpretation of the concrete, and the clearest translation of the abstract. In Ingres we have the first draughtsman since the old men. Not the picturesque—but the profound ideal of form. Degas followed, and this ideal of form learned from Ingres he used to express in his powerful way, certain phases of modernism. He is perhaps the chief power of modern times. Monet, Pissarro, and the other French Impressionists, made an attempt to reconquer the active vital spirit, to connect the inner with the outer by means of a more spontaneous and intelligent understanding of the actual.

We come now to what is known as the Post Impressionist movement. This was an attempt by men of the deepest culture, and reverence for art, to see nature as a child might see it. However profound their ideas, however mixed with the multiplexity of modern life, their presentation of that idea must be a sort of detachment from all they know—it must be purely that one thing. We know that children see colours bright and unmixed. A drawing by a child of an animal running would express speed by lines that could mean nothing else. It is when we begin to think, and thought begins to modify all our perceptions of an object, that we can no longer see a thing as a thing without associated ideas. The presentation of an object then would be sentiment. It was in Chinese Art these men found similar aims, but joined to a perfect sense of craft, and in Rembrandt. Art to them was inspiration—not mere craft and secondhand enthusiasm, and this they strove to destroy. With a feverish impatience of the bonds of technique, in a vehement spontaneity, they poured on canvas their direct visions. Their attempt always for vital rhythms, more vehement and startling connections, their colour is perhaps too lyrical for the fiercer qualities of their design. In Cézanne, rose and green and pearl, in definite patterns of colour, make beautiful harmonies. To feel continuity in variety, both in colour and in form, to feel freshness and intimacy—life and genuine communion of man's spirit with the universal spirit, was the aim of these men. But a new being has arisen. Hitherto all Art has been an attempt to reconcile the present with the age of Artists, the standard has always been the highest achieved, the forms have always remained the same, though the content has changed. But the Futurist, the last spark struck from this seething modernism, this mechanical age of speed and convulsive machinery, must create a new form to completely express this entirely new and changed humanity. The old forms to him are useless, they served for the outworn creed that made the beauty of woman, or some quietist searching for ideal beauty its object, always taking some commonly recognised symbol to express this. This quietist detachment from life to watch from outside is not for the Futurist. Violence and perpetual struggle—this is life. Dynamic force, the constantaneous rush of electricity, the swift fierce power of steam, the endless contortions and deadly logic of machinery; and this can only be expressed by lines that are violent and struggle, that are mechanical and purely abstract. Theirs is an ideal of strength and scorn. The tiger must battle with the tiger. The world must be cleansed of the useless old and weak, for the splendour of battle must rage between the strong and the strong. Theirs is the terrible beauty of destruction and the furious energy in destroying. They would burn up the past, they would destroy all standards. They have wearied of this unfair competition of the dead with the living. To express these new ideals, they have invented forms abstract and mechanical, remote from and unassociated with natural objects, and by the rhythmic arrangement of these forms, to convey sensation. This presupposes a sympathetic intuition—an understanding of the symbols in the spectator.

We can only see ingenuity. The forms are not new, but dead and mechanical. There is no subtlety nor infinity. The only sensation I have ever got from a Futurist picture is that of a house falling, and however unlike the pictures were, that has always been the sensation. We can never strip ourselves completely from associated ideas; and art, being in its form at least, descriptive, the cubes and abrupt angles call to mind falling bricks. It is too purely abstract and devoid of any human basis to ever become intelligible to anybody outside the creator's self. The symbols they use are symbols of symbols. But they have introduced urgency—energy into Art, and striven to connect it more with life.

Art is now, as it were, a volcano. Eruptions are continual, and immense cities of culture at its foot are shaken and shivered. The roots of a dead universe are torn up by hands, feverish and consuming with an exuberant vitality—and amid dynamic threatenings we watch the hastening of the corroding doom.

But we believe that the Gioconda will endure, and Albrecht Dürer will never be forgotten, and that the reign of Blake is yet to begin.

I have said nothing of Art in England. We have never had a tradition, Gainsborough in a small charming way, Blake in his magnificent great way, Alfred Stevens[1] in his noble reminiscent way, and Rossetti in a romantic way, with Turner and Constable, are perhaps all the English artists who count at all, and of all these, only Blake can be ranked amongst the highest order. But lately Art has sprung into flower. In Augustus John, we have a power; the first English artist with a genuine conception of Art.

About 30 years ago the Slade school was started. Before the Slade, with the exception of Alfred Stevens and Legros[2], both of whom learnt abroad, and were unrecognised here, no drawings worthy of the name had been done by an English artist. Blake was not a good draughtsman, but he had a noble idea of form. It was a great pity he had Flaxman for a teacher instead of Dürer. I here mean drawing as we understand it in the classic sense. Blake knew the end but grasped at it too quickly; he recognised a result and conceived too simple a cause. What else could he do? The unbroken tradition that runs right from Egypt through Da Vinci, Dürer to John, passed by him; there were none to hand it on to him. Drawing is a science, the final result of a slow growth, and continual criticism of ages, and no man however divine can be expected to invent it. I hold Blake to be the highest artist England has ever had, as high above the next highest as this to the lowest. No other artist that ever lived possessed in so high a degree, that inspired quality; that unimpaired divinity that shines from all things mortal when looked [at] through the eye of imagination. Each touch is interpenetrated with sense, with life that breathes from the reachless and obscure heights and depths, deep, profound, and all embracing. And this in spite of a bad and mannered way of drawing, which sometimes obtrudes and obscures our pure appreciation. I will not enter into the claims of Leighton,[3] Watts, Millais as draughtsmen. In England they have been forgotten long ago and nobody dreams of disturbing their memories. Whiles these men were still alive and England mute and wondering at their powers, real drawings were being done by students at the Slade. John burst upon London with amazing drawings, some that could be hung side by side with da Vinci without suffering. At last we were able to boast of a draughtsman, such as Italy once had, and France now possessed. A man who could apprehend a fact, its significance, and translate into terms of expressive line the visual substance of things. You look at a drawing. Can I read it? Is it clear, concise, definite? It cannot be too harsh for me. The lines must cut into my consciousness;

---

[1] Alfred Stevens (1817-75) was a precocious and versatile artist whose early promise was nearly wrecked by his being sent to Naples almost penniless, at the age of 16, by a well-meaning but misguided patron. After various adventures in Rome and Florence he returned to England in 1842, and eventually established a considerable reputation as draughtsman, occasional portrait painter, and sculptor.

[2] Alphonse Legros (1837-1911), French painter and etcher, exhibited in the Paris *Salon* 1859-63 but in 1866 settled in London. In 1876 he was appointed Slade Professor, a post he held for the next 18 years.

[3] Lord Leighton, R.A. (1830-1896), as a young man travelled widely in Europe, where he studied art under the leading Continental teachers. An academic rather than an inspired painter and sculptor, he achieved early and lasting success, becoming President of the Royal Academy, a knight, a baronet and finally a peer.

the waves of life must be disturbed, sharp, and unhesitating. It is nature's consent, her agreement that what we can wrest from her we keep. Truth, structural veracity, clearness of thought and utterance, the intelligent understanding of what is essential. I should like to make the distinction between the picturesque and the profound, the swagger and the stately. Rubens, Vandyke, Watteau are considered good but not serious enough. They are the 'knuts' of the Renaissance. These glib and aristocratic hunger marchers, who were too clever to sweat, are as shallow as they are fertile. Compare an etching of Rembrandt with Vandyke, a drawing by Ingres or Degas with Rubens or Watteau. It is the difference of the Temple to the Playhouse, of the Prophet to the ballad monger. It is the difference between the accessory and the essential, the accidental and the inevitable. The difference between the pretty plausible and the fierce straightforward.

The French Impressionists were the reaction from the traditional and lifeless. Art somehow had lost touch with nature and lay simpering, cosy and snug, propped up by sweet anecdote and delicious armchair sentiment. It was the day of Dickens' slime and slush. Then Baudelaire published 'The Flowers of Evil', Swinburne his ballads, and Meredith 'Modern Love', while at the same time Degas, Manet, Pissarro, Puvis de Chavannes tried to get at the core of nature with paint. In their anxiety to get at truth, the Impressionists, unlike Puvis and Degas, overlooked one great point, which was, the form by which truth is to be conveyed must be concise and arbitrary, to isolate and impress its significance. Post Impressionism is that criticism of Impressionism. Vitality is expressed by patterns of clear form.

In England Impressionism manifested itself in Wilson Steer, Professor Brown, Sargent, Walter Sickert, Henry Tonks. To my mind the personality of Sickert is the most interesting of this school. It is very forbidding and sombre and stands alone in its ruthless philosophy. Steer is more lyrical and gay, and has recaptured the golden splendour of Turner. Clausen[1] serves as a good populariser of other men while Sargent pains one by his smartness. Then we have a group of artists whose ideal is mixed up with Dutch Art, with Vermeer and Van Hooch, William Rothenstein, Orpen[2] and Walter Russell.[3] Rothenstein's picture of 'The Doll's House' is very beautiful and haunting.

[1] Sir George Clausen (1852-1944), rural landscape painter, was at the Royal College of Art 1873-5 and became a founder member of the N.E.A.C. in 1886. He was Professor of Painting at the Royal Academy Schools 1904-6, and made an R.A. in 1908.

[2] Sir William Orpen, R.A. (1878-1931), was of Irish descent. After showing exceptional early promise and winning an important Slade prize in 1899, he became a successful portrait painter and thereafter exploited rather than developed his talent. He was an official War Artist in the 1914 war, and attended the Peace Conference as official painter.

[3] Sir Walter Russell (1867-1949), painter of portraits, landscapes and interiors, was Assistant Professor at the Slade 1895-1927. He served in the Royal Engineers from 1916-19 doing camouflage. A worthy though uninspired painter, he was made an R.A. in 1926.

But the young men have been taught by John that a sharp contour means more than the blending of tone into tone. Nature can be a lure and a snare and be used as an end and not as a means to an end. The concise pregnant quality of poetry rather than prose.

Henry Lamb is shy, a tremulous and ever-shaken life in shadow. Compared to Lamb, John is the broad ocean with the sun on it, and Lamb the sea with the moon. Innes paints landscapes very much like the Chinese and Mantegna. They have the vague beauty of perfumes and luxuriant reverie. Mark Gertler has a deep understanding of nature and sometimes achieves to that intensity we call imagination. John Currie has painted lovely things without being very convincing as a draughtsman. David Bomberg has crude power of a too calculated violence—and is mechanical, but undoubtedly interesting. Roberts,[1] who is yet a boy[,] is a remarkable draughtsman in a stodgy academic way, clear, logical, and fervent. But the finest of all is Stanley Spencer. He is too independent for contemporary influence and goes back to Giotto and Blake as his masters. He strikes even a deeper note than John, and his pictures have that sense of everlastingness[,] of no beginning and no end[,] that we get in all masterpieces.[2]

SHORTER FRAGMENTS OF PROSE

I

We have hints, suggestions—as if we have just woken up in time to note the passing; there are moments in thought where thought almost knows—words are not delicate or intimate enough; that instant we have died—our souls truly etherialised—that instant we have truly lived.

We all build the tower of Babel to reach to God and he has stricken us [with] confusion of speech who understand each other.

Is not each soul solitary, condemned in its separate prison? Yet when all the prisoners assemble in the courtyard we suspect each other and talk guardedly and opposite, fearing to be betrayed.

If I could die and leave no trace, ah, that thought of mine must live, incomplete and imperfect, maimed. Could I destroy all I have ever thought and done . . .

You the world, will sneer: 'Young fool—mad . . .' But my quiet undisturbed serenity rebukes your despairs and vexations and the joys that pass. I go to meet Moses who assuredly was a suicide, and the young

[1] William Roberts (b. 1895) was originally apprenticed to a printer as a commercial artist, but attended the Slade 1910-13. He subsequently worked under Roger Fry in the Omega workshops before joining Wyndham Lewis at the Rebel Art Centre in 1914. After repudiating Futurism and espousing Vorticism he joined the Royal Field Artillery in 1916 and was an official War Artist 1917-18. He was made an A.R.A. in 1958.

[2] For biographical details of the other modern painters see pp. 194n1, 204n, and 206n3.

Christ who invited death, I who have striven to preach the gospel of beauty—

How small a thing is art. A little pain; disappointment, and any man feels a depth—a boundlessness of emotion, inarticulate thoughts no poet has ever succeeded in imaging.

Death does not conquer me, I conquer death, I am the master.

II

THE PRE-RAPHAELITES AND IMAGINATION IN PAINT

We are apt to confuse imagination with literature, with the psychological interest of a picture, as a quality apart from its technical qualities. Literature, I think, is permissible if it enhances the interest of a picture, but it only increases the difficulties of imagination. A picture must be a perfect consistency of thought and execution, of colour and design and conception; the more dramatic or psychological a picture is the more intense must be the imagination of colour and design to harmonise with the idea. The psychology is helpless without the other elements; the psychology itself is only part of the imagination and perhaps the smallest. Whatever the subject, nature is always our resort, a basis for creation. To feel and interpret nature, to project ourself beyond nature through nature, and yet convince of the veracity of the sensation,[1] is imagination.

The ultimate end of all the arts should be beauty. Poetry and music achieve that end through the intellect and the ear; painting and sculpture through the eye. The former possess advantages which the latter do not; and the latter, *vice versa*. Painting is stationary while poetry is motion. Through the intellect the emotion is enchained; feeling made articulate transmits its exact state to the reader. Each word adapts itself to the phase of emotion, (I include sensation of the soul) and carries one along from degree to degree. Painting can only give the moment, the visual aspect, and only suggest the spiritual consciousness; not even a mood, but the phase of a mood. By imagination in paint we do not encroach on the domain of the writer; we give what the writer cannot give, with all his advantages, the visible aspect of things, which the writer can only suggest, and give that aspect a poetic interest; and by that a more intensely human interest: for here the body and the soul are one, and beauty the crown thereof.

[1] CW has 'convince of our faithfulness to the sensation'. The holograph is obscure at this point.

III

ON MODERN ART

We are not affected by Art in the same way as life. The spiritual consciousness is stirred to aesthetic emotion. Colour being more imitative is responded to by the senses. Form has a greater interest for the mind. Here nature becomes an abstraction, an essence. Mere representation is unreal, is fragmentary. The bone taken from Adam remains a bone.

To create is to apply pulsating rhythmical principles to the part, a unity, another nature is created.

The renaissance was the revival of learning. Civilization has been tamed by the commercial spirit, a logic without imagination, mechanical, scientific, practical. Impetuous ideals, Art has become too self-conscious.

The sky stagnates, life becomes inert, arid, a perishing tomb for itself. Dust are the stars, dust the sun, the whole world dust. Obscured and effaced, the life force fails and like a pricked balloon subsides. Out of this nothingness, out of this dust, art is born and philosophies.

*

Life stales and dulls, the mind demands noble excitement, half apprehended surprises, the eternal desire, the beautiful. It is a vain belief that Art and life go hand in hand. Art is as it were another planet, which does indeed reflect the rays of life, but is nevertheless a distinct and separate planet.

Passivity and detachment is a need, even as a mirror to reflect truly must be calm and undimmed. The vivifying organism[1] that is the pulse of a work of art does not come from the ardour of the limbs, or the impulse to mix with men, and do what men do (an external life) but from the imaginative understanding, a necessary consequence of having something genuine to express. We all experience all emotions possible to be experienced. Similar sentiments may dwell in dissimilar conditions,[2] and qualities that appear to be unapprehensible, because their activities are possible only in certain conditions, have their corresponding elements in apparently [?dissimilar situations.] though the connection would be difficult to trace.

[1] Another version has for l. 2: 'The vivifying organism $\left.\begin{array}{l}\text{activates,} \\ \text{animates,}\end{array}\right\}$ does not come from the ardour of the limbs, but the imaginative understanding.'

[2] And for l.7: 'Sentiments transferred to another sphere of action.' The alternative paragraph ends: 'The artist intuitively apprehends them, transfers them dramatically, disguised, and renamed objectives. Some artists take a delight in showing their delight in showing their ingenuity this way, but as a rule, what is gained is loss'.

N.B. The above text differs somewhat from CW, which did not include the last sentence of para 3, and did include part of para 5 which R appears to have deleted. But the holograph is very confused and difficult to elucidate.

IV

THE SLADE AND ITS RELATIONS TO THE UNIVERSE

[1911-1912]

'The Slade, what is the Slade?', nine-tenths of our readers will cry. Is it a building or a threshing machine? It is merely an art school. In Gower Street, concealed in a corner of that noble edifice the University, the Slade reposes in promiscuous obscurity. You pass through the gate and take the small path to the left. You pass a building which you take no notice of, and then pause before a stately imposing [one], and on proceeding to enter you are intercepted by a buttoned authority and you find you have mistaken the porter's lodge for the Slade. You retrace your footsteps and hesitate before the insignificant building we passed before. Then you catch glimpses of girls in painting overalls through the glass doors, and are oppressed by an uncomfortable feeling of being watched by numberless eyes from rows and rows of windows. You pluck up courage and look, and you know then that it is the Slade. What is the Slade? You don't know yet. Well, I can't find it in my heart to blame you. I know what the Slade is. I have been a student there, and so I ought to know. The first day I came I thought I had wandered into a Seminary, and I spent the whole day in trying to find my way out without being seen, but I only succeeded in getting myself grabbed by a student—a male luckily— the first I had seen, who told me the model was taken ill and they generally had new students [to take their place]. Afterward I ran across some stray waifs of youthful males descending to the lower regions [where] the atmosphere distinctly became more masculine.[1]

V

THE SLADE AND MODERN CULTURE

If we consider the Slade as it stands related to modern culture we will find one fundamental principle exemplified—one guiding law, one fact that is of paramount interest in our endeavour. We find that the law of change only proves the futility of change, that it is a circle revolving round the rock of fixity.

*　　　　*　　　　*

The Slade marks an era in the history of Art. Constable, [the] French Impressionists, had given flashes to the world of an attempt to wrest her secret from her; of the endeavour to show to the world the beauty that lies around us if our souls will only see; with more or less adequate power and concentration of vision. Whistler, exquisite, dainty and superficial, dandied[2] through the slushy sentimentalism that had saturated English

---

[1] The men's Life-Room was in the basement.

[2] R originally wrote 'breathed upon' and then 'tripped through' for 'dandied through'.

art, and taught Art not to despise the moods of nature; that a pigsty in twilight was a poem, and even a church could be hallowed—by a fog.

But these, though they were forces, were not as one might say an organized force, they were flashes; the final culmination, the concentration of the blaze is the Slade.

*   *   *

This is the paradox of the Slade: to be ourselves we must not forget others—but forget ourselves. We must not look at nature with the self-conscious, mannered eye of a stylist, whose vision is limited by his own personal outlook, but assimilate the multifarious and widened vision of masters to widen our outlook to the natural, to attain to a completeness of vision which simply means a total sinking of all conscious personality, a complete absorption and forgetfulness in nature, to bring out one's personality.

VI

An age that believes in Blake and tolerates Tennyson, that has forgotten Pope and worships Shelley, to whom Keats is simply sensuous and Shakespeare not subtle or intense enough—this is our age of poetry. Rossetti I think is the keynote of the demand, and in the 'Monochord' and 'The Song of the Bower'—in the first all poignancy—a richness and variety, a purity of imagination—a truth, far beyond wit, or thought. There are poets who delight in the morbid, for whom life always is arrayed in crepe; whose very vigour and energy find its outlet in a perverse and insistent plucking at the wings of death. The poet is so not because he is weak but because he is perverse. His life is a paradox—he does not live, if what other men do is life. This poet will make a song out of sorrow and find in a tear a jewel of perpetual delight. Love is his theme, life is the background, and the beauty of woman stands to him as the manifestation of the beauty of spiritual nature and all outer aspects of the workings of nature.

VII

Hidden in air, in nature, are unexplored powers which the earlier masters had no hint of. We are immeasurably in advance of them in range and scope of subject. The spirit of inquiry wrestled with superstition; Luther brought to bear upon the moral world what Darwin has upon the physical world. Marlowe foreshadows Nietzsche. Tamburlaine, the towering colossus, symbolises the subjection of matter to will—the huge blind forces of nature shrink terrorised before this indomitable energy of purpose, clay for some colossal plastic shaping.

We of this age stand in the same relation to things as they, but with a sharpened curiosity. Religious freedom, freedom of thought, has prepared the way for heights of daring and speculation. Social freedom is still as far off as ever, but we dare dream of it.

301

VIII

We never excuse the absolute want of spirit and dignity of character, or a proper sense of what is due to oneself, in society and the common intercourse of life. This vice constitutes what we properly call *meanness*; when a man can submit to the basest slavery, in order to gain his ends; fawn upon those who abuse him, and degrade himself by intimacies and familiarities with undeserving inferiors. A certain degree of generous pride or self-value is so requisite that the absence of it in the mind displeases.

IX

An artist who depends on his art for his living must be an advertiser.

X

Poor people are born in troubles and spend all their lives trying to get out of them. But, born free, all try to get into them.

XI

Very few people say what they mean, though they may say what they think. Few can shape their feelings into words, and in the hurry of conversation say the first words that come. Few people's actions are expressions even of their nature—we are different with different persons.

XII

Youth is still childhood. When we cast off every cloudy vesture and our thoughts are clear and mature; when every act is a conscious thought, every thought an attempt to arrest feelings; our feelings strong and overwhelming, our sensitiveness awakened by insignificant things in life . . . When the skies race tumultuously with our blood and the earth shines and laughs, when our blood hangs suspended at the rustling of a dress . . . Our vanity loves to subdue—battle, aggressive . . . How we despise those older and duller—we want life, newness, excitement.

XIII

'Crossing the Bar' has this consistency, this perfect oneness of tone. A sense of unutterable life in quiet, a depth of yearning, the fading greyness of the whole piece . . .

XIV

Art to be great must be unforgettable. Leaving the picture or poem, the impression remains, the quintessence, epitome. Suggestiveness, mystery, vagueness, something underlying what is actually put down, a hauntingness of . . .

XV

ON NOSES

It has often struck me as a fact of paramount significance in life that noise projectivity and ostentation, though always in themselves signs of uselessness and the superficial, are generally the echoes and heralds of the great, the useful and substantial. If we take religion as an instance, or a great cause like dandyism or women's suffrage, is not the spouting, the shouting, the foppishness but the effervescence, the first dribblings of a solid and profound idea, of an earnest soul-enthralling basis? Nature has constructed each of us, rightly or wrongly, as an individual demonstration of this principle. The apparent important feature, the centre, the arresting portion of the face, the part that stands before all others in singleness of leadership, ostentatious and projecting, is the nose. Whereever it leads the face, the entire body must follow after it. There is no protesting, no argufying, we must endure. The eyes may close in chagrin, mortification, the mouth may howl in disgust, the ears twitch in agony, but still we must endure. Yet what is this apparent leadership? It is only a station it has appropriated to secure a position, a prominence which otherwise it had not got, and it only heralds the will.

The following fragment, not in CW, clearly belongs with the above and seems worth preserving.

. . . The larger, the grander [the] beauty of the face. Be this as it may, in itself the nose's shape and quality has exercised remarkable influence on the fate of not only individuals but world movements, conquests, death and life. We owe all our heritage of sin and shame to the extraordinary length of Eve's nose, which lost us the world. Columbus discovered a world for that very same reason, [and] Polonius lost his life . . .

JOY [1]

And when we had seen Time die, and passed through the porches of silence, we came to a land where joy spread its boughs, and we knew that the dreams we had dreamed before Time were but the shadows of the tree of joy mirrored in the waters of life. For the roots of joy lie beyond the valleys and hills of life, and the branches thereof blossom where weeping earth mists come not near, and only the sounds of the laughing of ripples, the running of happy streams, and the rapturous singing of birds is heard. Where delight lies coolly shadowed, overburdened by the weariness of joy, lulled by the songs of joy. Joy—joy the birds sing, joy— the rivers, joy—the happy leaves, for the fear of Time haunts not, and the hands of fate are afar.

[1] R produced an oil painting called Joy for the Slade Summer Competition of 1912. It has disappeared.

INDICES

*

I Poetry and Plays
(a) INDEX OF TITLES

(b) INDEX OF FIRST LINES

313

II Letters

III General Index